Poverty in Affluence

Under the General Editorship of
Robert K. Merton
Columbia University

Poverty in Affluence

The Social, Political, and Economic Dimensions of Poverty in the United States

SECOND EDITION

Edited by

Robert E. Will
Carleton College

and

Harold G. Vatter
Portland State University

Harcourt, Brace & World, Inc.

New York   Chicago   San Francisco   Atlanta

To GUNNAR MYRDAL, *Social Scientist*

Like preventable disease, economic want persists as a social ill only because men do not desire sufficiently that it shall cease. There is still much mumbling of old commonplaces, and it has seemed worth while to emphasize anew this definite corollary of modern political economy, that the essential causes of poverty are determinable and its considerable presence unnecessary.

—Jacob Hollander

ISBN: 0-15-570751-5

Library of Congress Catalog Card Number: 70-115866

Printed in the United States of America

ACKNOWLEDGMENTS

"Poverty as a Way of Life," reprinted from *Poverty and Progress* (1941) by B. Seebohn Rowntree, p. 103, by permission of the Joseph Rowntree Charitable Trust, York, England.

"The Advantages of Poverty," reprinted from *The Gospel of Wealth and Other Essays* by Andrew Carnegie, edited by E. C. Kirkland (1962). Reprinted by permission of the Belknap Press of Harvard University Press, Cambridge, Mass.

"Family on Relief: Puerto Ricans in New York" reprinted from "Family on Relief: Study in Poverty" by Philip Dougherty, The New York *Times* (April 5, 1964). © 1964 by the New York Times Company. Reprinted by permission.

"Homer Burleigh: How Many Problems Can a Man Have?" and "Harry Martin: The Dreams of a Six-year-old," reprinted from *In the Midst of Plenty: The Poor in America* (1964) by Ben H. Bagdikian, Chapters 3 and 11. Reprinted by permission of the Beacon Press. Copyright © 1964 by Ben H. Bagdikian.

"Never To Be Employed," reprinted from "Unemployment in America," *Newsweek* (April 1, 1963), pp. 58–60. Copyright Newsweek, Inc. Reprinted by permission.

"Backlash, Privilege, and Pressure," reprinted from "Gunnar Myrdal on Poor People's March" (interview by Mike McGrady), Boston Sunday *Globe* (May 26, 1968). Reprinted with permission from Newsday, Inc.

Cover photograph by Meryl Sussman

Preface

Over five years have passed since President Johnson launched the War on Poverty on March 16, 1964. Yet many Americans, and especially American youth of the present college generation, still need to be informed about what that commitment involves and what the brief historical anti-poverty record shows.

This book is an attempt to fill that information gap. The first edition was published within a year of the Poverty War's inauguration. It is not at all surprising, however, that half a decade can make both data and ideas obsolete. A case in point is Michael Harrington's hypothesis that the poor are politically invisible, inarticulate, and powerless. In a few short years, the situation has become quite the opposite.

This is one way of saying that the present book, while retaining a basically similar format, has a very different content. Indeed the only section that has remained intact is the popular one on intellectual history, "Ideologies of Poverty." The rest of the book is almost all new, taken from a large pool of books, articles, government documents, pamphlets, and newspaper clippings that we have carefully assembled, perused, and sifted since 1965. All the headnotes except that for the ideologies section have been completely rewritten. Our frustration in having to reject many fine pieces is alleviated by our belief that the reader is somewhat guaranteed that he is getting the best that experienced judgment can provide.

A book of this size cannot analyze any one aspect of poverty in depth but will give the reader a sound basis for more detailed study. We suggest that such further study might well start with the complete texts from which these selections have been taken.

Although *Poverty in Affluence* is not confined to one approach, its editors are dedicated to the abolition of poverty in all its forms; they favor amelioration only as a transitional policy until the social disease of poverty can be completely eradicated.

This book is for the student and the nonprofessional reader who is interested in social problems in general and the problem of poverty in particular. It should be useful in adult education courses and in discussion groups. College and university courses in which it can be, and has been, used include the following: introductory sociology, economics, and political science; social science area or survey courses; economic problems and policies; American society and contemporary American social problems; American studies; and other interdisciplinary courses.

The final choice of materials is, of course, the responsibility of the editors, but we are grateful for the many helpful ideas conveyed to us by Professor William Hartley, Department of Economics, Carleton College; Mr. Gelvin Stevenson, Department of Economics, Washington University; and Mr. Thomas Gerity, Librarian, Portland State University. We wish also to acknowledge the many constructive suggestions from Professor Martin Rein of Bryn Mawr College. And we are deeply indebted to our wives for their numerous suggestions and copious time away from home and family and in conflict with their own intellectual activities. For typing and work requiring imaginative detail we wish to thank Mrs. Virginia Tibbetts.

Robert E. Will
Harold G. Vatter

Contents

• indicates a table or chart

III. The Economics of Poverty

IV. The Anatomy of Poverty

Contents

VII. Poverty and Political Action

VIII. Perspectives on Poverty

Introduction

POVERTY as a social, economic, and emotional condition has long been with us. For many, however, it has been nearly invisible, and our closest personal involvement has been an occasional gift to charity or the more regular payment of taxes, a portion of which we know to be used for public welfare. As a source of social and political unrest, on the other hand, poverty has recently become sharply registered in the consciousness of almost everybody—especially with the rise of the civil-rights movement as a significant political force in the 1960s. It is noteworthy that as early as 1956 W. Averell Harriman, then governor of New York, called for an "attack on poverty" in his annual message to the state legislature.

A powerful popular consensus has created the opportunity in the United States to secure in the near future a decent life for those considerable numbers of impoverished people whom the brooding genius Thorstein Veblen included in his rich term "the underlying masses." Americans have not yet by any means fully exploited their self-created opportunity to transform poverty into an "unpleasant memory," as optimistically foreseen by the President's Council of Economic Advisers, although progress has been made during the 1960s. The anti-poverty effort has many enemies—a conservative coalition, the supporters of a large military budget, exponents of the "Protestant ethic" —and its fate in the 1970s is conjectural. Yet we have progressed immensely from the nineteenth-century view of Bishop William Lawrence that wealth is in happy league with godliness. Today there is an abiding determination, despite cyclical and episodic fluctuations in public opinion, to make this the century of the common man.

The attack on involuntary poverty throughout those major areas of the world where human misery and degradation still prevail will not have proved fully victorious when the century draws to a close, but in the United States poverty could be eliminated within a decade. Perhaps at last we will vindicate Herbert Hoover's assertion in a 1928 campaign speech—an assertion that rang hollow in the subsequent decades—that "we in America today are nearer to the final triumph over poverty than ever before in the history of any land." The record will no doubt show that the good war has been escalated and that the good life is being increasingly shared by those rising out of poverty to a level of at least minimum health and decency.

Poverty, as this book shows, has many faces: lack of material necessities and comforts, psychic travail, the multiproblem family and individual, dysfunctional behavior. But it is the first of these above all; as Carlyle so penetratingly wrote, "it is to live miserable we know not why; to work sore and yet gain nothing." William Dean Howells described it as "the fear and dread of want." While poverty may indeed be associated in specific cases with virtue and possibly happiness, twentieth-century humanism assumes that virtue or happiness generally arises from wellsprings other than poverty. Unlike the nineteenth and earlier centuries, the twentieth-century enlightenment finds little that is good in a life of poverty.

The Industrial Revolution shattered the age-old continuum of human poverty by ushering in an epoch of rising income per capita which has culminated in recent decades in the abundant economy of the United States and much of Europe. It is true that the achievement of abundance for many in the United States has so far scarcely touched most of the world's peoples; nevertheless, the historical breakthrough in man's economic and social evolution represented by the Industrial Revolution is still enormously significant. As the eminent geographer Erich Zimmerman has shown, that revolution brought mankind across the great divide separating scarcity from abundance, largely because impressive technological achievements enlarged man's physical resource base and vastly improved our efficiency in the use of human and machine skills.

Not surprisingly, the first breakthroughs in reducing poverty have occurred in those regions of the world where the Industrial Revolution began. In most of the Western world, technological constraints no longer limit the eradication of poverty. What remains to be seen, however, is the extent to which Western social structures will take advantage of the technological potential of our high-capacity economy. It is striking that a number of European countries have already gone far toward the complete elimination of poverty despite having per capita incomes well below those of the United States.

Dean John C. Bennett of Union Theological Seminary has called attention to the great chasm between contemporary and traditional ethical attitudes toward poverty and wealth distribution—a split that has resulted from the emergence of abundant economies. He quotes in part the report of the Oxford Conference in 1937:

> The abolition of such poverty now seems to depend on the human organization of economic life, rather than on favors given in nature or on what might be called the inevitable constitution of every economic order. But the possibility of economic "plenty" has this moral importance, that to an increasing extent it makes the persistence of poverty a matter for which men are morally responsible. This possibility marks off our time from the period of the New Testament and from other periods in which Christian thinking about economic life has been formulated. In the light of it the direction of Christian effort in relation to the economic order should henceforth be turned from charitable paternalism to the realization of more equal justice in the distribution of wealth.

Today even in less developed countries, in remote corners of the globe, there is a revolution of rising expectations as more and more people resolve to share the fruits of technological advance. Thus, an adequate perspective on the task of dispelling poverty requires both a historical and a cross-cultural appreciation of its nature and extent.

Each major section of this book begins with an introduction describing the contents of the section and explaining the main controversies or areas of agreement about a particular aspect of poverty. Where appropriate we indicate our own approach to the matter. In many cases the introductions draw upon the wealth of material that could not be included in this short anthology. The introductions and selections show that poverty is a multidimensional phenomenon and thus poverty policy cannot be narrow in range, limited in emphasis, or simple in solution. Indeed, the diverse facets of poverty may require seemingly inconsistent strategies, disturbing those who yearn for clear-cut, simple answers.

This country's current official definition of "poverty" is based on the amount of income required to provide an arbitrarily stipulated minimum living level *in the United States*. This "line of poverty" approach has its historical roots in two groups of studies begun at the turn of the century, one seeking to establish minimum family budgets in real terms at different levels of living and the other attempting to measure the cost of living. The concepts necessary for analyzing family budgets and living levels were later refined by the Heller Committee in California. At the same time, economists and statisticians were expanding and improving techniques for measuring the cost of living and changes in it. When price data provided by the extensive cost-of-living studies of the Federal Bureau of Labor Statistics are combined with each budget level, it is possible to determine the annual income with which a family can achieve a level of living providing minimum health and decency.

The United States is preeminent in its capacity to underwrite the commitment to eliminate want for the great numbers of Americans living in poverty, and it is the country best equipped to attack impoverishment elsewhere in the world. No other people have such a high ratio of discretionary income to total income. Unfortunately, there is a vast gap between our capability and our programmatic execution, and it remains to be seen whether Bernard Nossiter was correct or just gloomy when he prognosticated in March 1964 that the attack on poverty "will be a long war."

I

Definitions and the Nature of Poverty

Poverty as a Way of Life

A family living [in poverty] must never spend a penny on railway fare or omnibus. They must never go into the country unless they walk. They must never purchase a halfpenny newspaper or spend a penny to buy a ticket for a popular concert. They must write no letters to absent children, for they cannot afford to pay the postage. They must never contribute anything to their church or chapel, or give any help to a neighbour which costs them money. They cannot save, nor can they join sick club or trade union, because they cannot pay the necessary subscriptions. The children must have no pocket money for dolls, marbles or sweets. The father must smoke no tobacco, and must drink no beer. The mother must never buy any pretty clothes for herself or for her children, the character of the family wardrobe, as for the family diet, being governed by the regulation, "Nothing must be bought but that which is absolutely necessary for the maintenance of physical health, and what is bought must be of the plainest and most economical description." Should a child fall ill, it must be attended by the parish doctor; should it die, it must be buried by the parish. Finally, the wage-earner must never be absent from his work for a single day.

If any of these conditions are broken, the extra expenditure involved is met, *and can only be met,* by limiting the diet; or, in other words, by sacrificing physical efficiency. . . . It cannot therefore be too clearly understood, nor too emphatically repeated, *that whenever a worker having three children dependent on him, and receiving not more than 21s. 8d. per week, indulges in any expenditure beyond that required for the barest physical needs, he can do so only at the cost of his own physical efficiency, or of that of some members of his family.*

FROM B. Seebohm Rowntree, *Poverty and Progress* (1941).

WHO are the poor in the United States today? According to today's social consensus, there *are* poor people in a significant, policy-centered sense of the term. This consensus exists at a time when this country's employment rate is much higher than it was in 1937, when FDR defined "one-third of a nation" as poor. Largely because of the rise in our employment rates and the long-run growth in per capita income, the proportion of the American population designated as poor has been reduced to approximately one-fifth. This proportion also reflects a social consensus, for it represents an arbitrarily selected cutoff point, a so-called poverty line. Academicians and experts may disagree over the appropriate definition of poverty, but all (or almost all) recognize that any policy or program directed toward a goal *must draw arbitrary lines to delineate the groups toward which policy is directed.* Thus programs and policies designed to ameliorate and eradicate poverty must be based on an official definition of "the poor" who are the object of the "War on Poverty."

In this volume we have used the current official definition of the poor, but since we are deliberately policy oriented, we strongly believe that the reader should be exposed to alternative concepts as well. We favor Victor Fuchs' definition as by far the most suggestive and potentially useful alternative to the official concept. It is eminent in its simplicity, historically dynamic, and practical for policy. However, it allows for only limited progress toward the elimination of poverty.

The varied social indicators used by S. M. Miller *et al.* to define "the poor" point to a notion quite different from that of Fuchs, and they are valuable reminders of the complexities of poverty. The precise definition and measurement of these social indicators would be a major task of a President's Council of Social Advisers, proposed at the academic level by Bertram Gross and others and at the congressional level by Senator Mondale. The work of such a council would greatly assist the formulation of an official definition of poverty that would be more useful than the current one in shaping policy.

We introduce the "poverty gap" notion early because we believe that, although simplistic, it is the best overall indicator of what public and private policy must still accomplish, even in terms of the limited objectives set by the current official definition. The poverty gap concept also indicates the costs of meeting the problem relative to the approaching trillion dollar gross national product of the United States. We thus begin the book with policy, and we will end with policy.

All the definitions and the problems of poverty presented in this book are based upon an arbitrarily determined, *relative* phenomenon. However, we believe that *absolute* poverty—that is, material means insufficient to sustain life—also exists in the United States today, although its incidence is far smaller than that of less developed countries, where absolute poverty frequently afflicts the majority of the population. But that it is permitted to exist at all in an affluent society should be sufficiently shocking to impel immediate action. *Hunger, U.S.A.,* a report by physicians and other citizens on hunger and malnutrition in our society, appeared in the summer of 1968. Readers of *Poverty in Affluence* will be able to determine whether its revelations have been heeded and appropriate steps taken.

Americans can take pride in the fact that they have added the removal of both absolute and relative poverty to their array of humanistic national goals. But this pride must be tempered by the recognition that it is largely the growth of technology that has made the goal feasible and that now only an insufficient willingness to achieve this goal stands in the way of its attainment.

I See One-third of a Nation
Ill-housed, Ill-clad, Ill-nourished

FRANKLIN D. ROOSEVELT

To hold to progress today . . . is . . . difficult. Dulled conscience, irresponsibility, and ruthless self-interest already reappear. Such symptoms of prosperity may become portents of disaster! Prosperity already tests the persistence of our progressive purpose.

Let us ask again: Have we reached the goal of our vision of that fourth day of March, 1933? Have we found our happy valley?

I see a great nation, upon a great continent, blessed with a great wealth of natural resources. Its hundred and thirty million people are at peace among themselves; they are making their country a good neighbor among the nations. I see a United States which can demonstrate that, under democratic methods of government, national wealth can be translated into a spreading volume of human comforts hitherto unknown, and the lowest standard of living can be raised far above the level of mere subsistence.

But here is the challenge to our democracy: In this nation I see

FROM President Roosevelt's Second Inaugural Address (January 20, 1937).

tens of millions of its citizens—a substantial part of its whole population—who at this very moment are denied the greater part of what
the very lowest standards of today call the necessities of life.

I see millions of families trying to live on incomes so meager that
the pall of family disaster hangs over them day by day.

I see millions whose daily lives in city and on farm continue under
conditions labeled indecent by a so-called polite society half a century
ago.

I see millions denied education, recreation, and the opportunity to
better their lot and the lot of their children.

I see millions lacking the means to buy the products of farm and
factory and by their poverty denying work and productiveness to
many other millions.

I see one-third of a nation ill-housed, ill-clad, ill-nourished.

It is not in despair that I paint you that picture. I paint it for you
in hope—because the Nation, seeing and understanding the injustice
in it, proposes to paint it out. We are determined to make every
American citizen the subject of his country's interest and concern;
and we will never regard any faithful, law-abiding group within our
borders as superfluous. The test of our progress is not whether we
add more to the abundance of those who have much; it is whether we
provide enough for those who have too little.

If I know aught of the spirit and purpose of our Nation, we will
not listen to Comfort, Opportunism, and Timidity. We will carry on.

Overwhelmingly, we of the Republic are men and women of good
will; men and women who have more than warm hearts of dedication;
men and women who have cool heads and willing hands of practical
purpose as well. They will insist that every agency of popular government use effective instruments to carry out their will.

Government is competent when all who compose it work as trust-
ees for the whole people. It can make constant progress when it
keeps abreast of all the facts. It can obtain justified support and legiti-
mate criticism when the people receive true information of all that
government does.

If I know aught of the will of our people, they will demand that
these conditions of effective government shall be created and maintained. They will demand a nation uncorrupted by cancers of injustice
and, therefore, strong among the nations in its example of the will
to peace.

Today we reconsecrate our country to long-cherished ideals in a
suddenly changed civilization. In every land there are always at work
forces that drive men apart and forces that draw men together. In our

personal ambitions we are individualists. But in our seeking for economic and political progress as a nation, we all go up, or else we all go down, as one people.

To maintain a democracy of effort requires a vast amount of patience in dealing with differing methods, a vast amount of humility. But out of the confusion of many voices rises an understanding of dominant public need. Then political leadership can voice common ideals, and aid in their realization.

The Great Unfinished Work
of Our Society

~ LYNDON B. JOHNSON

We are citizens of the richest and most fortunate nation in the history of the world.

One hundred and eighty years ago we were a small country struggling for survival on the margin of a hostile land.

Today we have established a civilization of free men which spans an entire continent.

With the growth of our country has come opportunity for our people—opportunity to educate our children, to use our energies in productive work, to increase our leisure—opportunity for almost every American to hope that through work and talent he could create a better life for himself and his family.

The path forward has not been an easy one.

But we have never lost sight of our goal: an America in which every citizen shares all the opportunities of his society, in which every man has a chance to advance his welfare to the limit of his capacities.

We have come a long way toward this goal.

We still have a long way to go.

The distance which remains is the measure of the great unfinished work of our society.

To finish that work I have called for a national war on poverty. Our objective: total victory.

There are millions of Americans—one fifth of our people—who

FROM President Johnson's Message on Poverty (March 16, 1964).

have not shared in the abundance which has been granted to most of us, and on whom the gates of opportunity have been closed.

What does this poverty mean to those who endure it?

It means a daily struggle to secure the necessities for even a meager existence. It means that the abundance, the comforts, the opportunities they see all around them are beyond their grasp.

Worst of all, it means hopelessness for the young.

The young man or woman who grows up without a decent education, in a broken home, in a hostile and squalid environment, in ill health or in the face of racial injustice—that young man or woman is often trapped in a life of poverty.

He does not have the skills demanded by a complex society. He does not know how to acquire those skills. He faces a mounting sense of despair which drains initiative and ambition and energy.

Our tax cut will create millions of new jobs—new exits from poverty.

But we must also strike down all the barriers which keep many from using those exits.

The war on poverty is not a struggle simply to support people, to make them dependent on the generosity of others.

It is a struggle to give people a chance.

It is an effort to allow them to develop and use their capacities, as we have been allowed to develop and use ours, so that they can share, as others share, in the promise of this nation.

We do this, first of all, because it is right that we should.

From the establishment of public education and land grant colleges through agricultural extension and encouragement to industry, we have pursued the goal of a nation with full and increasing opportunities for all its citizens.

The war on poverty is a further step in that pursuit.

We do it also because helping some will increase the prosperity of all.

Our fight against poverty will be an investment in the most valuable of our resources—the skills and strength of our people.

And in the future, as in the past, this investment will return its cost many fold to our entire economy.

If we can raise the annual earnings of 10 million among the poor by only $1,000 we will have added 14 billion dollars a year to our national output. In addition we can make important reductions in public assistance payments which now cost us 4 billion dollars a year, and in the large costs of fighting crime and delinquency, disease and hunger.

This is only part of the story.

Our history has proved that each time we broaden the base of abundance, giving more people the chance to produce and consume, we create new industry, higher production, increased earnings and better income for all.

Giving new opportunity to those who have little will enrich the lives of all the rest.

Because it is right, because it is wise, and because, for the first time in our history, it is possible to conquer poverty, I submit, for the consideration of the Congress and the country, the Economic Opportunity Act of 1964.

An Official Definition of Poverty

MOLLIE ORSHANSKY

When the Council of Economic Advisors used annual income of less than $3,000 to define families living in poverty, it noted that this was a crude and approximate measure. Obviously the amount of cash income required to maintain any given level of living will be different for the family of two and the family of eight, for the person living in a large metropolitan area and a person of the same age and sex living on a farm.

There is not, and indeed in a rapidly changing pluralistic society there cannot be, one standard universally accepted and uniformly applicable by which it can be decided who is poor. Almost inevitably a single criterion applied across the board must either leave out of the count some who should be there or include some who, all things considered, ought not be classed as indigent. There can be, however, agreement on some of the considerations to be taken into account in arriving at a standard. And if it is not possible to state unequivocally "how much is enough," it should be possible to assert with confidence how much, on an average, is too little. Whatever the level at which we peg the concept of "too little," the measure of income used should

FROM Mollie Orshansky, Division of Research and Statistics, Social Security Administration, "Counting the Poor: Another Look at the Poverty Profile," *Social Security Bulletin* (January 1965), pp. 3–13.

reflect at least roughly an equivalent level of living for individuals and families of different size and composition.

In such terms, it is the purpose of this paper to sketch a profile of poverty based on a particular income standard that makes allowance for the different needs of families with varying numbers of adults and children to support. It recognizes, too, that a family on a farm normally is able to manage on somewhat less cash income than a family living in a city. As an example, a family of father, mother, two young children, and no other relatives is assumed on the average to need a minimum of $1,860 today if living on a farm and $3,100 elsewhere. It should go without saying that, although such cutoff points have their place when the economic well-being of the population at large is being assessed, they do not necessarily apply with equal validity to each individual family in its own special setting.

The standard itself is admittedly arbitrary, but not unreasonable. It is based essentially on the amount of income remaining after allowance for an adequate diet at minimum cost. . . .

When applied to the Census income distributions the cutoff points are being related to income before income taxes, although they were derived on an after-tax basis. At the economy level the incomes are so low that for most families of more than two persons and for aged unrelated individuals no tax would be required. . . .

Much of the recent discussion of the poor has centered about an ad hoc definition adopted in 1963. Under this definition a family of two persons or more with income of less than $3,000 and one person alone with less than $1,500 were considered poor. . . .

The present analysis pivots about a standard of roughly $3,130 for a family of four persons (all types combined) and $1,540 for an unrelated individual—a level in itself not materially different from the earlier one. The standard assumes in addition that families with fewer than four persons will, on the average, require less and that larger families will need more, despite the fact that in actuality they do not always have incomes to correspond. The resulting count of the poor therefore includes fewer small families and more large ones, many of them with children. Moreover, the preceding standard treats farm and nonfarm families alike, but the one discussed here assumes a lower cash requirement for families receiving some food and housing without direct outlay, as part of a farming operation. Accordingly, farm families, despite their low cash income, have a somewhat smaller representation in the current count of the poor for 1963 than in the earlier statistic.

The gross number of the population counted as poor will reflect, in

Poverty Income Levels by Types of Families, March 1967

Number of family members	Weighted average of incomes at poverty level						Weighted average of incomes at low-income level					
	Nonfarm			Farm			Nonfarm			Farm		
	Total	Male head	Female head	Total	Male head	Female head	Total	Male head	Female head	Total	Male head	Female head
1 member	$1,635	$1,710	$1,595	$1,145	$1,180	$1,110	$1,985	$2,080	$1,930	$1,390	$1,440	$1,340
Head under age 65	1,685	1,760	1,625	1,195	1,230	1,140	2,045	2,140	1,975	1,450	1,495	1,380
Head aged 65 or over	1,565	1,580	1,560	1,095	1,105	1,090	1,890	1,925	1,880	1,330	1,350	1,315
2 members	2,115	2,130	2,055	1,475	1,480	1,400	2,855	2,875	2,735	1,990	2,000	1,870
Head under age 65	2,185	2,200	2,105	1,535	1,540	1,465	2,945	2,970	2,790	2,075	2,080	1,945
Head aged 65 or over	1,970	1,975	1,955	1,380	1,380	1,370	2,665	2,675	2,615	1,870	1,875	1,835
3 members	2,600	2,610	2,515	1,815	1,820	1,725	3,425	3,440	3,330	2,400	2,400	2,325
4 members	3,335	3,335	3,320	2,345	2,345	2,320	4,345	4,355	4,255	3,060	3,060	3,000
5 members	3,930	3,930	3,895	2,755	2,755	2,775	5,080	5,085	4,970	3,565	3,565	3,560
6 members	4,410	4,410	4,395	3,090	3,090	3,075	5,700	5,710	5,600	3,995	4,000	3,920
7 or more members	5,430	5,440	5,310	3,790	3,795	3,760	6,945	6,960	6,780	4,850	4,850	4,815

FROM Mollie Orshansky, "The Shape of Poverty in 1966." *Social Security Bulletin* (March 1968), p. 4.

the main, the level of living used as the basis. In this respect the old definition and the present one are much alike: Twenty-eight and one-half million persons in families would be called poor today because their families have income less than $3,000; 29¾ million persons in families would be poor because their family income is considered too low in relation to the number it must support. What is more telling, however, is the composition of the groups selected, for in considerable measure they are not the same.

To the extent that families differing in composition tend also to differ in income, the power of the poverty line to approximate an equivalent measure of need determines how accurately the selected group reflects the economic well-being of families of different composition. It may be that the consistency of the measure of economic well-being applied to different types of families is even more important than the level itself. . . .

Clearly a profile of the poor that includes large numbers of farm families and aged couples may raise different questions and evoke different answers than when the group is characterized by relatively more young nonfarm families—many of them with several children. Nonwhite families, generally larger than white families, account for about 2 million of the poor units by either definition. Because the total number of families counted among the poor by the economy standard is smaller, however, the nonwhite families make up a larger part of them. . . .

An Alternative Income-oriented Definition

VICTOR R. FUCHS

I propose that we define as poor *any family whose income is less than one-half the median family income*. No special claim is made for the precise figure of one-half; but the advantages of using a poverty standard that changes with the growth of real national income are considerable.

First, it explicitly recognizes that all so-called "minimum" or "sub-

FROM Victor R. Fuchs, National Bureau of Economic Research, "Redefining Poverty and Redistributing Income," *The Public Interest* (Summer 1967), pp. 89–94.

sistence" budgets are based on contemporary standards which will soon be out of date.

Second, it focuses attention on what seems to be a fundamental factor underlying the present concern about poverty—i.e., it represents a tentative groping toward a national policy with respect to the distribution of income.

Finally, it provides a more realistic basis for appraising the success or failure of anti-poverty programs.

TABLE 1

Percentage of U.S. Families Classified Poor
by Changing and Fixed Standards, 1947–65

(in 1965 dollars)

		Percentage of families with income		
Year	*Median income*	*Less than one-half the median*[1]	*Less than $3,000*	*Less than $2,000*
1947	$4,275	18.9	30.0	17.2
1948	4,178	19.1	31.2	18.1
1949	4,116	20.2	32.3	19.5
1950	4,351	20.0	29.9	18.1
1951	4,507	18.9	27.8	16.3
1952	4,625	18.9	26.3	15.8
1953	5,002	19.8	24.6	15.4
1954	4,889	20.9	26.2	16.7
1955	5,223	20.0	23.6	14.6
1956	5,561	19.6	21.5	13.0
1957	5,554	19.7	21.7	13.0
1958	5,543	19.8	21.8	12.8
1959	5,856	20.0	20.6	12.1
1960	5,991	20.3	20.3	12.1
1961	6,054	20.3	20.1	11.9
1962	6,220	19.8	18.9	10.9
1963	6,444	19.9	18.0	10.2
1964	6,676	19.9	17.1	9.2
1965	6,882	20.0	16.5	9.1

[1] Estimated by interpolation.

Source: U.S. Bureau of the Census, *Current Population Reports* Series P-60, No. 51, "Income in 1965 of Families and Persons in the United States," January, 1967.

These points will be developed below. Table 1, which shows the percentage of families classified as poor under various definitions, provides a useful statistical background. We see that the fraction of families with less than half the median income has remained constant —at about 20 percent—throughout the postwar period. The highest level ever reached was 20.9 percent in the recession year of 1954; the lowest was 18.9 in 1947, and in the Korean War years 1951 and 1952. Throughout the period there is no evidence of either an upward or downward trend.

The constancy of poverty so defined contrasts sharply with the decline of poverty defined by a fixed standard, as shown in columns 4 and 5. Whether we use $3,000 or $2,000 (in 1965 dollars) as the standard of poverty, we see that the number of poor families has shrunk considerably in the post-war period. The percentage has been cut almost in half, and there is every reason to believe that continued growth of national income would bring about further reductions in the years ahead. The record on this point is unmistakable. In those years when the nation's median income rose rapidly, there were substantial decreases in the percentage of families with incomes under $3,000. In those years when the median income declined, the percentage increased.

Provided we cling to a fixed standard, it is not difficult to foresee the virtual elimination of poverty. But standards will move upwards, so long as ours is a progressive society. And column 3 is a sobering reminder that, when poverty is consistently defined in relation to contemporary standards, there has not been any decrease in the entire postwar period.[1]

Ever since poverty has been an object of study and a focus for policy, there have been attempts to set standards to identify the poor. These standards have varied enormously with time and place; the search for a single fixed standard, when the society is getting richer and is changing itself in all sorts of ways, is like the pursuit of a will-o'-the-wisp. A brief look at U.S. poverty now as compared with poverty thirty years ago is instructive. If the current standard of $3,000 had been set back in the 1930s, President Roosevelt's estimate of "one-third of a nation" would have been far off the mark. We do not have accurate data on family income for that period, but it is probable that *close to two-thirds of all American families then had incomes (adjusted for price change) below $3,000*. But the point is that

---

[1] The above picture is based on the total money income of families, including Social Security and unemployment benefits, and public assistance payments. The picture would be modified only slightly if account could be taken of the distribution of non-money benefits—such as subsidized housing and food stamps —to the poor. Medicare and Medicaid will have some impact, but will not alter the basic pattern.

$3,000 in 1933—even $3,000 1967 dollars—was not at all the same as $3,000 in 1967. It was a different world, inhabited by people with different habits, different needs, and different life-styles.

Recent surveys of low income families have reported a high percentage owning television sets, washing machines, telephones, and other consumer goods that would be considered luxuries by most of the world's population—and would have been considered luxuries by most Americans thirty years ago. By the standards that have prevailed over most of history, and still prevail over large areas of the world, there are very few poor in the United States today. Nevertheless, there are millions of American families who, both in their own eyes and in those of others, are poor. As our nation prospers, our judgment as to what constitutes poverty will inevitably change. When we talk about poverty in America, we are talking about families and individuals who have much less income than most of us. When we talk about reducing or eliminating poverty, we are really talking about changing the distribution of income. . . .

There are, to be sure, several questions that can be raised about the proposed definition. First, isn't the figure of one-half the median just as subjective and arbitrary as $3,000? In some ways it is, but there are important differences. It makes no pretense of being objective and therefore is not subject to political manipulation under the guise of "technical budget studies." The selection of the fraction, be it one-half, two-fifths, three-fifths, or some other, would be recognized as a national value judgment and would be arrived at openly through the political process.

A second question arises concerning the use of a single national median for all families. The answer is that in implementing such a measure it would be possible and probably desirable to modify the national standard to take account of family size and composition, place of residence, and other relevant variables. But again, the basic advantages of this approach are unaffected by such modifications.

A third question is whether we need bother with any policy at all—won't the problem of poverty seem less urgent as the median income rises in the years to come, as the consequence of economic growth? The assumption underlying this question is that there are some things that can be identified as "necessities," and that they remain relatively unchanged over time. Recent experience indicates that such an assumption is unwarranted. The median income (in constant dollars) in 1965 was 60 percent higher than in 1947, but there is no evidence that the problem of poverty is regarded as less serious now than twenty years ago. Today's comfort or convenience is yesterday's luxury and tomorrow's necessity. In a dynamic society it could hardly be otherwise. . . .

A Social Indicators Definition

S. M. MILLER, MARTIN REIN,
PAMELA ROBY, AND BERTRAM M. GROSS

. . . Much of the current discussion of poverty is posed in terms of an income line: How many families and individuals are living below this line, adjusted for family size and other conditions? At what rate is this number being reduced? The availability of these figures and the historic view of poverty in terms of pauperism lead to the emphasis on the income figures. But income is only *one* of the dimensions of poverty and inequality today.

In the last third of this century, we need new approaches to the quality of life in every country. We suggest that *a minimum approach by government in any society with significant inequalities must provide for rising minimum levels not only of incomes, assets, and basic services, but also of self-respect and opportunities for social mobility and participation in many forms of decision-making.*

The approach which we suggest broadens the economic perspective from a narrow concern with "income." The starting point is Titmuss' conceptualization of income as the "command over resources over time." This moves us to a growing concern with assets as disguised income and as the source of future income (pensions) and with services as an increasingly important ingredient of a standard of life. But even this expanded perspective fails to measure all the concerns that we have today in dealing with poverty and inequality. The concern is also with the individual's political role, the opportunities for his children, and his self-respect. This broadened view of "the command over resources" requires us to range beyond the economic. Many of the hesitations about "the war on poverty" in the United States have

FROM S. M. Miller, professor of education and sociology, New York University: Martin Rein, associate professor of social work, Bryn Mawr College; Pamela Roby, Russell Sage Foundation; and Bertram M. Gross, professor of political science, Syracuse University, "Poverty, Inequality, and Conflict," *The Annals of The American Academy of Political and Social Science* (September 1967), pp. 18–52.

occurred because it has been viewed through an exceedingly narrow income lens. Poverty is not only a condition of economic insufficiency; it is also social and political exclusion. . . .

Current income is an inadequate indicator of the economic position of a family. First, it does not provide an adequate basis for comparing poor and nonpoor groups, since some of the income of the nonpoor is received in ways (for example, capital gains) purposely designated to appear as nonincome in order to reduce taxation. Second, current income inadequately reflects the future command over resources. Savings and pension accumulations are important in the future picture. Further, they affect present satisfactions by providing confidence about the future. Third, past expenditures affect present well-being, as in the case of household furnishings. Fourth, income does not always adequately reflect the character of housing. Fifth, the aged with low incomes (and others temporarily with low income) may have nonpoverty levels of living because of the use of their accumulated assets. . . .

Income and assets are important components of the command over resources, but they do not include the increasingly important area of services. These services include education and training, health, neighborhood amenities, protection, social services, and transportation. In the high-income society, services compose a high and increasing proportion of expenditures and furnish important segments of total satisfaction and well-being.

The connection between family income and basic services is close but incomplete. . . .

Education is increasingly the route to social mobility in our credential-oriented society. Educational sophistication is also protection against bureaucratic manipulation. It is an aid in learning how to get services. And, for Negroes in particular, it is a barrier to offhand humiliating treatment, especially by police.

. . . Does not improvement in family income *automatically* result in improvement in social mobility chances? The data . . . do not support this conclusion. The education of a family, in most situations, is more important than the income of the family in affecting how far the youth goes in school. Furthermore, two families of the same income obviously fare quite differently in other respects if the offspring of one have a much better chance of higher education and resulting better job prospects than the other. To some extent, then, social mobility is a dimension of well-being deserving of separate attention. It is one of most crucial indicators of a socially democratic society. . . .

Why is status important? . . . A gain in income that is stigmatized diminishes the satisfactions of the income-recipients. Further, it may be that a major issue of the poor today is their social exclusion, rather than their income level. Being included in society—which means being accorded respect and accepted in social and political relations with others—is increasingly an important part of the issue of inequality.

Status refers to the views that others hold of an individual. This view affects the way in which individuals are treated—with approval or with disapprobation, with respect or dishonor. The "two nations" of Disraeli and Harrington, the have's and the have-not's, are divided not only by income and hope, but by respect as well. . . .

Discrimination is the most striking case of status barriers. But it is not the main dimension today. The more important dimensions surround the prestige of various groupings in society and the nature of the interactions among groups. Data are lacking on the ways in which low-income groups are rated by others. The most common data available are those on occupational prestige; they uniformly show that the occupations held by the low-income are at the bottom. In 1947 and 1963, janitors, bartenders, sharecroppers, garbage-collectors, streetsweepers, and shoeshiners were ranked among the bottom ten in prestige of ninety occupations in nationwide samples. . . .

The basis for and the way in which one receives income affect the satisfactions derived from income. In American society, income that is not obtained directly or indirectly from work or education (for example, scholarships) is likely to be demeaned. Some 15 per cent of adult units with under $1,000 income received payments in the form of public welfare, accompanied by demeaning means tests.

Transfer payments to upper, unlike lower, income groups generally have the seal of social acceptance. Social security, government payments to farmers, and indirect subsidies in the form of tax deductions, allowances, and exemptions are generally accepted forms of government transfers. Fifty-five per cent of total 1963 government payments to farmers went to the top 11 per cent of all farmers, those with farm sales of $20,000 and over.

Many of the discussions of the reform of the welfare system are concerned with the importance of removing the stigma associated with receiving income in this way. The concern is largely, though not exclusively, with the degradation of the means-test ceremonials. In effect, then, we are in the midst of a *politicalization of status* where the distribution of stigma through the distribution of income and services is being challenged. Stigma is now a political issue; the demand is for mechanisms, like the negative income tax, welfare rights, or family allowances, which reduce the possibilities of families' having low status because of the way that they procure income. (In part, too, . . . the effort is to change the recipients' views of themselves by removing the stigmatizing procedures.) While it would be difficult to construct, an index of income stigma would be a useful indicator in measuring poverty movement.

. . . A very important area is the way that the poor look upon themselves. A significant aspect of satisfactory life is the degree of acceptance of self, the agreeability of self-image, the satisfactions with life. In addition to statistical data of actual inequalities, indicators are needed of individuals' perceptions of inequalities in each dimension of well-being: incomes, assets, basic services, social mobility and education, political position, and status. . . .

In contrast to the "good savage, healthy and free" view of the poor, most measures show that they enjoy life less than do other groups. As one would expect in an industrial, instrumentally oriented society, the available data are largely about job satisfaction and morale. Here, the results are almost all in the same direction: the higher the job level, the greater the degree of job satisfaction: for example, only 16 per cent of unskilled auto workers as compared with over 90 per cent of mathematicians and urban university professors reported that they would try to get into a similar type of work if they could start over again.

According to the findings of Bradburn and Caplovitz' study on happiness, job dissatisfaction is an instance of relative deprivation. Men in a low socioeconomic position in prosperous communities were found more dissatified with their jobs than similar men in depressed communities.

. . . More complex assessments of mental health show that the bottommost class is characterized by more emotional instability than higher-placed groups. . . .

The Bradburn-Caplovitz study of happiness in four medium-size communities demonstrates the importance of many items which are not included in the definitions of an "adequate level of income." Going for a ride in a car as well as eating in a restaurant several times a week and participating in or watching games or sports activities are related to positive feelings. . . .

The fact that many of the poor in the United States would be well off in low-income societies suggests that more is involved in "poverty" than just low levels of the physical conditions of life. The issues of relative deprivation appear to be more important. In that perspective, we must increasingly turn to the indicators of inequality as well as of "poverty," which implies a scientific standard of subsistence. The second half of the twentieth century requires more sensitive instruments than the nineteenth century. . . .

We believe that greater awareness of the extent of inequalities, an awareness which would be deepened by the presentation of the kinds of indicators suggested here, would make possible more useful discussions of inequality: How many differences and what kind are we really willing to live with? . . .

The Poverty Gap

MOLLIE ORSHANSKY

The latest statistics on the aggregate dollar amount by which poor households fell short of their estimated income need are for 1965 when the total poverty roster numbered 31.9 million persons, of whom 14 million were under age 18. At that time the total dollar poverty gap—the aggregate difference between required and actual income—stood at $11 billion. This figure represented an overall reduction of 20 percent since 1959, but now one-fifth of the gap represented unmet need of families with children and headed by a woman, compared with one-sixth then. In contrast, the share of the total gap accounted for by families with children and a man at the head dropped from 37 percent in 1959 to 34 percent in 1965.

It must be remembered that aggregate deficits as computed represent a needs-resources gap, still remaining after payments of public assistance, OASDHI benefits, and any other public programs aiming to help families with insufficient income of their own. Many receive no such help. It has been estimated that only about a fourth of all persons counted poor receive any public assistance, and the proportion of poor households who receive assistance is even less. In 1965, only a fourth of all households whose income for the year was below the poverty line had received any public assistance payments.

FROM Mollie Orshansky, Division of Research and Statistics, Social Security Administration, "The Shape of Poverty in 1966," *Social Security Bulletin* (March 1968), pp. 18–21.

Because, as a rule, women's families have fewer persons than men's families, the income needed for the women's families to stay above poverty is lower. But even allowing for this lesser need the families headed by women had incomes proportionately less in relation to estimated requirements than was true of families headed by a man.

For example, the median income deficit for poor families with children—that is, the difference between the family's actual money income and the minimum amount appropriate for a household of that size and composition—was $1,150 for the families headed by a man and $1,380 where the head was a woman. As a parallel to the fact that the larger the family the more likely it was to be poor, it was also true that irrespective of the sex of the head, the more children in the poor family the greater the dollar gap between the income it had to live on and what it should have had. . . .

Absolute Poverty

CITIZENS' BOARD OF INQUIRY INTO
HUNGER AND MALNUTRITION IN THE
UNITED STATES

In issuing this report, we find ourselves somewhat startled by our own findings, for we too had been lulled into the comforting belief that at least the extremes of privation had been eliminated in the process of becoming the world's wealthiest nation. Even the most concerned, aware, and informed of us were not prepared to take issue with the presumption stated by Michael Harrington on the opening page of his classic, *The Other America:* "to be sure, the other America is not impoverished in the same sense as those poor nations where millions cling to hunger as a defense against starvation. This country has escaped such extremes."

But starting from this premise, we found ourselves compelled to conclude that America has not escaped such extremes. For it became

FROM Citizens' Board of Inquiry into Hunger and Malnutrition in the United States, *Hunger, U.S.A.* (Washington, D.C.: New Community Press, 1968), pp. 8–9.

increasingly difficult, and eventually impossible, to reconcile our pre-conceptions with statements we heard everywhere we went:

- that substantial numbers of new-born, who survive the hazards of birth and live through the first month, die between the second month and their second birthday from causes which can be traced directly and primarily to malnutrition.
- that protein deprivation between the ages of six months and a year and one-half causes permanent and irreversible brain damage to some young infants.
- that nutritional anemia, stemming primarily from protein deficiency and iron deficiency, was commonly found in percentages ranging from 30 to 70 percent among children from poverty backgrounds.
- that teachers report children who come to school without breakfast, who are too hungry to learn, and in such pain that they must be taken home or sent to the school nurse.
- that mother after mother in region after region reported that the cupboard was bare, sometimes at the beginning and throughout the month, sometimes only the last week of the month.
- that doctors personally testified to seeing case after case of premature death, infant deaths, and vulnerability to secondary infection, all of which were attributable to or indicative of malnutrition.
- that in some communities people band together to share the little food they have, living from hand to mouth.
- that the aged living alone, subsist on liquid foods that provide inadequate sustenance.

We also found ourselves surrounded by myths which were all too easy to believe because they are so comforting. We number among these:

MYTH: The really poor and needy have access to adequate surplus commodities and food stamps if they are in danger of starving.

FACT: Only 5.4 million of the more than 29 million poor participate in these two government food programs, and the majority of those participating are not the poorest of the poor.

MYTH: Progress is being made as a result of massive federal efforts in which multimillion dollar food programs take care of more people now than ever before.

FACT: Participation in government food programs has dropped 1.4 million in the last six years. Malnutrition among the poor has risen sharply over the past decade.

MYTH: Hunger and starvation must be restricted to terrible places of need, such as Mississippi, which will not institute programs to take adequate care of its people.

FACT: Mississippi makes more extensive use of the two federal food programs than any state in the United States. . . .

Prior to our efforts, the presumption was against hunger, against malnutrition; now the presumption has shifted. The burden of proof has shifted. It rests with those who would deny the following words of one of our members, "there is sufficient evidence to indict" on the following charges:

1. Hunger and malnutrition exist in this country, affecting millions of our fellow Americans and increasing in severity and extent from year to year.

2. Hunger and malnutrition take their toll in this country in the form of infant deaths, organic brain damage, retarded growth and learning rates, increased vulnerability to disease, withdrawal, apathy, alienation, frustration and violence.

3. There is a shocking absence of knowledge in this country about the extent and severity of malnutrition—a lack of information and action which stands in marked contrast to our recorded knowledge in other countries.

4. Federal efforts aimed at securing adequate nutrition for the needy have failed to reach a significant portion of the poor and to help those it did reach in any substantial and satisfactory degree.

5. The failure of federal efforts to feed the poor cannot be divorced from our nation's agricultural policy, the congressional committees that dictate that policy and the Department of Agriculture that implements it; for hunger and malnutrition in a country of abundance must be seen as consequences of a political and economic system that spends billions to remove food from the market, to limit productions, to retire land from production, to guarantee and sustain profits for the producer. . . .

II

Ideologies of Poverty

The Advantages of Poverty

Poor boys reared directly by their parents possess such advantages over those watched and taught by hired strangers, and exposed to the temptations of wealth and position, that it is not surprising they become the leaders in every branch of human action. They appear upon the stage, athletes trained for the contest, with sinews braced, indomitable wills, resolved to do or die. Such boys always have marched, and always will march, straight to the front and lead the world; they are the epoch-makers. Let one select the three or four foremost names, the supremely great in every field of human triumph, and note how small is the contribution of hereditary rank and wealth to the short list of immortals who have lifted and advanced the race. It will, I think, be seen that the possession of these is almost fatal to greatness and goodness, and that the greatest and best of our race have necessarily been nurtured in the bracing school of poverty—the only school capable of producing the supremely great, the genius.

FROM Andrew Carnegie, *The Gospel of Wealth and Other Essays* (1901).

MANY leading social theorists of the past have been sensitive to the existence of poverty. But contact with poverty for them, unlike their counterparts in the contemporary United States, was intimate to their daily lives, even though they sometimes belonged to the upper social strata. Despite their familiarity with poverty, however, what some of these theorists had to say about it was obsolete even in their own times. Other theorists were ahead of their times. It is the task of today's students to winnow these early doctrines to discover what is appropriate for our own day. This section and some selections in other sections present a number of classical statements for the reader to evaluate.

Although our concern is with involuntary poverty, it is important to recognize that virtuous poverty, as conceived by St. Francis, may have become confused with involuntary poverty as a virtue, as in the later conceptualization of Carnegie. This insidious conversion, no doubt abhorrent to the followers of St. Francis, has in recent centuries been given powerful intellectual support by the subsistence doctrine, or "iron law," of real wages. According to this view, eminently represented by Malthus, only the need for the bare necessities of life induced the laboring poor to produce luxuries—indeed, to work at all. Laborers were considered a subhuman species that would work only if driven by what Howells called the "dread of want." Fortified by the Malthusian population postulate that poverty stimulated high birth rates and the spurious psychology that laborers had an innately high propensity toward indolence, the classical subsistence doctrine implied that all productive effort exerted by the working classes was the result of workers' being forced to overcome their laziness by the need to maintain a bare level of subsistence. If laborers as a class rose above this level, indolence would reign supreme. Furthermore, the provision for subsistence living through public policy such as poor laws or even through private charity would, by destroying the fear of want, destroy the incentive to work.

The poor "deserved what they got," according to this traditional perspective, because of their own individual deficiencies, which, in all likelihood, stemmed from the individual's *innate* defects. Such individuals were *inherently* unfit, perhaps even unfit to survive, as the Social Darwinist put it. On the less dismal side of this Horatio Alger coin were, of course, the fit, whose material achievements provided sufficient proof of fitness.

The ruggedly individualistic presuppositions of the doctrine did contain a germ of truth—just enough to establish the dominance of the spuriously valid doctrine of laissez faire and the concomitant principle that society was not responsible for human deprivation. The poor were expected to help themselves, and the private charity of the conscience-stricken well-to-do was tolerated only as a last resort. In this orthodox view, the poor laws in any form were an infamous concoction of the devil because they invoked the concept of social responsibility for the poor and deprived, the ill and incapacitated, the unemployed and destitute.

Perhaps the greatest deficiency on the part of the poor, according to the traditional view, was their presumed irrational propensity to proliferate. Indeed, this population "principle" guaranteed poverty for the masses. Endowed with the sanctity of a natural law, the principle asserted that poverty bred irrational proliferation (see footnote 1 on page 34), which assured the elimination of temporary material gains until the long-run equilibrium of a misery-level subsistence was again reestablished. Malthus' *First Essay,* written in response to Godwin's equalitarian views and to the threat to the Establishment by the French Revolution, offered no hope for these poor, "irrational animals." As the threat dimmed, Malthus introduced the softer notion of the "preventive check" in later editions of his population essay.

By contrast, John Stuart Mill, penetrating genius that he was, advocated that for an entire generation the state should arrange for the laboring classes to have a taste of higher levels of living. Mill sensed what we now more strongly hold: that rising living levels provide incentives to reduce the average family size among the wage-earning classes. This is why the germ of truth in Malthusianism applies today mainly in the "vicious circle" cultures of the depressed areas and the less developed regions.[1] More will be said about patterns of population growth later, but it is important to note here that the population argument was a cornerstone in the traditional doctrine of inevitable mass poverty. There are, of course, inconsistencies in the value system of this doctrine, such as the belief that poverty is both a virtue and a vice.

Nonetheless, the principles of this doctrine became so deeply rooted—at least in the culture of the North Atlantic world—that they still represent the dominant orthodoxy of the twentieth century. The frighteningly large percentage of "lack of effort" responses in the Gallup Poll and the results of Lane's scholarly survey undoubtedly express important vestiges of this traditional credo. This section gives

---

[1] Perhaps we should note that the emergence of affluent pockets in modern suburbia may have introduced another social law of large families, for indeed it is here that the large-sized average family is a new object of population study today.

the reader a chance to consider some of the classic projections of the eighteenth and nineteenth centuries—projections that remain part of the often subconscious attitudes of many Americans today.

Contemporary reformers, on the other hand, share with the socialists the notion that poverty is primarily an institutionally generated phenomenon calling for a social approach to its eradication. The social-reform approach differs from the socialist, of course, in its acceptance of existing institutional arrangements. In the United States today it is extremely doubtful that a massive antipoverty program would be a political threat to the established order.

Poverty itself may have represented such a threat early in the Great Depression of the 1930s, as many of the more frightened New Dealers believed. The extent to which today's poverty threatens the existing order will be examined in a later section, but we would argue that our society's present commitment to develop and expand our public and private antipoverty programs comes as much from humanism as from fear.

Overpopulation and the Distress
of the Lower Classes

THOMAS R. MALTHUS

The principal object of the present essay is to examine the effects of one great cause intimately united with the very nature of man; which, though it has been constantly and powerfully operating since the commencement of society, has been little noticed by the writers who have treated this subject. The facts which establish the existence of this cause have, indeed, been repeatedly stated and acknowledged; but its natural and necessary effects have been almost totally overlooked; though probably among these effects may be reckoned a very considerable portion of that vice and misery, and of that unequal distribution of the bounties of nature, which it has been the unceasing object of the enlightened philanthropist in all ages to correct.

FROM Thomas R. Malthus, English economist, population theorist, and utilitarian moralist, *An Essay on the Principle of Population* (New York: E. P. Dutton, Everyman's Library, 1914; first published 1798), pp. 5–16.

The cause to which I allude is the constant tendency in all animated life to increase beyond the nourishment prepared for it. . . .

It may safely be pronounced . . . that population, when unchecked, goes on doubling itself every twenty-five years, or increases in a geometrical ratio.

The rate according to which the productions of the earth may be supposed to increase, it will not be so easy to determine. Of this, however, we may be perfectly certain, that the ratio of their increase in a limited territory must be of a totally different nature from the ratio of the increase of population. A thousand millions are just as easily doubled every twenty-five years by the power of population as a thousand. But the food to support the increase from the greater number will by no means be obtained with the same facility. Man is necessarily confined in room. When acre has been added to acre till all the fertile land is occupied, the yearly increase of food must depend upon the melioration of the land already in possession. This is a fund, which, from the nature of all soils, instead of increasing, must be gradually diminishing. But population, could it be supplied with food, would go on with unexhausted vigour; and the increase of one period would furnish the power of a greater increase the next, and this without any limit. . . .

The ultimate check to population appears then to be a want of food, arising necessarily from the different ratios according to which population and food increase. But this ultimate check is never the immediate check, except in cases of actual famine.

The immediate check may be stated to consist in all those customs, and all those diseases, which seem to be generated by a scarcity of the means of subsistence; and all those causes, independent of this scarcity, whether of a moral or physical nature, which tend prematurely to weaken and destroy the human frame.

These checks to population, which are constantly operating with more or less force in every society, and keep down the number to the level of the means of subsistence, may be classed under two general heads—the preventive and the positive checks.

The preventive check, as far as it is voluntary, is peculiar to man, and arises from that distinctive superiority in his reasoning faculties which enables him to calculate distant consequences. The checks to the indefinite increase of plants and irrational animals are all either positive, or, if preventive, involuntary. But man cannot look around him and see the distress which frequently presses upon those who have large families; he cannot contemplate his present possessions or earnings, which he now nearly consumes himself, and calculate the amount of each share, when with very little addition they must be divided, perhaps, among seven or eight, without feeling a doubt whether, if he follow the bent of his inclinations, he may be able to support the offspring which he will probably bring into the world. . . .

These considerations are calculated to prevent, and certainly do prevent, a great number of persons in all civilised nations from pursuing the dictate of nature in an early attachment to one woman. . . .

The positive checks to population are extremely various, and include every cause, whether arising from vice or misery, which in any degree contributes to shorten the natural duration of human life. Under this head, therefore, may be enumerated all unwholesome occupations, severe labour and exposure to the seasons, extreme poverty, bad nursing of children, great towns, excesses of all kinds, the whole train of common diseases and epidemics, wars, plague, and famine. . . .

In every country some of these checks are, with more or less force, in constant operation; yet, notwithstanding their general prevalence, there are few states in which there is not a constant effort in the population to increase beyond the means of subsistence. This constant effort as constantly tends to subject the lower classes of society to distress, and to prevent any great permanent melioration of their condition.

These effects, in the present state of society, seem to be produced in the following manner. We will suppose the means of subsistence in any country just equal to the easy support of its inhabitants. The constant effort towards population, which is found to act even in the most vicious societies, increases the number of people before the means of subsistence are increased. The food, therefore, which before supported eleven millions, must now be divided among eleven millions and a half. The poor consequently must live much worse, and many of them be reduced to severe distress. The number of labourers also being above the proportion of work in the market, the price of labour must tend to fall, while the price of provisions would at the same time tend to rise. The labourer therefore must do more work to earn the same as he did before. During this season of distress, the discouragements to marriage and the difficulty of rearing a family are so great that the progress of population is retarded. In the meantime, the cheapness of labour, the plenty of labourers, and the necessity of an increased industry among them, encourage cultivators to employ more labour upon their land, to turn up fresh soil, and to manure and improve more completely what is already in tillage, till ultimately the means of subsistence may become in the same proportion to the population as at the period from which we set out. The situation of the labourer being then again tolerably comfortable, the restraints to population are in some degree loosened; and, after a short period, the same retrograde and progressive movements, with respect to happiness, are repeated.

Exploitation and the Accumulation of Misery

KARL MARX

The relative surplus-population exists in every possible form. Every labourer belongs to it during the time when he is only partially employed or wholly unemployed. Not taking into account the great periodically recurring forms that the changing phases of the industrial cycle impress on it, now an acute form during the crisis, then again a chronic form during dull times—it has always three forms, the floating, the latent, the stagnant.

In the centres of modern industry—factories, manufactures, ironworks, mines, &c.—the labourers are sometimes repelled, sometimes attracted again in greater masses, the number of those employed increasing on the whole, although in a constantly decreasing proportion to the scale of production. Here the surplus-population exists in the floating form. . . .

The consumption of labour-power by capital is, besides, so rapid that the labourer, half-way through his life, has already more or less completely lived himself out. He falls into the ranks of the supernumeraries, or is thrust down from a higher to a lower step in the scale. It is precisely among the workpeople of modern industry that we meet with the shortest duration of life. Dr. Lee, Medical Officer of Health for Manchester, stated "that the average age at death of the Manchester . . . upper middle class was 38 years, while the average age at death of the labouring class was 17; while at Liverpool those figures were represented as 35 against 15. It thus appeared that

FROM Karl Marx, social philosopher, revolutionary leader, and founder of "scientific" socialism, *Capital,* Vol. 1 (Moscow: Foreign Languages Publishing House, 1959; first published 1867), pp. 640–45.

the well-to-do classes had a lease of life which was more than double the value of that which fell to the lot of the less favoured citizens." In order to conform to these circumstances, the absolute increase of this section of the proletariat must take place under conditions that shall swell their numbers, although the individual elements are used up rapidly. Hence, rapid renewal of the generations of labourers (this law does not hold for the other classes of the population). This social need is met by early marriages, a necessary consequence of the conditions in which the labourers of modern industry live, and by the premium that the exploitation of children sets on their production. . . .

The third category of the relative surplus-population, the stagnant, forms a part of the active labour army, but with extremely irregular employment. Hence it furnishes to capital an inexhaustible reservoir of disposable labour-power. Its conditions of life sink below the average normal level of the working-class; this makes it at once the broad basis of special branches of capitalist exploitation. It is characterised by maximum of working-time, and minimum of wages. We have learnt to know its chief form under the rubric of "domestic industry." It recruits itself constantly from the supernumerary forces of modern industry and agriculture, and specially from those decaying branches of industry where handicraft is yielding to manufacture, manfacture to machinery. Its extent grows, as with the extent and energy of accumulation, the creation of a surplus-population advances. But it forms at the same time a self-reproducing and self-perpetuating element of the working-class, taking a proportionally greater part in the general increase of that class than the other elements. In fact, not only the number of births and deaths, but the absolute size of the families stand in inverse proportion to the height of wages, and therefore to the amount of means of subsistence of which the different categories of labourers dispose. This law of capitalistic society would sound absurd to savages, or even civilised colonists. It calls to mind the boundless reproduction of animals individually weak and constantly hunted down.[1]

The lowest sediment of the relative surplus-population finally dwells in the sphere of pauperism. Exclusive of vagabonds, criminals, prosti-

---

[1] "Poverty seems favourable to generation." (A. Smith.) This is even a specially wise arrangement of God, according to the gallant and witty Abbé Galiani. "Iddio af che gli uomini che esercitano mestieri di prima utilità nascono abbondantemente." (Galiani, 1. c., p. 78.) "Misery up to the extreme point of famine and pestilence, instead of checking, tends to increase population." (S. Laing, "National Distress," 1844, p. 69.) After Laing has illustrated this by statistics, he continues: "If the people were all in easy circumstances, the world would soon be depopulated."

tutes, in a word, the "dangerous" classes, this layer of society consists of three categories. First, those able to work. One need only glance superficially at the statistics of English pauperism to find that the quantity of paupers increases with every crisis, and diminishes with every revival of trade. Second, orphans and pauper children. These are candidates for the industrial reserve army, and are, in times of great prosperity, as 1860, *e.g.,* speedily and in large numbers enrolled in the active army of labourers. Third, the demoralised and ragged and those unable to work, chiefly people who succumb to their incapacity for adaptation, due to the division of labour; people who have passed the normal age of the labourer; the victims of industry, whose number increases with the increase of dangerous machinery, of mines, chemical works, &c., the mutilated, the sickly, the widows, &c. Pauperism is the hospital of the active labour-army and the dead weight of the industrial reserve army. Its production is included in that of the relative surplus-population, its necessity in theirs; along with the surplus-population, pauperism forms a condition of capitalist production, and of the capitalist development of wealth. It enters into the *faux frais* of capitalist production; but capital knows how to throw these, for the most part, from its own shoulders on to those of the working-class and the lower middle class.

The greater the social wealth, the functioning capital, the extent and energy of its growth, and, therefore, also the absolute mass of the proletariat and the productiveness of its labour, the greater is the industrial reserve army. The same causes which develop the expansive power of capital, develop also the labour-power at its disposal. The relative mass of the industrial reserve army increases therefore with the potential energy of wealth. But the greater this reserve army in proportion to the active labour-army, the greater is the mass of a consolidated surplus-population, whose misery is in inverse ratio to its torment of labour. The more extensive, finally, the lazarus-layers of the working-class, and the industrial reserve army, the greater is official pauperism. *This is the absolute general law of capitalist accumulation. . . .*

Within the capitalist system all methods for raising the social productiveness of labour are brought about at the cost of the individual labourer; all means for the development of production transform themselves into means of domination over, and exploitation of, the producers; they mutilate the labourer into a fragment of a man, degrade him to the level of an appendage of a machine, destroy every remnant of charm in his work and turn it into a hated toil; they estrange from him the intellectual potentialities of the labour-process in the same proportion as science is incorporated in it as an independent power; they distort the conditions under which he works, subject him during the labour-process to a despotism the more hateful for its meanness; they transform his life-time into working-time, and drag his wife and child beneath the wheels of the Juggernaut of capital. But all methods for the production of surplus-value are at the same time methods of accumulation; and every extension of accumulation becomes again a means for the development of those methods. It follows therefore that in proportion as capital accumulates, the lot of the labourer, be his payment high or low, must grow worse. The law, finally, that always equilibrates the relative surplus-population, or industrial reserve army, to the extent and energy of accumulation, this law rivets the labourer to capital more firmly than the wedges of Vulcan did Prometheus to the rock. It establishes an accumulation of misery, corresponding with accumulation of capital. Accumulation of wealth at one pole is, therefore, at the same time accumulation of misery, agony of toil, slavery, ignorance, brutality, mental degradation, at the opposite pole, *i.e.,* on the sides of the class that produces its own product in the form of capital.

Poverty Purifies Society

HERBERT SPENCER

The well-being of existing humanity, and the unfolding of it into this ultimate perfection, are both secured by that same beneficent, though severe discipline, to which the animate creation at large is subject: a discipline which is pitiless in the working out of good: a felicity-pursuing law which never swerves for the avoidance of partial and temporary suffering. The poverty of the incapable, the distresses that come upon the imprudent, the starvation of the idle, and those shoulderings aside of the weak by the strong, which leave so many "in shallows and in miseries," are the decrees of a large, far-seeing benevolence. It seems hard that an unskilfulness which with all his efforts he cannot overcome, should entail hunger upon the artisan. It seems hard that a labourer incapacitated by sickness

FROM Herbert Spencer, English social philosopher, *Social Statics* (New York: D. Appleton and Company, 1880; first published 1850), pp. 353–56.

from competing with his stronger fellows, should have to bear the resulting privations. It seems hard that widows and orphans should be left to struggle for life or death. Nevertheless, when regarded not separately, but in connection with the interests of universal humanity, these harsh fatalities are seen to be full of the highest beneficence—the same beneficence which brings to early graves the children of diseased parents, and singles out the low-spirited, the intemperate, and the debilitated as the victims of an epidemic.

There are many very amiable people—people over whom in so far as their feelings are concerned we may fitly rejoice—who have not the nerve to look this matter fairly in the face. Disabled as they are by their sympathies with present suffering, from duly regarding ultimate consequences, they pursue a course which is very injudicious, and in the end even cruel. We do not consider it true kindness in a mother to gratify her child with sweetmeats that are certain to make it ill. We should think it a very foolish sort of benevolence which led a surgeon to let his patient's disease progress to a fatal issue, rather than inflict pain by an operation. Similarly, we must call those spurious philanthropists, who, to prevent present misery, would entail greater misery upon future generations. All defenders of a poor-law must, however, be classed amongst such. That rigorous necessity which, when allowed to act on them, becomes so sharp a spur to the lazy, and so strong a bridle to the random, these paupers' friends would repeal, because of the wailings it here and there produces. Blind to the fact, that under the natural order of things society is constantly excreting its unhealthy, imbecile, slow, vacillating, faithless members, these unthinking, though well-meaning, men advocate an interference which not only stops the purifying process, but even increases the vitiation—absolutely encourages the multiplication of the reckless and incompetent by offering them an unfailing provision, and *dis*courages the multiplication of the competent and provident by heightening the prospective difficulty of maintaining a family. And thus, in their eagerness to prevent the really salutary sufferings that surround us, these sigh-wise and groan-foolish people bequeath to posterity a continually increasing curse.

Returning again to the highest point of view, we find that there is a second and still more injurious mode in which law-enforced charity checks the process of adaptation. To become fit for the social state, man has not only to lose his savageness, but he has to acquire the capacities needful for civilized life. Power of application must be developed; such modification of the intellect as shall qualify it for its new tasks must take place; and, above all, there must be gained the ability to sacrifice a small immediate gratification for a future great one. The state of transition will of course be an unhappy state. Misery inevitably results from incongruity between constitution and conditions. All these evils, which afflict us, and seem to the uninitiated the obvious consequences of this or that removable cause, are unavoidable attendants on the adaptation now in progress. Humanity is being pressed against the inexorable necessities of its new position—is being moulded into harmony with them, and has to bear the resulting unhappiness as best it can. The process *must* be undergone, and the sufferings *must* be endured. No power on earth, no cunningly-devised laws of statesmen, no world-rectifying schemes of the humane, no communist panaceas, no reforms that men ever did broach or ever will broach, can diminish them one jot. Intensified they may be, and are; and in preventing their intensification, the philanthropic will find ample scope for exertion. But there is bound up with the change a *normal* amount of suffering, which cannot be lessened without altering the very laws of life. Every attempt at mitigation of this eventuates in exacerbation of it. All that a poor-law, or any kindred institution can do, is to partially suspend the transition—to take off for awhile, from certain members of society, the painful pressure which is effecting their transformation. At best this is merely to postpone what must ultimately be borne. But it is more than this: it is to undo what has already been done. For the circumstances to which adaptation is taking place cannot be superseded without causing a retrogression—a partial loss of the adaptation previously effected; and as the whole process must some time or other be passed through, the lost ground must be gone over again, and the attendant pain borne afresh. Thus, besides retarding adaptation, a poor-law adds to the distresses inevitably attending it.

Survival of the Fittest

WILLIAM GRAHAM SUMNER

Many of them [the economists] seem to be terrified to find that distress and misery still remain on earth and promise to remain as long as the vices of human nature remain. Many of them are frightened at liberty, especially under the form of competition, which they elevate into a bugbear. They think that it bears harshly on the weak. They do not perceive that here "the strong" and "the weak" are terms which admit of no definition unless they are made equivalent to the industrious and the idle, the frugal and the extravagant. They do not perceive, furthermore, that if we do not like the survival of the fittest, we have only one possible alternative, and that is the survival of the unfittest. The former is the law of civilization; the latter is the law of anticivilization. We have our choice between the two, or we can go on, as in the past, vacillating between the two, but a third plan—the socialist desideratum—a plan for nourishing the unfittest and yet advancing in civilization, no man will ever find.

FROM William Graham Sumner, professor of political and social science, Yale University, "The Influence of Commercial Crisis on Opinions About Economic Doctrines," address before The Free Trade Club, New York City, May 15, 1879, in *Essays of William Graham Sumner,* ed. A. G. Keller and M. R. Davie, Vol. 2 (New Haven: Yale University Press, 1934), p. 56.

Survival of the Unfittest

THOMAS H. HUXLEY

It strikes me that men who are accustomed to contemplate the active or passive extirpation of the weak, the unfortunate, and the superfluous; who justify that conduct on the ground that it has the sanction of the cosmic process, and is the only way of ensuring the

FROM Thomas H. Huxley, English biologist and proponent of the theory of evolution, *Evolution and Ethics and Other Essays* (New York: D. Appleton and Company, 1902; first published 1894), pp. 36–37.

progress of the race; who, if they are consistent, must rank medicine among the black arts and count the physician a mischievous pre-server of the unfit; on whose matrimonial undertakings the principles of the stud have the chief influence; whose whole lives, therefore, are an education in the noble art of suppressing natural affection and sympathy, are not likely to have any large stock of these commodi-ties left. But, without them, there is no conscience, nor any restraint on the conduct of men, except the calculation of self-interest, the balancing of certain present gratifications against doubtful future pains; and experience tells us how much that is worth.

Caring for the Unfit:
The Poor Law

JOHN STUART MILL

It would be possible for the state to guarantee employment at ample wages to all who are born. But if it does this, it is bound in self-protection, and for the sake of every purpose for which govern-ment exists, to provide that no person shall be born without its consent. If the ordinary and spontaneous motives to self-restraint are removed, others must be substituted. Restrictions on marriage, at least equivalent to those existing [1848] in some of the German states, or severe penalties on those who have children when unable to support them, would then be indispensable. Society can feed the necessitous, if it takes their multiplication under its control: or (if destitute of all moral feelings for the wretched offspring) it can leave the last to their discretion, abandoning the first to their own care. But it cannot with impunity take the feeding upon itself, and leave the multiplying free.

To give profusely to the people, whether under the name of charity or of employment, without placing them under such influences that prudential motives shall act powerfully upon them, is to lavish the means of benefiting mankind, without attaining the object. Leave the

FROM John Stuart Mill, English social philosopher and economist, *Principles of Political Economy,* John Stuart Mill, ed. W. J. Ashley (London: Longmans, Green and Company, 1909; first published 1848), pp. 365–66.

people in a situation in which their condition manifestly depends upon their numbers, and the greatest permanent benefit may be derived from any sacrifice made to improve the physical well-being of the present generation, and raise, by that means, the habits of their children. But remove the regulation of their wages from their own control; guarantee to them a certain payment, either by law, or by the feeling of the community; and no amount of comfort that you can give them will make either them or their descendants look to their own self-restraint as the proper means of preserving them in that state. You will only make them indignantly claim the continuance of your guarantee to themselves and their full complement of possible posterity.

On these grounds some writers have altogether condemned the English poor-law, and any system of relief to the able-bodied, at least when uncombined with systematic legal precautions against over-population. The famous Act of the 43rd of Elizabeth undertook, on the part of the public, to provide work and wages for all the destitute able-bodied: and there is little doubt that if the intent of that Act had been fully carried out, and no means had been adopted by the administrators of relief to neutralize its natural tendencies, the poor-rate would by this time have absorbed the whole net produce of the land and labour of the country. It is not at all surprising, therefore, that Mr. Malthus and others should at first have concluded against all poor laws whatever. It required much experience, and careful examination of different modes of poor-law management, to give assurance that the admission of an absolute right to be supported at the cost of other people, could exist in law and in fact, without fatally relaxing the springs of industry and the restraints of prudence. This, however, was fully substantiated by the investigations of the original Poor Law Commissioners. Hostile as they are unjustly accused of being to the principle of legal relief, they are the first who fully proved the compatibility of any Poor Law, in which a right to relief was recognised, with the permanent interests of the labouring class and of posterity. By a collection of facts, experimentally ascertained in parishes scattered throughout England, it was shown that the guarantee of support could be freed from its injurious effects upon the minds and habits of the people, if the relief, though ample in respect to necessaries, was accompanied with conditions which they disliked, consisting of some restraints on their freedom, and the privation of some indulgences. Under this proviso, it may be regarded as irrevocably established, that the fate of no member of the community needs be abandoned to chance; that society can and therefore ought to insure every individual belonging to it against the extreme of want; that the condition even of those who are unable to find their own support, needs not be one of physical suffering, or the dread of it, but only of restricted indulgence, and enforced rigidity of discipline. This is surely something gained for humanity, important in itself, and still more so as a step to something beyond; and humanity has no worse enemies than those who lend themselves, either knowingly or unintentionally, to bring odium on this law, or on the principles in which it originated.

The Lower Classes Deserve
No Better than They Get[1]

ROBERT E. LANE

By and large those in the lower orders are those who are paid daily (not weekly) or are on relief; they live in slums or in public housing projects (but not middle-income projects); they do not live respectable lives; they have only grammar-school education; they may have no regular jobs. Closer to home, those slightly lower in status are people like "the lady next door who has a little less than I have," the man who can't afford to take care of his kids properly in the project, people who spend their money on liquor, the person with less skill in the same line of work.

The rationale for their lower status turns chiefly on two things: their lack of education, and therefore failure to know what they want or failure to understand lifesmanship, and their general indifference. It is particularly this "not caring" that seems so salient in the upper-working-class mind. This is consonant with the general view that success is a triumph of the will and a reflection of ability. Poverty is for lazy people, just as middle status is for struggling people. Thus,

FROM Robert E. Lane, professor of political science, Yale University, *Political Ideology: Why the American Common Man Believes What He Does* (Glencoe, Ill.: Free Press, 1962), pp. 71–72, 330–31.
[1] The specific and general conclusions Lane draws in this selection are based on his intensive study of attitudes toward political, economic, and social issues held by a selected group of adults in an Atlantic seaboard community of 100,000 which Lane has called "Eastport."

Ruggiero, a building maintenance man, accounts for poverty by saying, "There's laziness, you'll always have lazy people." DeAngelo, a
factory operative, sees it this way:

> A guy gets married and, you know, he's not educated too well, he
> doesn't have a good job and he gets a large family and he's in bad
> shape, y'know what I mean. It's tough; he's got to live in a lousy rent
> —he can't afford anything better.

But DeAngelo takes away some of this sympathy the next moment
when he goes on to say:

> But then you get a lot of people who don't want to work; you got
> welfare. People will go on living on that welfare—they're happier than
> hell. Why should they work if the city will support them?

In general, there is little sympathy given to those lower in the scale,
little reference to the overpowering forces of circumstance, only rare
mention of sickness, death of a breadwinner, senility, factories moving out of town, and so forth. The only major cause of poverty to
which no moral blame attaches is depression or "unemployment"—
but this is not considered a strikingly important cause in the minds of
the Eastport men. They are Christian in the sense that they believe
"The poor ye have with you always," but there is no trace of a belief
that the poor are in any way "blessed." . . .

If the Eastport common man is unmoralistic, he is not amoral;
if he thinks more easily in terms of error than of evil, he does not
forget about good and bad; if he is slow to blame, yet he knows what
blame is. He has a moral code that he follows—and applies to the
situations confronting him.

In a lower-middle stratum of the population one can reach upward
and engage the behavior of the ruling classes in a moral grip, or
downward and prick out the violations of the moral code of the un-
respectable, the *outré*, the failures. There is gratification to be had
either way, but Eastport's common man chooses to moralize downward, not upward. He spends more time condemning the failures of
the poor than in condemning the extravagance, the sinful living, the
exploitative behavior of the rich. The poor are under his nose, while
the rich are not; but the activities of the rich are reported, while those
of the poor receive less public notice. (Yet it is true that the misbe-
havior of the stars of the entertainment world attracts a kind of lip-
licking moralistic attention.)

It is the *economic* failure of the poor that occasions comment,
not their loose living or indulgence or self-gratification. This eco-

nomic criticism cannot be made of the rich, for they are successes. On the other hand the rich might be criticized for their shady practices, their exploitation, their monopolistic controls, their conspiracies against the people, their withholding from labor the fruits of its effort, and their deliberate organization of recessions. These things are said, but they are said infrequently—more as explanations than as moral judgments. No, the relief chiseler is morally worse than the price fixer; the person unable to hold a steady job is worse than the landlord who does not fix his broken railings. In general the moral defections of the upper-status groups are more tolerable in Eastport than the moral defections of the poor and lowly.

The relation between morality and success may assume many shapes in men's minds; one of them, greatly feared by Tocqueville, is that men will, upon seeing a successful man, "impute his success mainly to some of his vices." This has the grave consequence that "an odious connection is thus formed between the ideas of turpitude and power, unworthiness and success, utility and dishonor." In spite of the widespread recognition of corruption in government, Eastport does not make this "odious connection"—on the contrary, there is a tendency to believe that men in high places deserve the power and honor and responsibility; otherwise they wouldn't be there. They deserve it, it is true, because of talent, not virtue—but had they been notably unvirtuous they would have been found out. At the other end of the social scale, those who are notably unsuccessful are indeed thought to have failed, in considerable part, because of "playing the ponies," drink, laziness, or shiftlessness. The net consequences of this framework of relationships is a reinforcement of the moral idea; it pays to be good, a premise they follow out in their own lives. Of course, here we speak of the majority; three or four believe, in some degree, that it is otherwise, and have themselves sought to shade the moral code in business dealings where it was too restrictive.

Two Basically Different Views
Held on Causes of Poverty

GEORGE GALLUP

President Johnson's legislative attack on poverty must take account of two basically different views: one, that poverty is primarily due to circumstances beyond an individual's control; the other, that poverty is due to lack of individual effort.

Views on this subject go deep to the roots of the political philosophy of American voters. If you hold the belief that poverty is primarily due to lack of individual effort, you are more likely to be a Republican than a Democrat. If you believe it is due more to circumstances, then you are more likely to be a Democrat than a Republican.

Gallup Poll reporters asked this question of persons across the country:

"In your opinion, which is more often to blame if a person is poor —lack of effort on his own part, or circumstances beyond his control?"

Here are the nationwide findings:

TABLE 1
Cause of Poverty?

Lack of effort	33%
Circumstances	29
Equal	32
No opinion	6

When those who could not make up their mind or could make no choice between the two are excluded, the results are as follows:

TABLE 2
Cause of Poverty?

Lack of effort	54%
Circumstances	46

FROM George Gallup, American Institute of Public Opinion, *Gallup Poll Report* (Spring 1964).

The rather sharp difference between Republicans, Democrats and Independents on this subject of poverty is shown as follows, excluding those who did not make a choice between the alternatives.

TABLE 3
Cause of Poverty?

	Republicans	*Democrats*	*Independents*
Lack of effort	64%	47%	62%
Circumstances	36	53	38

Among those persons with income of $10,000 and over, more blame lack of effort than blame circumstances.

Among those persons with incomes under $3,000, more cite circumstances as the cause of poverty than blame lack of effort.

Those persons with the most education, who perhaps have had better opportunities, tend to cite lack of effort as the major reason for a person being in poverty.

III

The Economics of Poverty

Family on Relief: Puerto Ricans in New York

Antonia Matos is a tall, overweight, 26-year-old with a pretty face, large warm brown eyes, three small children and no husband. She is also a special sort of poverty statistic—an entry on the relief rolls. . . .

The only money that comes into the family's three-room apartment, which is badly in need of paint and floor covering, is a $94 check from the city every 15 days. Life depends on this check, on the monthly free Federal surplus foods and free medical care.

The very existence of Miss Matos and her family, a 7-year-old son and two daughters, rests with her welfare investigator and his little black book—the omnipresent Manual of Policies and Procedures. The book tells the agent in minute detail what an individual's "entitlement" is, depending on age, sex, employment and physical condition.

Exclusive of rent, utilities and a few other recurring items, the official daily budget, which is required by state law, comes to $1 for the mother, 90 cents for the son, 74 cents for the 4-year-old daughter and 66 cents for the baby. These allowances must provide food, clothing, personal care and household supplies. . . .

Each month she gets about 19 packages of food with a retail value of $17.50—eight pounds of meat, two pounds of peanut butter, 10 pounds of flour, five pounds of cheese, four pounds of butter and two pounds of lard. There is also rice, cereal, cornmeal and powdered milk. Next month a pound of powdered eggs will be added.

The investigator arranges for the check-like voucher for these staples. He also arranges for grants for such items as suits, overcoats and overshoes.

When the investigator visits he always checks on the receipts for rent and utilities. Many persons on relief fall behind on gas and electricity payments because the bills come bimonthly and they have failed to save for them.

"I don't owe nobody," Miss Matos said with pride.

FROM Philip Dougherty, "Family on Relief: Study in Poverty," *The New York Times* (April 5, 1964).

IF poverty is primarily a relative term, then as real income per capita rises historically, the distribution of that income among various groups in society becomes relevant in analyzing the status of the poor. Whether the poor receive a greater share of this gradually increasing real income becomes significant not only for them but for society as a whole, because this share is an indicator of the effectiveness of ameliorative policies. We say that poverty exists where people's command over resources (their income plus their assets) is less than that required to provide some socially determined standard of living.

The use of a poverty line concept through time changes the proportion of the population in poverty through the interaction of three factors: the socially determined minimum standard of living or needs, the level of income per capita, and the distribution of income by size. The socially determined minimum is itself an income-per-capita concept, so with a given distribution of income the proportion of the population in poverty over time is determined by a race between the rate of increase in per capita income of the total population and the rate of increase in the income per person at the poverty line.

Assume that the standard of needs does not rise at the same rate as per capita income does, and assume further that the distribution of income is constant over time. If so, the proportion of the population in poverty falls (case 1). That proportion would fall even more if the income distribution became more nearly equal (case 2).

If the standard of minimum needs rose at the same rate as the long-run rise in per capita income, the only way that the proportion of the total households in poverty could fall would be for the distribution of income to become more nearly equal—with respect to the lowest bracket, of course (case 3).[1] Now in fact, the American social consensus has tended to define the "minimum level of living," or the poverty line, at higher and higher levels over time, as the whole society has moved toward higher total output and higher output per capita. But the poverty line has risen at a slower rate than the rate of growth for per capita income.

The question, therefore, is whether this country's historical experience meets the conditions of case 1 or case 2, in both of which the proportion of poor people in society falls. The extent of the fall depends in part upon what has happened to the distribution of income. The following discussions of income patterns through time indicate

---

[1] We ignore for empirical reasons a possible case 4, in which the distribution of income becomes more unequal.

that income distribution in the United States tended to become slightly more even up to World War II, but that this trend has been arrested since 1949–50. Hence we must conclude that since World War II the United States has experienced case 1, a fall in the proportion of all income receivers who are in poverty, and that this decline has been due to a lag in the rising standard of needs in relation to the rise in per capita income. Projections of the population in poverty or near it in the 1970s are only mildly comforting.

The discussion of transfer payments (for example, social insurance, public assistance, employee fringe benefits) by Lampman is vital in understanding why the relative position of the lower income groups has remained fixed. (The share of the lowest quintile has been constant.) Roughly one-half of the income of the poor consists of transfer payments! Lampman estimates that in 1964 the nonpoor lost $30 billion in transfers of income to the poor.

In the selections on the spatial distribution of poverty, some focal aspects of the central city versus the suburbs are presented. These metropolitan contrasts clearly cut across categories of poor versus nonpoor. They throw light on the origins of social upheaval in the central cities and point to the transportation, housing, and other barriers tending to block policies to reduce the growing disparities between the two worlds within our metropolitan centers. The opening vignette on the life of a Puerto Rican family on relief in New York illustrates succinctly the nature of transfer payments and the great difference between middle-class America and the world of the urban poor.

Poverty in rural areas is given recognition in the report of the President's National Advisory Commission on Rural Poverty. The Commission advances the challenging hypothesis that urban riots have their roots partly in rural poverty because of the significant stream of migration from rural areas to the great cities.

There is still a distinct regional bent to the geographic distribution of poverty in the United States, an aspect historically represented in particular by the lower per capita income of the South. Nevertheless, it is clear that a convergence toward the national pattern is occurring; the South's per capita income has for several decades been approaching the national average. Furthermore, the South's rural population, long a source of poverty and backwardness, has been whittled down to the point where its declining numbers will within a decade or two cease to provide masses of new troops for the poor people's army, whether Southern rural or Northern urban. The same trend seems to apply to the South's Negro population. Nevertheless, Ornati shows that there is still a problem; even if the rural and race influences were to become statistically neutralized, the South would retain a disproportionate share of our nation's poor.

Poverty and Income Patterns Through Time

Income and Inequality:
The 1930s to the 1960s

ROBERT J. LAMPMAN

Size distribution data are hard to compare over time because what is comprehended in the key definitions of income, income period, and income-receiving unit changes over time. Careful working and re-working of all available data by numerous scholars have produced a consensus that there was indeed a lessening of inequality in the 1938–1948 period and no clear trend one way or another since 1948. The lessening of inequality seems to be confined to those groups within the top half of the income distribution, with no great change in the income share of, and no change in inequality within, the bottom half. The lowest one-fifth of the consumer units (families and unattached individuals) got 4.1 per cent of the total family personal income in 1935, 5.0 per cent in 1947, and 4.6 per cent in 1962.

Over the period from the prewar to the postwar years, so many

FROM Robert J. Lampman, professor of economics, University of Wisconsin, "Income Distribution and Poverty," *Poverty in America,* Margaret S. Gordon, ed. (San Francisco: Chandler, 1965), pp. 105–06.

variables have been in the picture that one needs to be cautious about any easy generalization on changes in income inequality. For example, size of family moved into closer positive association with level of income (there was a doubling of middle and lower income families, earlier marriage, and a rise in number of children for upper income families), thus suggesting that the decline in inequality is understated by a simple consumer-unit distribution. On the other hand, home-produced services fell in importance and capital gains and expense-account living increased, suggesting that the decline in inequality is overstated.

· . . . There are a few straws in the wind which suggest that 1949–1950 was a turning point toward more economic inequality among persons. These straws include the following:

1. In my study of top wealth-holders, I found that the share of wealth held by the top two per cent of families fell steadily from 1929 to 1949, but then rose between 1949 and 1956. This finding is confirmed and extended by data from the Survey of Consumer Finances which show that, between 1953 and 1962, the share of net worth of the top decile of wealth-holders rose from 58 to 61 per cent, and that of the bottom fifth of income receivers fell from 11 to 7 per cent.

2. The narrowing trend in the Negro-white differential was halted and reversed about 1950, in spite of a continued closing of the education difference between the two groups.

3. There seems to be an increasing association between extremely large families and very low incomes.

4. Fringe benefits won by organized and highly paid workers have not been extended to lower-income workers.

5. Earnings of young men aged 20–24 years were more unequal in distribution in 1961 than they were in 1951 or 1941, according to an unpublished study by Dorothy S. Brady and F. G. Adams. However, this is not reflected in over-all income for the younger age groups as reported by Herman Miller.

6. Increasing numbers of highly educated married women are adding to middle or higher incomes of their husbands.

7. Early retirement of low-income men seems to be increasing.

8. It may be that inequality in the distribution of skill and of educational attainment is increasing.

9. Progressivity of federal, state, and local taxes combined has been decreased.

I would emphasize that these facts and surmises about facts are only straws which have not yet been reflected in income data—and may not be. I would conclude that we have not had and are not currently experiencing an increase in income inequality. . . .

The Demography
of Poverty

COUNCIL OF
ECONOMIC ADVISERS

Poverty is not evenly distributed throughout the population. The aged, nonwhites, and members of households headed by a woman constitute larger fractions of the poor than of the general population. Moreover, the rate of progress in reducing poverty has varied widely among these and other groups. Between 1959 and 1966, the number of poor nonfarm households headed by a man declined 20 percent, while the poor nonfarm households headed by women increased by 2 percent. As a result, households headed by a woman constitute a growing proportion—now nearly half—of all poor households.

The most impressive reductions in poverty have occurred among households headed by a working-age male. The number of such households declined by one-third between 1959 and 1966 as a direct result of the increasing availability of good jobs at high wages. While the number of nonfarm households in this group declined 27 percent, there was a drop of two-thirds in the number of farm households. Among the nonfarm group the decline was as rapid for nonwhites as for whites.

High employment is essential to further reduction of poverty among households with an actual or potential wage earner. Yet many poor men of working age must first receive training or other special assistance to enable them to raise their earnings. For those who cannot

FROM Council of Economic Advisers, *Economic Report of the President, 1968* (Washington, D.C.: U.S. Government Printing Office, 1968), pp. 142–43.

TABLE 1

Number of Poor Households and Incidence of Poverty, 1959 and 1966

Characteristics of head of household	Poor households (millions)[1]		Incidence of poverty (percent)[2]	
	1959	1966	1959	1966
Nonfarm	11.6	10.3	22.5	17.6
White	9.0	7.9	19.6	15.3
Male head	5.0	3.9	13.4	9.4
Under 65 years	3.3	2.4	10.2	6.8
Aged (65 years and over)	1.7	1.5	34.0	24.7
Female head	4.0	4.0	45.2	37.7
Under 65 years	2.2	2.0	37.8	30.5
Aged (65 years and over)	1.8	2.0	59.3	48.9
Nonwhite	2.6	2.4	48.9	37.5
Male head	1.4	1.2	39.7	26.9
Under 65 years	1.2	.9	36.7	23.3
Aged (65 years and over)	.2	.3	64.4	51.4
Female head	1.1	1.2	69.4	60.8
Under 65 years	.9	.9	68.1	58.8
Aged (65 years and over)	.2	.2	76.3	69.9
Farm	1.8	.6	40.9	20.8
White	1.3	.5	34.7	16.9
Nonwhite	.4	.2	85.0	69.7

[1] Households are defined here as the total of families and unrelated individuals.

[2] Poor households as a percent of the total number of households in the category.

Note: Poverty is defined by the Social Security Administration poverty-income standard; it takes into account family size, composition, and place of residence. Poverty-income lines are adjusted to take account of price changes during the period. Detail will not necessarily add to totals because of rounding.

Source: Department of Commerce and Department of Health, Education, and Welfare.

work, or who—despite training and other services—still cannot earn enough to emerge from poverty by their own efforts, adequate income maintenance programs are needed. . . .

Characteristics of Families with Incomes Under $3,000, 1951 and 1960

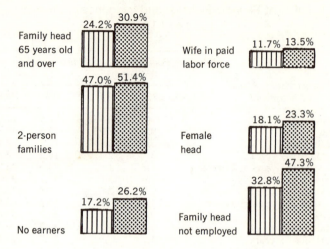

Family head 65 years old and over — 24.2% 30.9%

2-person families — 47.0% 51.4%

No earners — 17.2% 26.2%

Wife in paid labor force — 11.7% 13.5%

Female head — 18.1% 23.3%

Family head not employed — 32.8% 47.3%

Characteristics of Families with Income Under $3,000, 1951 and 1960

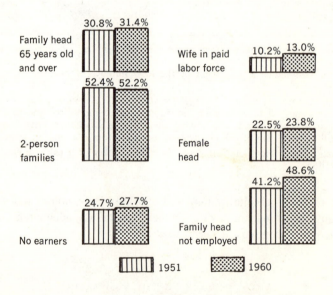

Family head 65 years old and over — 30.8% 31.4%

2-person families — 52.4% 52.2%

No earners — 24.7% 27.7%

Wife in paid labor force — 10.2% 13.0%

Female head — 22.5% 23.8%

Family head not employed — 41.2% 48.6%

1951   1960

FROM Herman P. Miller, *Trends in the Income of Families and Persons in the United States, 1947 to 1960* (Washington, D.C.: U.S. Department of Commerce, Bureau of the Budget, 1963), pp. 3, 14.

Income Distribution Changes
in the 1960s

LESTER C. THUROW

The 1966 median family income was $7,436, but this average masks a wide dispersion. Fourteen percent of American families had less than $3,000; thirty percent had incomes over $10,000. Among unrelated individuals the median income was $2,270. Thirty-seven percent had less than $1,500; four percent had incomes over $10,000. Since 1947 family incomes have risen from $4,401 (1966 dollars). Although incomes have risen, measures of income dispersion indicate no progress to a more egalitarian income distribution since World War II. In 1947 the bottom fifth of the families received five percent of aggregate income; in 1966 the bottom fifth of the families received five percent of aggregate income.

The impact of racial inequality can be seen in the differences between the income distributions for whites and nonwhites. In 1966 the median family income was $7,722 for whites and $4,628 for nonwhites. Nonwhite incomes were 60 percent of white incomes. Although only 12.4 percent of the white families had incomes of less than $3,000, 30.4 percent of the nonwhite families had incomes less than $3,000. At the upper end of the income distribution, 31.6 percent of all white families had incomes above $10,000. Only 12.2 percent of nonwhite families had similar incomes. While there have been cyclical changes in the ratio of nonwhite to white family incomes there have been no discernible secular trends toward closing the gap between white and nonwhite incomes. In terms of their income distribution, the nonwhite population is lagging approximately thirty years behind the white population. This was true in 1947; it is true in 1966.

Although relative measures of income dispersion were constant in the postwar period, they imply widening absolute differences in income. In 1947 the difference between white and nonwhite median

FROM Lester C. Thurow, professor of economics, Harvard University, "The American Income Distribution," *Employment and Manpower Problems in the Cities: Implications of the Report of the National Advisory Commission on Civil Disorders* (Washington, D.C.: Joint Economic Committee, 1968), pp. 143–45.

family incomes was $2,249 (1966 dollars); in 1966 the difference was $3,094. In 1947 the difference between the median family incomes of the lowest fifth of the population and the highest fifth of the population was $8,569 (1966 dollars); in 1966 the difference was $12,083.

Given twenty years of stability in relative measures of income dispersion and twenty years of widening absolute differences, there is no reason to suppose that the nature of the American economy is about to change. The burden of proof is certainly on those that think the income distribution will take care of itself. Unless positive evidence can be found of structural factors that will alter the nature of the American economy, there is no reason to think that our income distribution problems will solve themselves. Without specific government programs to change the income distribution, the present trends will continue.

Poverty as it is now defined will slowly decline. If more realistic long-run poverty definitions such as fifty percent of median incomes are used, there will be no progress in eliminating poverty. The gap between Negro and white incomes will remain constant in relative terms; it will widen in absolute terms.

The Poor's Share of Transfer Income

ROBERT J. LAMPMAN

Since almost $100 billion in money and nonmoney income is moved from hand to hand, how can we explain the fact that there is any poverty left in the United States? Some light is shed on this question by Table 1, which provides estimates of how the "pretransfer poor" —that is, those families with earned incomes lower than poverty-line incomes (where the poverty line is set at $1,500 for a one-person unit, $2,000 for a two-person unit, and with $500 added for each additional person)—share in the distribution of the $97 billion fringe-transfer benefits and of the offsetting $97 billion cost.

Background for these estimates includes the following. The "post-transfer poor" were about 18 percent of the total population in 1964,

FROM Robert J. Lampman, professor of economics, University of Wisconsin, "How Much Does the American System of Transfers Benefit the Poor?" *Economic Progress and Social Welfare,* Leonard H. Goodman, ed. (New York: Columbia University Press, 1966), pp. 130–33.

and the "pretransfer poor" were about 28 percent of the population. The latter group had about 5 percent of the factor income. We have had only a few clues to follow in making the allocations shown in Table 1, and some of them are offered only as rough guesses. For items 3, 8, 9, and 10 we have good evidence from the Bureau of Labor Statistics Consumer Expenditure Survey and from the special survey conducted by Morgan and others at the Survey Research Center, University of Michigan. For items 11 and 12 we have relied upon our own observations. For item 13, education, we are saying that although the pretransfer poor are 28 percent of the total population,

TABLE 1

Estimates of Pretransfer Poor's Share of
Fringes, Transfers, and Taxes, 1964

| | | Shares of pretransfer poor | |
Item	Total (billions of dollars)	Percent	Amount (billions of dollars)
1. Employee fringe benefits	11	10	1.1
2. Factor income due to public purchase for no use	1	10	0.1
3. Direct interfamily gifts	3	50	1.5
4. Philanthropic welfare service	1	50	0.5
5. Philanthropic education	2	20	0.4
6. Philanthropic health care	1	50	0.5
7. Subtotal (1–6)	19	22	4.1
8. Social insurance benefits	28	55	15.4
9. Public assistance benefits	6	93	5.6
10. Veterans benefits	6	46	2.8
11. Other welfare services and public housing	3	50	1.5
12. Health benefits (public)	7	50	3.5
13. Education benefits (public)	28	10	5.1
14. Subtotal (8–13)	78	43	33.9
15. Total (1–14)	97	39	38.0
16. Employee contribution to fringe benefits	5	5	0.3
17. Employer contribution to fringe benefits (net)	5	0	0
18. Private contributions to gifts and philanthropy (net)	6	5	0.3
19. Subtotal (16–18)	16	4	0.6
20. Taxes	81	9	7.5
21. Total (16–20)	97	8	8.1

they get only 18 percent of the benefits of public expenditure for education. This is based on the assumption that the poor get 20 percent of the benefits of expenditure for primary and secondary education and 10 percent of higher education benefits. For taxes (item 20), we have assumed a proportional tax system at a 15 percent rate against total posttransfer money income. That tax rate would raise the $81 billion in taxes, $7.5 billion of which would come from an estimated $50 billion of total money income ($25 billion factor income and $25 billion of money transfers) of the pretransfer poor.

According to these rough estimates the pretransfer poor received $38 billion worth of fringes and transfers, over half of which come to them in the form of social insurance and public assistance. In return, they contributed $8.1 billion in private-public contributions. The pretransfer poor received 39 percent of fringe transfers (22 percent of private and 42 percent of public) and paid 8 percent of the costs. The other side of the coin is that the nonpoor majority received 61 percent of the fringe transfers and paid 92 percent of the cost. These relationships are further set forth in Table 2, which presents the startling estimate that while the pretransfer poor start with only 5 percent of factor income, they end up with 11 percent of factor income plus fringes and transfers net of the transfer costs. In the process, the nonpoor lose, and the poor gain, $30 billion.

TABLE 2

Estimates of Receipt of Income and Payment of Cost of
Transfer for Pretransfer Poor and Nonpoor, 1964

		Pretransfer poor		Nonpoor	
Type	Total (billions of dollars)	Per-cent	Billions of dollars	Per-cent	Billions of dollars
1. Factor income	500	5	25	95	475
2. Fringes and transfers	97	39	38	61	59
3. Private	19	22	4	78	15
4. Public	78	42	34	58	44
5. Money income	47	51	24	55	23
6. In kind	50	28	14	72	36
7. Factor income plus fringe and transfer income	597	10	63	89	534
8. Cost of fringes and transfers	97	8	8	92	89
9. Row 7 less 8	500	11	55	89	445
10. Net transfer (9 less 1)	0	0	30	0	− 30

Poor and Near Poor:
Projections for the 1970s

U.S. DEPARTMENT OF
HEALTH, EDUCATION AND WELFARE

The generally accepted federal government definition of poverty (Social Security Administration indexes) is a formula based on three times the minimum dollars required to feed a family of given size and location (rural-urban). Thirty million people in 1966 fall within the poor category. (By this definition, an urban family of four requires $3,335 to be non-poor). There is another version of this same formula defining a population called "low-income" which adds the "near-poor" and results in a universe of some 45 million persons. An urban family of four requires $4,345 by this index.

Other definitions of poverty are based on minimum consumer expenditures; still others include non-economic criteria. These definitions result in different numbers of poor, slightly different populations, or both. A poverty definition based specifically on health needs embodies still another set of concepts. Neither the Social Security Administration Index nor any others specifically take medical care costs into account. . . .

In developing the Social Security Administration Index, it was assumed that persons at or below the poverty line would have to rely on public or privately provided free care to meet their medical needs —that any outlay for other than the most rudimentary supplies could not be made except at the risk of cutting down on some necessity.

. . . The universe of need is determined by the number of individuals who fall within the Social Security Administration's low income definition (a combination of the "poor" and "near-poor" categories). In view of the general rise in standard of living and the spectacular rise in prices of medical services, the "near-poor" line is a more realistic criterion of need for medical care and perhaps for an overall definition of poverty as well. . . .

Starting with the Census Bureau's *Current Population Survey,* the total "poor" poverty population (as distinct from the "near-poor")

FROM U.S. Department of Health, Education, and Welfare, *Delivery of Health Services for the Poor,* Human Investment Program (December 1967), pp. 7–8.

has been projected forward to 1972 by several sources. . . . Based on a preliminary figure of 32.9 million "poor" in 1965, it was estimated that there would be 28.5 million in 1972 (a drop of about 600,000 per year), and in 1973, 27.9 million "poor." With the poverty total for 1965 now revised down to 31.9 million, and the newly available tally for 1966 down to 29.7 million, it seems more reasonable to assume the number in 1973 would be no greater than 25–26 million if the present stringent definition remained in effect. With continued economic expansion and rising expectations this of course may not be plausible.

The number of total "poor" plus "near-poor" for 1959–1966 parallels the number of "poor," at a difference of about 15 million. In determining the universe of need for this analysis, the number of "poor" plus "near-poor" through 1973 is assumed to be on a parallel line to the projections of the "poor" population alone. The analysts who worked on various "poor" poverty population projections believe this to be a reliable assumption. It is felt that overall income distributions in this country will continue to be fairly constant over the next six or seven years, and the number of "near-poor" escaping poverty will be replenished in about the same numbers as those "poor" graduating to the "near-poor" category plus those coming into the world to live in poverty and those falling from non-poverty to poverty.

Limited data are available on what the "poor" portion of the low income population might look like in the early 1970s. For the total low income population, much depends on the state of the economy, the existence or non-existence of anti-poverty programs, and the effectiveness of present measures. Projections over this relatively short period of time, as far as detailed characteristics are concerned, are difficult and somewhat questionable. However, some generalizations can be made. It is likely that the poverty program emphasis will continue to be in the area of employment, the economy itself is likely to produce more jobs, with the result that a large percentage of the decrease in low income will be for men of working age and their families. But in the absence of new programs, the number of large families (with five or more children) in poverty will decline very slowly, if at all. Assuming no basic changes in attitudes toward non-whites, the disproportionately higher number of non-white poor will continue. Similarly, the demonstration scale anti-poverty educational programs are not expected to result in measurable reduction of poor youth by the early 1970s, but rather the numbers are expected to increase, if for no other reason than that of their projected increased proportion of the total population. The rural poor migration will probably continue, although at a slower pace than during the 1960s. Assuming an increase in Social Security benefits, the total number of elderly poor will certainly be reduced.

Spatial Patterns

The Deterioration of Central Cities

AFL–CIO ECONOMIC POLICY COMMITTEE

The growth of the American population has increased sharply—from several hundred thousand a year in the 1930s to an average yearly rise of 2.7 million since World War II. Moreover, the number of people in rural areas has been declining, while metropolitan area growth has been booming. Each year, the population of America's metropolitan areas grows by over 3 million, the size of a very large city.

Under the impact of the technological revolution in agriculture, employment in farming has dropped—it fell 3.2 million between 1950 and 1966. Hundreds of thousands of farmers, farm workers and their families—several million people—have been leaving the rural areas in search of jobs and homes in the cities.

Many of those who seek their future in the cities are Negroes. Between 1940 and 1967, probably about 4 million Negroes moved from the South—primarily rural areas—to the cities of the North and West. In 1960, according to the Department of Labor, about 40 percent to nearly 50 percent of the Negro population of 10 major northern and western cities was born in the South.

The Department of Labor estimates that almost 1.5 million Negroes left the South in 1950–1960, following a similar migration of

FROM AFL–CIO Economic Policy Committee, "The Urban Crisis: An Analysis, An Answer," *American Federationist* (October 1967), pp. 1–4.

1.6 million Negroes in the wartime decade, 1940–1950. This historic migration is continuing at about that rate in the 1960s.

For the country as a whole, the proportion of Negroes in city populations rose from less than 10 percent in 1940 to over 20 percent in 1965. In most of the large northern and western cities the rise was greater.

All of the new migrants to America's cities of the past quarter of a century—whites and Negroes, Puerto Ricans and Mexican Americans —have faced the difficulties of adjusting to a new and strange environment. But these difficulties have been especially harsh for Negroes.

The Negro migrants to the cities of the past quarter of a century have brought with them a history of slavery, segregation, lack of education and, frequently, poor health, as well as suspicion of government authorities. On coming to the cities of the North and the West, the new migrants have faced the discriminatory practices of those areas, lack of adequate housing and the impact of automation on job opportunities for uneducated, unskilled workers. . . .

The northern and western cities are suffering, in part, from the social ills and delinquencies of the South—including color bars in private, state and local government employment; backward standards of education, vocational training and public welfare generally, with particularly low standards for Negroes and Mexican Americans; social patterns to enforce the dependency of both poor whites and Negroes.

Since World War II and particularly since the early 1950s, the spread of automation has been reducing the number of unskilled and semi-skilled jobs that require little or no education or training. The types of jobs that helped to adjust previous generations of foreign immigrants and rural American migrants to America's urban areas have not been expanding.

In ghetto areas in the cities, about 10 percent to 15 percent of the adult men and about 40 percent to 50 percent of out-of-school teenagers (including an estimate of those usually not counted by the Labor Department) are unemployed. In addition, a Labor Department survey of slum areas in November 1966 found that nearly 7 percent of those with jobs were employed only part-time although they wanted full-time work, and 20 percent of those working full-time earned less than $60 a week. This same Labor Department survey found that nearly 40 percent of the families and unrelated individuals in big city slum areas earn less than $3,000 a year.

However, it costs about $7,000, at present prices, to maintain a modest standard of living, including a few amenities but no luxuries, for a family of four in America's metropolitan areas—more for a larger family and less for a smaller family. Elimination of the amenities would result in a cost of about $5,000 to maintain a minimum decent standard of living for a family of four in our urban areas— scaled up and down for different family sizes.

Yet government reports indicate that probably about 20 percent of the population, within city limits, earn less than the amount necessary for a minimum decent standard of living. Within ghetto areas, perhaps 60 percent to 70 percent or more of the families are in that category. The result is badly overcrowded housing, inadequate diet, poor medical care, few books and magazines for about 20 percent of city families and about 60 to 70 percent of those who live in ghetto slums.

The hardcore slum areas continue to deteriorate. People with jobs, some skills and some regular incomes have been moving out. They are replaced with new migrants from the rural South—adding to the remaining lowest-income families, the jobless, the aged and fatherless families.

A large proportion of these slum residents depend on welfare payments, often to mothers with dependent children and no father present. The Labor Department survey of November 1966 found that 30 percent of the population of East Harlem, 30 percent of the Watts population, 40 percent of the Bedford-Stuyvesant children and 25 percent of the adults receive welfare payments. Moreover, the lack of adequate child-care facilities in slum areas is a barrier to employment for women with children.

Trapped by a history of degradation and the recent impact of automation, these new migrants to the city are also trapped by the unavailability of low- and moderate-cost housing, as well as by discrimination against colored peoples.

The peak home construction year before World War II was 1925. From 1926 to 1945, a period of 20 years, home-building was in a slump. It wasn't until 1946 that the 1925-level of housing starts was reached.

Since 1945, the ups and downs of residential construction have followed conditions in the money market—interest rates and availability of money. Normal business operations and government programs have provided housing for families in the middle-income range and above (at present, about $7,000–$8,000 annual income and more).

The residential construction of the postwar period, however, has essentially ignored housing for the entire bottom half of our income distribution—for the lower middle-income group as well as the poor.

For lower middle-income families, with current incomes of about $5,000 to $8,000, the postwar years have seen only little new housing construction, with present rentals or carrying charges and taxes of about $85–$135 per month. This is particularly true for large families, with three or more children, in this income-range.

For the urban poor—families with current incomes of about $5,000 a year and less—there has been hardly any new housing construction during the 22 years since World War II and there was very little of such construction in the preceding 20 years from 1926 through 1945. Almost a half-century of rapid change in our cities—including the great Negro migration—has passed with hardly any housing construction for low-income families.

Realistic rentals for poor families would have to be concentrated around $40 to $70 a month. Since the private market cannot provide such housing, public housing and public rehabilitation are essential. But, in recent years, the total number of new public dwelling units has been only about 30,000–40,000 per year.

Moreover, the urban renewal program, which has bulldozed Negro slum areas, has concentrated on the construction of commercial buildings and luxury high-rise apartments. Relocation of families displaced from the slums has been neglected or ignored and there has been hardly any replacement of low-rental housing.

In addition, during the 1950s and early 1960s, the traditional conservative opposition to low-cost publicly subsidized housing for the poor was joined by many so-called liberals—the same coalition that debunked the impact of automation on unskilled and semi-skilled factory workers and on industrial location as a trade union myth.

At the same time, middle and upper-income families have been moving to the suburbs. This movement has opened up older housing in the cities. But, combined with the movement of industry to the suburbs and countryside, it has reduced the tax-base of the cities, when the demands on their financial resources for housing, welfare, education and public facilities are mounting. Moreover, the change of industrial location has compounded the problems of inadequate mass transportation facilities for low-income city-dwellers to get to the new areas of employment growth. And most suburban communities have rather rigid color-bar restrictions, as well as an absence of low-cost housing.

The New Deal's beginnings to provide low-cost public housing nearly perished between 1952 and 1966. And much of the long-delayed legislation of the 1960s to achieve partial adjustments to the radical changes in American life were first steps, without previous experience, precedents and trained personnel. Moreover, federal appropriations for even these purposes were kept down by public apathy. Yet, they were greatly oversold and their adoption aroused expectations of overnight solutions that were impossible to achieve.

America's urban crisis is a national complex of social problems—rather than simple problems of individual communities. No city or state government can solve them in isolation. Neither can private enterprise, even with the promise of tax subsidies. Their solution requires nationwide social measures, with adequate federal funds and standards. . . .

America requires a national housing goal of 2½ million new dwelling units each year during the next decade, supplemented by a large-scale effort to rehabilitate substantial housing that is worth saving—to provide an ample supply of decent homes for our rapidly growing population, as well as for those who live in substandard housing. Such goal is in sharp contrast to the annual construction of only 1.2–1.6 million new housing units in recent years, accompanied by very little rehabilitation. . . .

The most urgent needs are: (1) to provide low-rent publicly subsidized housing—new and rehabilitated—for the approximately 20 percent of city families whose incomes are below the requirements for a minimum decent standard of living (about $5,000 a year for a family of four); (2) to provide adequate housing for lower middle-income families (between about $5,000 and $8,000 a year for a 4-person family) who are not eligible for public housing and cannot obtain decent dwellings in the standard, privately financed housing market; and (3) to provide expanded and improved community facilities and services—such as schools, hospitals, mass transit, day-care centers and playgrounds.

Construction of new, low-rent publicly-subsidized housing should be stepped up immediately from a yearly rate of 30,000–40,000 new starts of recent years to 200,000–300,000 per year in the next two years and stepped up, thereafter, to an annual rate of 500,000.

New public housing construction should be supplemented by large-scale publicly-subsidized rehabilitation to provide additional low-rent housing. Rentals of such new and rehabilitated housing should be concentrated in a range of $40 to $70 per month to meet the needs of the city poor. In order to maintain decent housing at low rentals, a partial government subsidy should be provided for adequate maintenance of the properties.

A major federal effort along these lines should include architectural designs and first-class construction for attractive homes and neighborhoods. It should also include an emphasis on people and services—with provision for nearby shopping, schools, transportation, playgrounds and the availability of social services. As part of an overall effort to rebuild our urban areas, new and rehabilitated low-rent public housing should be located in both the city and suburbs and interspersed with other types of rental and private housing for the creation of balanced neighborhoods.

The federal program should include provision for the potential sale of low-rent public housing developments or parts of such developments to tenant cooperatives or to tenants who meet the income requirements for home-ownership.

Suburban Jobs and
the Urban Unemployed

DOROTHY K. NEWMAN

. . . It appears that matching jobs with workers is one of the more intractable problems in the present economy.

One of the prime causes of this failure to match available jobs with available personnel is the movement of new jobs into the suburbs and out of large central cities. It is in these cities that unemployment, underemployment, and poverty are greatest.

The steady trend of this movement is illustrated by the concentration of new factory and commercial buildings in the ring of metropolitan areas rather than in the central city. . . . In the same periods, also, a relatively large proportion of community buildings, such as schools and hospitals, has been constructed in the suburbs instead of the city. These buildings represent a large capital investment, leading to substantial increases in suburban employment, especially in industry, retail and wholesale trade, and business, professional, and technical services. Many of the jobs created are within the capabilities of

FROM Dorothy K. Newman, Division of Economic Studies, Bureau of Labor Statistics, "The Decentralization of Jobs," *Monthly Labor Review* (May 1967), pp. 7–12.

the people who need employment opportunities, but most of the new jobs are too distant and difficult to reach.

The trend to place new structures in the suburbs—particularly those devoted to factories and trade, and, to a smaller extent, to schools and hospitals—is especially marked in the North, where central cities of the largest SMSA's tend to be old and the flight of population to the suburbs has been going on for many years. Northern cities are frequently handicapped by narrow streets, one-way traffic patterns, obsolescent structures, and rapidly changing neighborhoods. A metropolitan-area view of city planning is only beginning, that might, in the future, accommodate city industrial parks and shopping centers. At the same time, large cities are the locus of the largest and oldest urban slums, and the magnet of most Negroes migrating from the South to seek jobs and improved living conditions. . . .

This substantial outmigration of facilities precedes and also mirrors the huge increase of business and employment in the ring, where population growth is greatest also.

. . . Payroll employment has soared in the suburbs compared with the SMSA as a whole (and, therefore, compared with the central city) in virtually all the SMSA's studied for which estimates of change could be obtained. . . .

The differences in employment change between city and suburb are pronounced—and consistently greater in the ring—in manufacturing, wholesale and retail trade, and services. These industries account for 2 of 3 employees on nonagricultural payrolls. Their employees are concentrated in clerical and sales work, in skilled and semiskilled industrial production, and as service workers outside of private households. In 1964, over 3 of 5 of all heads of families in central cities were in such occupations. It is likely, therefore, that many central-city residents might qualify for new openings in the suburbs. Early in 1967, about 60 percent of those unemployed 15 weeks or more were last employed in such jobs. . . .

In 1964 (the latest year for which such figures are available), the median income of all nonwhite households in the central cities of SMSA's was $3,656 compared with $6,034 for white central-city households. Even among those who worked full time all year, the median for nonwhite households was $5,292 compared with $7,718 for the whites.

Getting to a suburban job, therefore, imposes a greater burden on central city residents than is experienced by the suburban commuter to the city. Thus, transportation difficulties particularly affect Negroes, who are frequently confronted with discriminatory housing practices in the ring.

Public transportation to the suburbs is usually expensive, often circuitous, or simply not available. Detailed fare schedules from the American Transit Association show that fares on public transit lines from the central city to the closest suburban area range from 30 cents one way in 1 of the 14 SMSA's studied to 65 cents in another. The distances for which public transportation is provided vary, but it is obvious that a minimum of $3 a week (or almost $15 a month), plus more than an hour a day, including transfer and waiting, would have to be spent by a city resident to work in the suburbs. Furthermore, rush-hour schedules are not usually arranged to speed transit users to the outside in the morning and to the inside in the evening, as is frequently done for commuters in the opposite direction.

There is substantial evidence that central city residents using public transport spend more money and time to reach suburban jobs than those commuting to the city. Those wanting jobs at a substantial distance, or beyond bus or rapid transit lines, pay an especially high price. According to estimates by the Traffic Commission of New York City, it would cost a worker in Harlem $40 a month to commute by public transportation to work in an aircraft plant in Farmingdale (Long Island), in a parts plant in Yonkers or Portchester (Westchester), or in a basic chemical plant or shipyard on Staten Island. The estimate includes $1.50 a week for the New York City subway, $30 a month for a commutation ticket on the Long Island or New Haven railroad, and $3 a week for transportation from the suburban station to the plant. The public transit cost for a Bedford-Stuyvesant resident to work in the same places would be nearly $50 a month.

Persons whose incomes are most limited are most likely to use public transportation to work. Also, public transit usage declines with auto ownership; auto ownership rises with earnings, even in the suburbs.

Most nonwhite families living in central cities do not have an automobile. Fewer than half owned a car in 8 of the 14 central cities in the SMSA's selected for study. . . .

Dependence on public transit among poor and relatively low-paid workers lends importance to the change in public transit costs as well as the level. Fares for public transportation have risen twice as fast as the cost of buying and operating an automobile since 1957–59. The rate of increase is more than for any other group of commodities or services in the Bureau of Labor Statistics Consumer Price Index, with the exception of medical care, and even exceeded medical care in Atlanta, Boston, Los Angeles, and Philadelphia.

Of all who traveled from home to work in 1960, the smallest journey-to-work group (less than 10 percent of the total) commuted from central city to the suburbs. This percentage is surprisingly small, considering that high unemployment rates and low-income populations are concentrated in the city, whereas employment opportunities are expanding in the outskirts. . . .

The People Left Behind

PRESIDENT'S ADVISORY COMMISSION
ON RURAL POVERTY

This report is about a problem which many in the United States do not realize exists. The problem is rural poverty. It affects some 14 million Americans. Rural poverty is so widespread, and so acute, as to be a national disgrace, and its consequences have swept into our cities, violently.

The urban riots during 1967 had their roots, in considerable part, in rural poverty. A high proportion of the people crowded into city slums today came there from rural slums. This fact alone makes clear how large a stake the people of this Nation have in an attack on rural poverty.

The total number of rural poor would be even larger than 14 million had not so many of them moved to the city. They made the move because they wanted a job and a decent place to live. Some have found them. Many have not. Many merely exchanged life in a rural slum for life in an urban slum, at an exorbitant cost to themselves, to the cities, and to rural America as well.

Even so, few migrants have returned to the rural areas they left. They have apparently concluded that bad as conditions are in an urban slum, they are worse in the rural slum they fled from. . . .

Rural poverty in the United States has no geographic boundaries. It is acute in the South, but it is present and serious in the East, the

FROM President's Advisory Commission on Rural Poverty, "The People Left Behind," *Employment Service Review* (April 1968), pp. 17–19.

West, and the North. Rural poverty is not limited to Negroes. It permeates all races and ethnic groups. Nor is poverty limited to the farm. Our farm population has declined until it is only a small fraction of our total rural population. Most of the rural poor do not live on farms. They live in the open country, in rural villages, and in small towns. Moreover, contrary to a common misconception, whites outnumber nonwhites among the rural poor by a wide margin. It is true, however, that an extremely high proportion of Negroes in the rural South and Indians on reservations are destitute.

Hunger, even among children, does exist among the rural poor, as a group of physicians discovered recently in a visit to the rural South. They found Negro children not getting enough food to sustain life, and so disease-ridden as to be beyond cure. Malnutrition is even more widespread. The evidence appears in bad diets and in diseases which often are a product of bad diets.

Disease and premature death are startlingly high among the rural poor. Infant mortality, for instance, is far higher among rural poor than among the least privileged group in urban areas. Chronic diseases also are common among both young and old. And medical and dental care is conspicuously absent.

Unemployment and underemployment are major problems in rural America. The rate of unemployment nationally is about 4 percent. The rate in rural areas averages about 18 percent. Among farmworkers, a recent study discovered that underemployment runs as high as 37 percent.

The rural poor have gone, and now go, to poor schools. One result is that more than 3 million rural adults are classified as illiterates. In both educational facilities and opportunities, the rural poor have been shortchanged.

Most of the rural poor live in atrocious houses. One in every 13 houses in rural America is officially classified as unfit to live in.

Many of the rural poor live in chronically depressed poverty-stricken rural communities. Most of the rural South is one vast poverty area. Indian reservations contain heavy concentrations of poverty. But there also are impoverished rural communities in the upper Great Lakes region, in New England, in Appalachia, in the Southwest, and in other sections.

The community in rural poverty areas has all but disappeared as an effective institution. In the past the rural community performed the services needed by farmers and other rural people. Technological progress brought sharp declines in the manpower needs of agriculture, forestry, fisheries, and mining. Other industries have not replaced the jobs lost, and they have supplied too few jobs for the young entries into the labor market. Larger towns and cities have taken over many of the economic and social functions of the villages and small towns.

The changes in rural America have rendered obsolete many of the political boundaries to villages and counties. Thus these units operate on too small a scale to be practicable. Their tax base has eroded as their more able-bodied wage earners left for jobs elsewhere. In consequence the public services in the typical poor rural community are grossly inadequate in number, magnitude, and quality. Local government is no longer able to cope with local needs.

As the communities ran downhill, they offered fewer and fewer opportunities for anyone to earn a living. The inadequately equipped young people left in search of better opportunities elsewhere. Those remaining behind have few resources with which to earn incomes adequate for a decent living and for revitalizing their communities.

For all practical purposes, then, most of the 14 million people in our poverty areas are outside our market economy. So far as they are concerned, the dramatic economic growth of the United States might as well never have happened. It has brought them few rewards. They are on the outside looking in, and they need help.

The South's Regional Disadvantage

OSCAR ORNATI

In spite of the fact that national forces clearly are dominant, regional economic differentials have been found to persist throughout the United States. . . .

That the South is poor has long been known. In a report prepared in 1938 by the National Emergency Council, the South—an underdeveloped area within the most developed country in the world—was labeled "the nation's economic problem No. 1." The Council's report recognized that much of southern poverty was the poverty of the social infrastructure—inadequate schooling and limited public ser-

FROM Oscar Ornati, professor of economics, New York University, *Poverty Amid Affluence* (New York: The Twentieth Century Fund, 1966), pp. 56–58.

vices, meager facilities for research which might lead to technological development and a population not as richly endowed as in the rest of the nation.

Since 1938 economic growth—"brought about not by the unseen hand of economic forces but by the long arm of national policy"— has helped the integration of the South into the American economy. The South is now a growing economy; it shares in the national efforts of "want creation" of the affluent society. Indeed, the growth rate of the South—since 1929—is higher than that of any other national region. Yet a century after the Civil War, poverty remains deeply ingrained in southern life. Whether measured by low income or by high functional illiteracy, by the quality of its housing or by the health of its people, the South lags behind the rest of the nation. It drags low income across one-third of the states. Within a "core" of seven southern states low income actually embraces a majority of the population.

One needs to define the term "South." In this study, two definitions were used, one the Census Bureau's definition and the other, a subgroup of "core" states. The following states are included in the Census definition: Alabama, Arkansas, Delaware, Florida, Georgia, Kentucky, Louisiana, Mississippi, Maryland, North Carolina, Oklahoma, South Carolina, Tennessee, Virginia, West Virginia, and the District of Columbia. Core states—referred to as "core-South"— include Mississippi, Arkansas, North and South Carolina, Alabama, Tennessee, and Kentucky. A first consideration leading to selection of these particular seven states was the fact that these states had roughly the highest proportions of families under our low-income points in 1960. The second consideration was that the core group showed less progress in reducing the low-income population during the 1950's than most other southern states.

Looking first at the broader, U.S. Census definition of the South, one concludes from the low-income data that there is a decided disadvantage associated with southern residence. Of the total number of families living in the southern region, slightly over 21 per cent had incomes below $2,000 in 1960. The comparable percentage for the United States was 13. The gap was somewhat narrower in the next two income classes. About a third of all southern family units had money incomes below $3,000 while only slightly more than a fifth of all U.S. families (which, of course, include southern families) were below this level. Under $4,000, the southern proportion approached 45 per cent, while the figure for the United States as a whole was 31 per cent. . . .

Any comparison of southern income with the national average

brings inevitable warnings that the racial and rural character of the region frustrates simple generalizations. Rural areas are poor and the South is the most rural area of the country. Negroes are poor and the South still has a higher proportion of Negroes than other regions. These factors can, however, be eliminated from the statistics. . . .

Comparing . . . the proportion of all families and of southern families with 1960 incomes under $2,000, the proportion is found to be greater by 63 per cent in the South and by 109 per cent in the core states. Similar calculations for white families only yield a figure of 52 per cent for the South and 89 per cent for the core group. Comparing urban families only, the results are 53 per cent and 81 per cent. When both race and residence variables are held constant and one deals only with comparisons of white urban families, the percentages are 35 and 40 respectively. The net effect of holding race and the urban-rural factor constant is to cut the difference between the nation as a whole and the South from 63 to 35 per cent; that is, a little over two-fifths of the difference is washed out. For the core states, roughly three-fifths of the difference disappears. In the "core-South," holding the urban-rural factor constant is even more revealing than in the South as defined by the Census Bureau. In these core states, the poorest non-whites obviously are rural residents. But differences between the general population and the "core-South" still remain, even in the white urban group. It is interesting to see that the relative advantage of white urban families over all families in the "core-South" is greater than in the whole South. It is perhaps an American parallel, in our area of underdevelopment, to the oft-cited polarization of rich and poor in underdeveloped countries.

IV

The Anatomy of Poverty

Homer Burleigh: How Many Problems Can a Man Have?

"You mean you want to take a look at a hillbilly!"

Homer Burleigh, thirty-three [and] immobile with resentment, blocked the doorway to his flat. Like 20,000 other Southern whites living in . . . Chicago's Uptown, he had his pride, his problems, and an innate suspicion of the Eastern city slicker.

Homer Burleigh finds it hard to stay angry for long and he led the way inside. Four of his five children, ages two, three, five, and seven (a ten-year-old boy was still in school), ran about in bare feet, dressed only in underpants. Mrs. Burleigh, a wan, hard, very pregnant woman, also was barefooted. . . .

He walked into a small kitchen, sat down, . . . and sighed. He was in trouble and he knew it. . . . Homer Burleigh was penniless, about to be evicted, maybe even jailed. Much of this was his own fault, the panicked response to crises. . . . Homer Burleigh made mistakes when the margin of safety with which he had to live permitted no mistakes whatever. . . . The day he talked at the kitchen table, the last of the final welfare payment had been spent and in four days he was to be evicted for non-payment of rent.

"If the arm continues this way, and if they don't give me assistance, I'm going to have to put the kids in a home." His eyes filled. . . .

And so the lines of failure seemed to converge for Homer Burleigh: a motherless home full of contention, almost no formal education, an impoverished landscape to grow in with no hope for a young man, . . . a drifting of life without heed for the consequences of more children. But he was not an evil man, or a lazy one. His was simply the fragile vessel of endemic poverty, never strong enough to withstand a prolonged storm. And his children seemed doomed to go forth in a similarly brittle craft.

FROM Ben H. Bagdikian, *In the Midst of Plenty: The Poor in America* (1964).

THE burden of poverty weighs most heavily upon minority groups, children, certain categories of youths, the unemployed, the rural population, the elderly, and the female family head. Thus the miseries of an unemployed black woman who is also the head of a family with several children are compounded accordingly. In this section we select a variety of descriptive and analytical discussions pertaining to the groups that bear the chief burdens of poverty. In addition, we briefly examine the special problems of those poor who are unfortunate enough to be sick also.

Because of space limitations, only the most prominent group aspects are dealt with in this section. For example, women, who are more likely to be in a poor household than men, are not explicitly represented here, although they are discussed in a number of other selections. Similarly, the rural poor, studied in the preceding section, do not receive special attention here. The breakdown into specific problem groups adopted in this section must be complemented by a study of the overlapping phenomena that compound the problems of millions of poor people and make poverty policy more complex than the simple breakdown implies. These complexities are evident in this section's opening vignette on the problems of Homer Burleigh and his family, and they are examined in the more scholarly study of the convergence of poverty-linked characteristics in Section V.

Some experts have argued that the War on Poverty was inaugurated to divert the civil rights movement into narrower channels and at the same time reduce its potential militancy. Riots in the ghettos lent plausibility to interpretations that connected riots with poverty or at least with the poverty-linked phenomena suffered by blacks. We consider the black minority first in this section partly in response to contemporary interest in this group's experience and partly because poverty among blacks is three or four times more widespread than it is among the population as a whole. The accompanying table on the incidence of poverty in 1966 shows, for example, that nonwhites, who are overwhelmingly blacks, accounted for about 28 per cent of all poor families although they represented only about 10 per cent of all families in the nation. Indeed, blacks are likely to be worse off than other nonwhite minorities. This is indicated, for example, by the concentration of black male employment in the low-paying occupations, as shown in the table on page 91, which compares the employment of different minority groups and whites by occupation and sex. Both the Batchelder and the Blau and Duncan discussions elaborate on the special problems of blacks and explore some of the major reasons for their persistence. (Material on the ghetto and on blacks in other sections sheds further light on their manifold problems in modern America.)

In examining poverty among the young we move chronologically, from childhood through the teenage period, cutting across racial and other lines. The fact that in the mid-1960s poor households averaged 4.1 persons and nonpoor households only 3.6 persons reflects the larger number of children in poor households; further family characteristics of the poor are found in the Orshansky table in this introduction. There is a growing and concerned literature on the subject of children in poverty, such as the excellent collection of essays by professors Nona Glazer and Carol Creedon. We hope that thoughtful discussion among readers will be stimulated by the overall perspective provided by the Orshansky selection and Kozol's report of the dreary school experience we give the children of the poor, sapping the inherent vitality of their early years, together with Chilman's controversial comparison of child-rearing patterns among the middle class and among the poor.

The problems of the mature young person who comes from a poverty-stricken background are factually and analytically treated in the discussions that follow on the difficulties of bridging the gap from school to work and the interrelationships among college training, income, other education, and occupation. We have emphasized education and employability as central to the determination of the older teenager's future.

In the absence of a guaranteed minimum annual money income, a person's earning power based on the sale of his personal services is of enormous importance in hoisting himself above the poverty line. The poor live to an inordinate degree in the "irregular economy" of low, discontinuous, and unpredictable earnings, where "the traditional distinctions between employment and unemployment, work and welfare become blurred, and extra-legal sources of income may be sought."[1] The selections on the unemployed and underpaid provide essential information on the origin of income inadequacy and its varied causes: unemployment of varying duration, low rates of remuneration, and failure to look for work even though work is desired. The first two causes are now often combined analytically because for many of the poor they are interlocked. Interrupted, casual, or migratory employment is frequently the experience of unskilled people, and the upper limit of their pay rates is about that of the minimum wage.

[1] *Manpower Report of the President, 1968,* page 94. See also "Life on the Streetcorner," from *Tally's Corner; A Study of Negro Streetcorner Men,* by Elliot Liebow, beginning on page 140.

Incidence of Family Poverty, 1966

(Numbers in thousands)

Characteristic	All families				With male head				With female head			
		Poor				Poor				Poor		
	Total	Number	Percent	Percentage distribution	Total	Number	Percent	Percentage distribution	Total	Number	Percent	Percentage distribution
Total	48,922	6,086	12.4	100.0	43,751	4,276	9.8	100.0	5,172	1,810	35.0	100.0
Residence												
Nonfarm	46,225	5,598	12.1	92.0	41,199	3,835	9.3	89.7	5,026	1,764	35.1	97.5
Farm	2,697	488	18.1	8.0	2,552	441	17.3	10.3	145	47	32.4	2.6
Race												
White	44,017	4,375	9.9	71.9	40,007	3,264	8.2	76.3	4,010	1,111	27.7	61.4
Nonwhite	4,905	1,711	34.9	28.1	3,744	1,012	27.0	23.7	1,162	699	60.2	38.6
Age of head												
14–24	3,011	510	16.9	8.4	2,761	347	12.6	8.1	250	163	65.2	9.0
25–34	9,560	1,139	11.9	18.7	8,753	668	7.6	15.6	806	472	58.6	26.1
35–44	11,113	1,180	10.6	19.4	10,026	737	7.4	17.2	1,087	444	40.8	24.5
45–54	10,620	919	8.7	15.1	9,503	587	6.2	13.7	1,116	333	29.8	18.4
55–64	7,689	800	10.4	13.1	6,900	635	9.2	14.9	789	166	21.0	9.2
65 and over	6,929	1,538	22.2	25.3	5,807	1,304	22.5	30.5	1,122	234	20.9	12.9
Number of persons in family												
2	16,354	2,271	13.9	37.3	13,978	1,693	12.1	39.6	2,376	578	24.3	31.9
3	10,098	889	8.8	14.6	8,901	532	6.0	12.4	1,197	357	29.8	19.7
4	9,400	793	8.4	13.0	8,687	488	5.6	11.4	712	305	42.8	16.9
5	6,189	649	10.5	10.7	5,808	440	7.6	10.3	382	209	54.7	11.5
6	3,438	501	14.6	8.2	3,230	362	11.2	8.5	209	138	66.0	7.6
7 or more	3,443	984	28.6	16.2	3,146	762	24.2	17.8	296	222	75.0	12.3

Region												
Northeast	12,039	1,037	8.6	17.0	10,650	675	6.3	15.8	1,389	362	26.1	20.0
North Central	13,617	1,259	9.2	20.7	12,400	874	7.0	20.4	1,216	385	31.7	21.3
South	14,978	2,950	19.7	48.5	13,251	2,186	16.5	51.1	1,727	763	44.2	42.2
West	8,288	840	10.1	13.8	7,448	540	7.2	12.6	839	300	35.8	16.6
Type of family												
Male head	43,751	4,276	9.8	70.3	43,751	4,276	9.8	100.0				
Married, wife present	42,553	4,069	9.6	66.9	42,553	4,069	9.6	95.2				
Wife in paid labor force	15,005	743	5.0	12.2	15,005	743	5.0	17.4				
Wife not in paid labor force	27,548	3,326	12.1	54.7	27,548	3,326	12.1	77.8				
Other marital status	1,197	207	17.3	3.4	1,197	207	17.3	4.8				
Female head	5,172	1,810	35.0	29.7	5,172				5,172	1,810	35.0	100.0
Employment status and occupation of head												
Employed, March 1967	38,885	3,020	7.8	49.6	36,293	2,376	6.5	55.6	2,593	641	24.7	35.4
Professional and technical workers	5,338	129	2.4	2.1	5,050	107	2.1	2.5	286	22	7.7	1.2
Farmers and farm managers	1,588	315	19.8	5.2	1,572	309	19.7	7.2	16	6	—	.3
Managers, officials, and proprietors (except farm)	5,759	233	4.0	3.8	5,643	216	3.8	5.1	118	17	14.4	.9
Clerical and sales workers	5,146	225	4.4	3.7	4,323	124	2.9	2.9	823	100	12.2	5.5
Craftsmen and foremen	8,050	353	4.4	5.8	8,013	349	4.4	8.2	36	3	—	.2
Operatives	7,696	746	8.4	10.6	7,230	544	7.5	12.7	466	102	21.9	5.6
Service workers	3,011	585	19.4	9.6	2,192	212	9.7	5.0	820	373	45.5	20.6
Private household workers	282	154	54.6	2.5	13	2		—	270	152	56.3	8.4
Laborers (except mine)	2,297	533	23.2	8.9	2,270	515	22.7	12.0	28	18	54.8	1.0
Unemployed	904	248	27.4	4.1	780	180	23.1	4.2	124	68	44.8	3.8
Not in labor force	9,132	2,817	30.8	46.3	6,678	1,718	25.7	40.2	2,454	1,100		60.8
Number of earners in 1966												
None	4,073	1,978	48.6	32.5	3,017	1,216	40.3	28.4	1,056	762	72.2	42.1
1	20,451	2,620	12.8	43.0	18,163	1,892	10.4	44.2	2,288	729	31.9	40.3
2	17,992	1,112	6.2	18.3	16,608	891	5.4	20.8	1,384	221	16.0	12.2
3 or more	6,405	376	5.9	6.2	5,961	278	4.7	6.5	443	100	22.8	5.5

FROM Mollie Orshansky, "The Shape of Poverty in 1966," *Social Security Bulletin* (March 1968), p. 11.

We are only beginning to collect quantitative information on the subemployed; but, with the reasonably good data available on unemployment duration and on money wages, it should soon be possible to discover enough about the magnitude of this problem to suggest policies for coping with it. Quantification of the newly recognized phenomenon of people not seeking but nevertheless desiring employment will no doubt prove a harder task. Furthermore, we still need to know why and to what extent subemployment is linked to poverty. The results so far yield a challenging new dimension to the anatomy of poverty and to our society's strategy in meeting the problem.

Advanced age is another poverty concentration point. The Orshansky table in this introduction tells us that as of 1966 slightly more than one-fourth of all poor family heads were sixty-five years old and over, and well over one-fifth of all family heads who were sixty-five or more were living in poverty. For individuals not in families but living by themselves, 56 per cent of those who were sixty-five or more were in poverty. Among the elderly, women seem by far the worst off; for example, about 59 per cent of all elderly women living by themselves were in poverty.

It has been argued that in order to establish the poverty line for the elderly, it is necessary to include assets as well as income (see the definitional discussion by S. M. Miller *et al.* in Section I). However, one study of this matter indicates that, if all assets other than the home were considered invested and prorated actuarially for use over the average remaining years of life, the adjustment would still leave five-sixths as many aged couples in poverty.[2]

The special medical problems of the poor and the failures of U.S. health services for the poor are analyzed by former Vice President Hubert H. Humphrey, a major architect of the Medicare program. We consider his selection by far the best available discussion on this subject. Additional information on the health status of the poor appears throughout this volume (such as in the selection on hunger and malnutrition in Section I).

---

[2] Mollie Orshansky, "Who's Who Among the Poor: A Demographic View of Poverty," *Social Security Bulletin,* vol. 28, no. 7 (July 1965), p. 13.

The Minority Poor

The Special Case of the Negro

ALAN BATCHELDER

. . . At least five economic considerations distinguish Negro from white poverty. As Wordsworth observed of the echo, "Like,—but oh how different."

First, $1,000 buys less for a poor Negro than for a poor white.

Second, the demographic cross section of the Negro poor is unlike that of the white poor.

Third, poor Negroes suffer though the general weal and poor whites benefit from secular changes in urban renewal, education medians, agriculture, manufacturing location, technology, and social minimum wages.

Fourth, the effect of government transfer payments is different for poor Negroes than for poor whites.

Fifth, discrimination operates against Negroes to restrict access to education and to the jobs that can provide an escape from poverty.

These considerations will be discussed in turn. . . .

The past decade's many admonitions and laws opposing discrimination could, by themselves, not raise the Negro's relative economic position in the face of rising unemployment. If Negroes are to approach economic and civil equality in the future, unemployment rates must fall.

. . . Attention now turns to the characteristics distinguishing poor Negro from poor white Americans.

When citing statistics of poverty, the portion of Negro families receiving incomes below a particular figure, e.g., $3,000, is often compared with the portion of white families receiving incomes below $3,000. Such comparisons implicitly assume the Negro's $3,000 buys as much as the white's $3,000.

It does not.

FROM Alan Batchelder, professor of economics, Kenyon College, "Poverty: The Special Case of the Negro" (unpublished paper), pp. 1–11.

American cities have two housing markets: the city-wide white market and the circumscribed Negro market. Because supply is restricted, Negroes receive less housing value for their dollars spent than do whites. Census statistics indicate that "non-white renters and home owners obtain fewer standard quality dwellings and frequently less space than do whites paying the same amounts." A Chicago welfare department study found "housing defects significantly greater for Negro than for white families, despite the fact that rents for Negro families are 28% a month higher than for whites in private dwellings."

Landlords are sometimes judged greedy extortionists for charging Negro tenants higher rents than whites. But they are operating in a market of restricted supply; high Negro rents reflect supply and demand relationships, not conspiratorial landlord greed. Since 15 percent of the consumption expenditures of urban Negro families is for shelter, real income is significantly reduced by relatively high rents.

Poor urban Negroes also pay more than whites for identical consumer durables bought on credit. Negroes pay more than whites for residential financing too. The difference may be due to white reluctance to sell to Negroes, to Negro immobility, or to the sellers' assumption that poor Negroes are poorer risks than poor whites. Whatever the cause, real income suffers.

Poor Negro families average a half person larger than poor white families. Consequently, per capita real income of poor Negroes is even farther below per capita real income of poor whites with the same money income.

If, then, $3,000 in Negro money buys only as much as $2,800 or even $2,500 in white money and is distributed over more people, one should keep in mind appropriate reservations when comparing percentage of whites with percentage of Negroes below some income level.

The Negro poor differ from the white poor in demographic characteristics. Remembering that Negro numbers will be understated, uniform dollar incomes can be used to identify non-white (not Negro) and white poor. Defining as poor, families with incomes under $3,000 and individuals living independently with incomes under $1,500 in 1959, four social-economic variables distinguish the non-white from the white poor.

First, the non-white poor are concentrated in the South. In 1960, 72 percent of poor non-white families and only four of ten poor white families lived in the South. The difference in Southern concentration resulted because, in 1960, the proportion of non-whites was double the proportion of whites living in the South.

Second, low income is more of a rural phenomenon for whites than for non-whites; 18 of every 100 poor white families, 12 of every 100 poor non-white families lived on farms in 1960. Most rural non-whites are poor.

Third, the aging of husbands is a much more important cause of white than of non-white poverty. Other forces are important in causing non-white poverty. In 1959, 29 percent of poor white families but only 13 percent of poor non-white families were headed by a man older than 64 years. Among unrelated individuals, 40 percent of the white poor, only 26 percent of the non-white poor were past 64.

Fourth, non-white poverty, far more than white, is associated with families headed by women. American Negro women have always borne exceptionally heavy family responsibility.

. . . So much for demographic differences involving regional residence, urban residence, age of men, and female heads of families.

The third difference between the Negro poor and the white poor is the collection of forces afoot today that give the affluent society and even poor whites the pleasure while injuring poor Negroes. One of these forces is urban renewal. It replaces slums with aesthetically attractive, commercially profitable structures, some of which provide low-income housing superior to that which the private market could provide.

Yet urban renewal seems to effect a net reduction in housing supply for poor Negroes. L. K. Northwood found "The supply of housing has been reduced in areas formerly occupied by Negro families. . . . 115,000 housing units were . . . planned to replace 190,500 . . . *a net loss of 75,000.*" Because many urban Negroes live in slums, 60 percent of the persons dispossessed by urban renewal demolition have been Negroes.

The long-run tendency to reduce the supply of low-cost housing is aggravated in the short run because time must elapse between demolition of old and dedication of new buildings. . . .

Poor whites may move elsewhere; poor Negroes must face reduced supply. Reduced supply should raise prices, and there is evidence that Negroes displaced by urban renewal pay rent 10 percent higher after relocation than before.

Until President Kennedy's November 1962 executive order, the supply-restriction effect was even greater, for no federal rule prohibited urban redevelopers from practicing racial discrimination. The 1962 order alleviated the problem but could not end the irony that poor Negroes suffer from programs designed to promote urban welfare.

The second force benefiting the rest of society but injuring poor

Negroes is rising education norms. E. F. Denison estimates that from 1929 to 1957 improved education "contributed 42 percent of the 1.60 percentage point growth rate in product per person employed." Improved education is manifested in rising median school years completed. 1950 Negro medians for men and for women, past age 24, lagged white medians by 2.8 years. By 1960, Negro medians had pushed up a year and a third. So had white medians. Average Negroes remained in the same relative position, but rising educational medians increased the comparative disadvantage of the 2,265,000 non-white functional illiterates (less than five years of school) making up 23.5 percent of the 1960 non-white population past age 24.

Many poor whites are illiterate, but figures on school years completed understate the number of illiterate Negroes and the size of their educational disadvantage. Understatements result for Negroes because so many attended inefficient segregated Southern schools. . . .

Of non-whites living North or West in 1960, 41 percent had been born in the South. These educationally deprived poor Southern Negroes are increasingly disadvantaged in regions where the median education of the local labor force and the quality of local schools rise each year. . . .

Left ever farther behind rising national educational norms, poor Negro families are ever less qualified to compete for jobs or to help their children acquire the education required to escape poverty. Improving education benefits the general public but injures poor Negroes moving from the South to the North and West.

The third force benefiting most Americans but particularly injuring poor Negroes has been agricultural change. Since 1945, the mechanization of cotton culture has revolutionized Southern agriculture. There has also been persistent change in crops grown and livestock raised. These changes raised agricultural productivity and expelled hand labor from Southern farms.

The economy benefits as productivity rises. The effect on Negroes is less favorable. As whites left, the white farms that averaged 130 acres in 1930 grew to average 249 acres in 1959. But Negro farms showed little growth. They averaged 43 acres in 1930, 52 acres in 1960; the remaining Negro farmers remained poor.

Change has not resulted in larger, more prosperous Negro farms. Change has expelled from Southern farms the most ill-educated Americans.

Looking ahead, the Negro reservoir is nearly exhausted. The number of rural farm Negroes in 1960 was only 47 percent of the number in 1950. The Negro exodus can never again approach the scale reached during the 1950's. Poor Negroes are already committed to the city.

The fourth change benefiting the general public and injuring poor Negroes has been manufacturing migration. Since 1950, Southern manufacturing has expanded more rapidly than Northern. . . .

Manufacturing's Southern migration to new markets and new sources of raw material has distributed American resources more efficiently. It has taken jobs to poor whites but not to poor Negro men. Between 1950 and 1960, the number of jobs in Southern manufacturing rose by 944,000. Of these 944,000 jobs, 12,000 went to Negro women (proportionately fewer than to white women); none went to Negro men.

During wartime, rural Southern Negroes proved themselves in manufacturing and developed vested interests in the growth of unskilled and semi-skilled manufacturing jobs.

Today, technological change benefits all by raising productivity. It also changes America's occupational cross section. In 1880 textile mechanization replaced skilled workers with unskilled rural immigrants. Negroes would prefer such changes today, but in 1964 skilled workers replaced unskilled.

In recent years, the occupations that during war gave Negroes a chance to get ahead have not grown as rapidly as the number of Negroes seeking work. Between 1947 and 1964, as male employment rose 10 percent, the number of manufacturing production jobs rose only 5½ percent. Between 1950 and 1960, male employment rose 6.9 percent; the number of semi-skilled jobs in manufacturing rose only 4.1 percent.

Most unfavorable for aspiring unskilled poor Negroes, the number of men's laboring jobs in manufacturing fell twenty percent (by 200,000) between 1950 and 1960.

These changes in America's occupational cross section result from technological developments that raise society's affluence. Poor whites are relatively free to enter other occupations, but, as present trends continue, manufacturing, the Negro's past ladder to escape from poverty, will offer fewer exits from poverty for Negroes handicapped by rural origins. . . .

Many Negroes transplanted to cities are unable to obtain steady work. Long's argument that America's social minimum wage rises above the marginal revenue product of society's least productive members applies especially to urban Negroes with rural Southern antecedents. Law and respectable custom press upward on the social minimum wage. The general welfare benefits as many low income persons receive more money and employers increase efficiency to off-set higher costs. But the first increase in the minimum causes the discharge of the least able persons employed. Successive increases cause the discharge of successively more able persons among the less able employed.

It is the function of the market to choose technology appropriate to available resources as reflected in flexible resource prices. But the market does not operate below the social minimum. Weighed down with their heritage from the Southern Way of Life, able-bodied Negroes with marginal revenue products below the social minimum wage must either find employers paying below the minimum or depend on transfers.

So much for [the] forces benefiting the general public but especially hurting poor Negroes.

A fourth kind of difference between poor Negroes and poor whites is in the effects of transfer payments. For 15 years, Negro unemployment rates have been double white rates. This distinguishes Negro from white need for transfers, but does not distinguish poor Negroes from poor whites.

Respecting government transfers, poor Negroes do differ from poor whites because proportionately more Negro households have feminine heads and proportionately fewer Negroes are past 64.

Relatively few Negroes receive OASDI (old age, survivors, and disability insurance). In 1962, 6.7 percent of the 12,500,000 recipients were non-white. This low figure was due to the non-white's shorter age span and the dissimilar work histories that led 73 percent of elderly whites but only 58 percent of elderly non-whites to qualify. In contrast, old age assistance goes to 38 percent of elderly non-whites, 12 percent of elderly whites.

OASDI brings elderly Negroes and whites close to income equality. For all persons, Negro income averages half of white income. Yet the average income of non-whites runs 80 percent the average total income of whites receiving OASDI. This happens because many Negroes continue in poverty while many whites sink into poverty after retiring.

Because Negro fathers so often decamp, Negro children receive a disproportionate share of ADC (aid to families with dependent children). Of 900,000 families (with 2,800,000 children) receiving ADC in 1963, 44 percent were Negro.

Per capita, ADC pays much less than retirement programs. Old age assistance meets 94 percent of the needs of the elderly; ADC supplies 58 percent of children's needs. Playing surrogate to absent fathers of poor Negro families, ADC never raises incomes or aspirations above

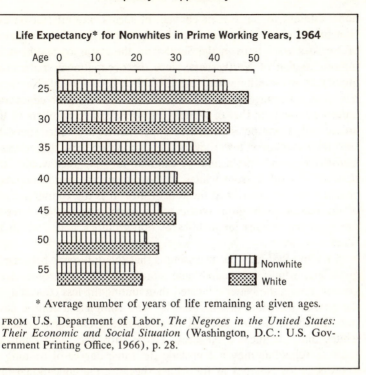

Life Expectancy* for Nonwhites in Prime Working Years, 1964

* Average number of years of life remaining at given ages.

FROM U.S. Department of Labor, *The Negroes in the United States: Their Economic and Social Situation* (Washington, D.C.: U.S. Government Printing Office, 1966), p. 28.

levels at which the mothers' and absent fathers', in the words of Mollie Orshansky, "only legacy to their children is the same one of poverty and deprivation that they received from their own parents."

Inequality of Opportunity

PETER M. BLAU
AND OTIS DUDLEY DUNCAN

It is hardly surprising that Negroes in the United States do not have the same occupational opportunities as whites. The lower occupational status of Negroes cannot be fully accounted for by their lower educa-

FROM Peter M. Blau, professor of sociology, University of Chicago; Otis Dudley Duncan, professor of sociology, Center for Population Studies, University of Michigan, *The American Occupational Structure* (New York: Wiley, 1967), pp. 238–41.

tional attainment, since their chances of success are inferior on every educational level. Neither is it attributable to the fact that the majority of Negroes were born in the South and the status of Southerners is inferior to that of Northerners, since the occupational status of Negroes remains inferior when region of birth is controlled. Negroes do have less advantageous social origins than whites; their education is indeed poorer than that of whites; disproportionate numbers of them are actually from the South where opportunities are inferior; and they start their careers on lower levels. Yet even when these differences are statistically standardized and we examine how Negroes would fare if they did not differ from whites in these respects, their occupational chances are still inferior to those of whites. It is the cumulative effect of the handicaps Negroes encounter at every step in their lives that produces the serious inequalities of opportunities under which they suffer.

A finding that may be surprising is that the difference between Negroes and whites in occupational status as well as income is even greater among the better educated than among the less educated, with the partial exception of the minority who complete a college education. In short, better educated Negroes fare even worse relative to whites than uneducated Negroes. To be sure, the same number of years of schooling may not provide the same degree of training and knowledge for Negroes as for whites, because the educational facilities that the white majority supplies for Negroes are usually inferior. But whether the discrimination against Negroes actually occurs in the educational system or subsequently in the occupational system—and it undoubtedly occurs to some extent in both—the fact remains that the results of this discrimination are more pronounced for the better than for the less educated Negro. This fact has some important implications.

Since Negroes receive less return in the form of superior occupational prestige and income for their educational investments than whites, they have less incentive to make such investments, that is, to make the sacrifices that staying in school to acquire more education entails, particularly for underprivileged youngsters. Acquiring an education is simply not very profitable for Negroes, which may explain why some Negroes exhibit little motivation to pursue their schooling. Negroes must be strongly imbued with the basic value of education for them to have improved their educational attainments in recent years despite the comparatively low rewards education brings them. Moreover, whereas educated persons are generally considered to be more enlightened and, specifically, to be less prejudiced against Negroes and other minorities than less educated ones, the data show that in actuality there is more discrimination against Negroes in highly than in less educated groups. It can hardly be a pattern of prejudice unique to the uneducated laborers and operatives that forces enlightened employers to discriminate against hiring Negroes on these levels, as is sometimes alleged, for there is even more discrimination on higher levels. Another anomaly implicit in these findings is that although it is the uneducated Negro who is the main object of the prejudiced stereotype, the educated one being often explicitly exempt from it, it is the better educated Negro who in practice suffers most from discrimination.

Men born in the South, white as well as Negro, have inferior occupational chances, whether they remain there or migrate north. The occupational handicaps of southern whites and of southern-born Negroes living in the North are due to their inferior preparation, as indicated by the finding that the differences between them and their northern counterparts disappear when education and other background factors are statistically controlled. The persisting residual difference for Negroes who have remained in the South is in all likelihood the result of discrimination in employment. There is some evidence that the discrimination against Negroes has declined in recent decades, but progress has been very slow. The improvements in the relative position of the Negro have been largely confined to minimum education and less discrimination in hiring at the point of entry into the labor market. In respect to higher education, necessary for advancement to more responsible positions, the gap between whites and Negroes not only has failed to narrow but actually has continued to widen in the last half-century.

Members of white ethnic minorities, in contrast to Negroes, fare as well as if not better than the dominant majority. This does not mean that there is no discrimination against any white ethnic minorities; as a matter of fact, the occupational differences between the second generation of northern European or western European descent and that of other origins suggests that there is some discrimination against descendants of the less prestigeful immigrant groups, such as Italians and Poles. Whatever discrimination against selected white minorities exists, however, is not so pronounced as to suppress the strong achievement motivation characteristic of many sons of immigrants, and their drive to succeed has apparently overcome their background handicap as well as such discrimination, as manifest in their high occupational achievements and rates of mobility. The finding that these sons of immigrants are more successful in their careers than the sons of the native-born majority who have remained near their homes but not than those sons of the majority group who have left their region of birth indicates that something the second generation and migrants have in common promotes occupational achievements. This may be the varied cultural experiences to which both sons of immigrants and men who live in a different part of the country from where they were raised are exposed, or it may be the fact that migration as well as immigration is selective of men with strong achievement motives that are passed on to sons.

The general conclusion to which these findings point is that the American occupational structure is largely governed by universalistic criteria of performance and achievement, with the notable exception of the influence of race. The close relationship between educational attainment and occupational achievement, with education being the most important determinant of occupational status that could be discovered, testifies to this universalism. So does the finding that there is little discrimination against white ethnic groups in occupational life, though discrimination against selected minorities unquestionably exists, concealed in our data due to the superior accomplishments of some members of the second generation. Most of the groups that are economically disadvantaged, such as those born in other countries and those born in the South, have lower educational attainments commensurate with their lower occupational positions. An important exception to this pervasive universalism is the severe discrimination the Negro suffers at every step in the process toward achieving occupational success. Although there is some indication that discrimination against Negroes has declined in this century, and hence that universalism has continued to spread, the trend is not consistent, does not encompass all areas of occupational life, and has only begun to penetrate into the South. But universalism cannot restore equality. Indeed, the data suggest that the relative position of the Negro in regard to higher levels of attainment has become worse in recent decades.

Employment of Minority Groups and Whites, 1966

(Numbers in thousands; percent distribution)

	Men					Women				
Occupation[1]	Negro	Oriental	American Indian[2]	Spanish American[3]	Anglo	Negro	Oriental	American Indian[2]	Spanish American[3]	Anglo
Total: Number	1,472	86	39	453	15,962	648	46	17	202	7,228
Percent	100.0	100.0	100.0	100.0	100.0	100.0	100.0	100.0	100.0	100.0
Professional and technical workers	2.0	29.3	6.6	4.7	13.9	6.1	18.2	5.6	3.6	7.4
Managers, officials, and proprietors	1.0	7.0	6.5	2.5	12.0	.7	1.9	2.2	.8	2.6
Clerical workers	2.7	8.3	3.9	5.1	7.1	17.5	41.1	21.7	24.1	40.8
Sales workers	1.3	4.8	4.7	3.0	7.4	4.0	5.9	12.5	6.9	9.3
Craftsmen	7.9	13.6	19.3	13.9	20.4	2.4	2.3	5.1	4.8	2.8
Operatives	37.2	14.0	29.9	32.1	25.5	24.9	11.4	24.2	29.8	21.7
Service workers	18.1	12.1	6.7	12.2	5.4	30.3	12.2	16.9	12.4	9.1
Laborers	29.8	10.9	22.3	26.4	8.4	14.1	7.0	11.8	17.6	6.4
Percent of total population (including Anglos) employed	8.2	.5	.2	2.5	88.6	7.9	.6	.2	2.5	88.9

[1] The data were collected from employers with 100 or more workers.
[2] Nonreservation Indians.
[3] Includes both Puerto Ricans and Mexican Americans.

FROM U.S. Department of Labor, *Manpower Report of the President, 1968* (Washington, D.C.: U.S. Government Printing Office, 1968), p. 64.

The Children

Children of the Poor

MOLLIE ORSHANSKY

Children generally do not contribute income of their own to a family but must rely instead on the support of others. As a result, after the aged—whose earning capacity is also likely to be limited if not lacking altogether—children are the poorest age group, particularly if the father is absent. Three out of 5 youngsters in families headed by women were being raised in poverty—a total of 4½ million poor children—but there were also 8 million other children who were poor in unbroken families. The mother of young children, whether she herself is the family head or shares the responsibility with a husband, finds it hard to take a job, but many families can escape poverty only if both parents work and some not even then. Twelve percent of the husband-wife families were poor when the wife did not work and 5 percent even when she did. Perhaps more to the point in assessing remedial action against poverty is the fact that 4½ million children were counted poor though they were in the home of a man who had worked throughout 1966 and nearly 1 million more were in the family of a woman who held a job all year. Children with a working mother but minus a father receive little help from existing public programs unless they are the orphans of veterans or workers who were covered under OASDHI, but the children with a father present and working receive almost no help at all. Youngsters in large families were particularly bad off, and if the large family had a woman at its head, the odds were better than 4 out of 5 that it was poor.

All told, close to half the Nation's poor children were in families with at least five youngsters present, but the size and current living arrangements of families, as the Census normally counts them, are

FROM Mollie Orshansky, Division of Research and Statistics, Social Security Administration, "The Shape of Poverty in 1966," *Social Security Bulletin* (March 1968), pp. 16–18.

sometimes the result of poverty; they are not always the cause. Family groups with insufficient income, particularly if there is no man at the head, may share living quarters with relatives to help meet living expenses. Thus in nonpoor families in 1966, only 1 in 25 of the children under age 18 were not the children of the head or wife but children of other relatives. In poor families as a group, 1 in 10 children were related rather than own children, and in poor families headed by a woman, the proportion was 1 in 8.

Many families with four or five youngsters had insufficient income to support even two or three, though all would be less poor if they spread their limited resources among fewer members. For example, of the families poor in 1966 with a woman at the head and four children, one-half had less than $2,300 income for the year. Even on the assumption that there was no one else in the family, this median was 40 percent less than the minimum of $3,900 required to enable a nonfarm family of this size to stay above the poverty line and was not even enough for a mother and two children.

Death at an Early Age

JONATHAN KOZOL

Perhaps a reader would like to know what it is like to go into a new classroom in the same way that I did and to see before you suddenly, and in terms you cannot avoid recognizing, the dreadful consequences of a year's wastage of real lives.

You walk into a narrow and old wood-smelling classroom and you see before you thirty-five curious, cautious and untrusting children, aged eight to thirteen, of whom about two-thirds are Negro. Three of the children are designated to you as special students. Thirty per cent of the class is reading at the Second Grade level in a year and in a month in which they should be reading at the height of Fourth Grade performance or at the beginning of the Fifth. Seven children out of the class are up to par. . . . Nobody seems to know

FROM Jonathan Kozol, erstwhile provisional teacher, Boston Public Schools, *Death at an Early Age: The Destruction of the Hearts and Minds of Negro Children in Boston Public Schools* (Boston: Houghton Mifflin, 1967), pp. 29–30, 61, 162–63, 190.

how many teachers they have had. Seven of their lifetime records are missing: symptomatic and emblematic at once of the chaos that has been with them all year long. Many more lives than just seven have already been wasted but the seven missing records become an embittering symbol of the lives behind them which, equally, have been lost or mislaid. (You have to spend the first three nights staying up until dawn trying to reconstruct these records out of notes and scraps.) On the first math test you give, the class average comes out to 36. The children tell you with embarrassment that it has been like that since fall. . . .

The room in which I taught my Fourth Grade was not a room at all, but the corner of an auditorium. . . . Three or four blackboards, two of them broken, made them seem a little bit set apart. Over at the other end of the auditorium there was another Fourth Grade class. Not much was happening at the other side at that minute so that for the moment the noise did not seem so bad. But it became a real nightmare of conflicting noises a little later on. Generally it was not until ten o'clock that the bad crossfire started. By ten-thirty it would have attained such a crescendo that the children in the back rows of my section often couldn't hear my questions and I could not hear their answers. There were no carpetings or sound-absorbers of any kind. The room, being large, and echoing, and wooden, added resonance to every sound. Sometimes the other teacher and I would stagger the lessons in which our classes would have to speak aloud, but this was a makeshift method and it also meant that our classes had to be induced to maintain an unnatural and otherwise unnecessary rule of silence during the rest of the time. We couldn't always do it anyway, and usually the only way out was to try to outshout each other so that both of us often left school hoarse or wheezing. While her class was reciting in unison you could not hear very much in mine. When she was talking alone I could be heard above her but the trouble then was that little bits of her talk got overheard by my class. . . .

Soon after I came into that auditorium, I discovered that it was not only our two Fourth Grades that were going to have their classes here. We were to share the space also with the glee club, with play rehearsals, special reading, special arithmetic, and also at certain times a Third or Fourth Grade phonics class. . . .

The first writing assignment that [my Fourth Grade] passed in emphasized what many of those children were thinking and feeling. . . .

"In my school," began a paper that was handed back to me a few days later, "I see dirty boards and I see papers on the floor. I see an old browken window with a sign on it saying, Do not unlock this window are browken. And I see cracks in the walls and I see old books with ink poured all over them and I see old painting hanging on the walls. I see old alfurbet letter hanging on one nail on the wall. I see a dirty fire exit I see a old closet with supplys for the class. I see pigons flying all over the school. I see old freght trains throgh the fence of the school yard. I see pictures of contryies hanging on the wall and I see desks with wrighting all over the top of the desks and insited of the desk."

Another child told me this: "I see lots of thinings in this room. I see new teachers omots every day. I can see flowers and children books and others things. I like the 100 papers I like allso cabnets. I don't like the drity windows. And the dusty window shallvalls . . ."

A little girl wrote this: "I can see old cars with gas in it and there is always people lighting fires old refrigartor an wood glass that comes from the old cars old trees and trash old weeds and people put there old chairs in there an flat tires and one thing there is up there is wood that you can make dog houses and there are beautiful flowers and there are dead dogs and cats . . . On some of the cars the weel is of and wisey bottles beer cans car seats are all out cars are all tip over and just the other day there was a fire and it was just blasting and whew in the back there is a big open space where Girl Scouts could mabe cook . . . this feild was a gas staition and the light pole is still up."

This was one more: "I see pictures in my school. I see pictures of Spain and a pictures of Portofino and a pictures of Chicago. I see arithmetic paper a spellings paper. I see a star chart. I see the flag of our Amerrica. The room is dirty . . . The auditorium dirty the seats are dusty. The light in the auditorium is brok. The curtains in the auditorium are ragged they took the curtains down because they was so ragged. The bathroom is dirty sometime the toilet is very hard. The cellar is dirty the hold school is dirty sometime . . . The flowers are dry every thing in my school is so so dirty."

. . . The place was ugly, noisy, rotten. Yet the children before me found it natural and automatic to accept as normal the school's structural inadequacies and to incorporate them, as it were, right into themselves: as if perhaps the rotting timbers might be not objective calamities but self-condemning configurations of their own making and as if the frenzied noise and overcrowding were a condition and an indictment not of the school building itself but rather of their own inadequate mentalities or of their own incapacitated souls. Other children were defiant but most of them were not. It was the tension between defiance and docility, and the need of a beleaguered teacher to justify something absolutely unjustifiable, which created the air of unreality, possible danger, intellectual hypocrisy and fear. The result of this atmosphere was that too many children became believers in their own responsibility for being ruined and they themselves, like the teachers, began somehow to believe that some human material is just biologically better and some of it worse. A former chairman and present member of the Boston School Committee, a person named William O'Connor, has publicly given utterance to this idea in words he must regret by this time. "We have no inferior education in our schools," he has let himself be quoted: "What we have been getting is an inferior type of student." Is it any wonder, with the heads of the school system believing this, that after a while some of the children come to believe they are inferior too?

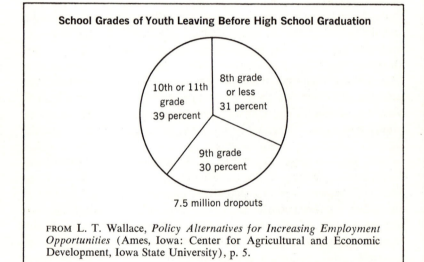

School Grades of Youth Leaving Before High School Graduation

10th or 11th grade
39 percent

8th grade or less
31 percent

9th grade
30 percent

7.5 million dropouts

FROM L. T. Wallace, *Policy Alternatives for Increasing Employment Opportunities* (Ames, Iowa: Center for Agricultural and Economic Development, Iowa State University), p. 5.

Strengths of the Children of the Poor

ROBERT COLES

Educators confirm what their brother social scientists have noted: ghetto children do not take to school, they are nasty—or plain lazy. (I wish they at least were described that way. Instead one meets up

FROM Robert Coles, research psychiatrist, Harvard University Health Services, "Children of the American Ghetto," *Harper's Magazine* (September 1967), pp. 16–22.

with the impossible jargon of educational psychologists, who talk about "motivational deficits" or "lowered achievement goals" or "self-esteem impairment.") They tell us that slum schools must be "enriched" with programs to suit children who live in a vast cultural wasteland. Machines, books, audio-visual equipment, special "curricula," smaller classes, trips to museums, contacts with suburban children, with trees and hillsides—the ghetto child needs all of it and more. He needs personal "guidance." He could benefit from knowing a VISTA volunteer, or a college student who wants to be a tutor, or a housewife from the other side of town who wants to give poor children the things her own children take for granted.

Though some of these assertions are obviously correct, their cumulative implication is misleading and unfair. It is about time the lives of ghetto children be seen as something more than a tangle of psychopathology and flawed performances in school. Children in the ghetto do need help, but not the kind that stems from an endless, condescending recital of their troubles and failures—and often ignores or caricatures the strength, intelligence, and considerable ingenuity they do possess. . . .

That people under stress can develop special strengths, while security tends to make one soft, has often been pointed out. However, no one in his right mind can *recommend* hardship or suffering as a way of life, nor does anyone with half a brain want to justify slavery, perpetuate segregation, or prove poverty "right"—make of them good things that produce strong, stubborn people. (Even so, I have no doubt that there are many people who would love a new and sophisticated way to tell the poor how wonderful their life is, after all.) Rather, the issue is one of justice—and not only to the Negro. The Negro deserves to be seen for who he is and what he has become. . . . If psychological or sociological labels are to be pinned on the Negro, then those who do so might at least be careful to mention the enormous, perplexing issues that plague the white, suburban middle class: a high divorce rate; juvenile delinquency; political indifference or inertia to match any rural Negro's; psychiatric clinics and child-guidance centers filled to the brim, and with waiting lists so long that some are called only after two or three years; greed and competitiveness that worried teachers see in the youngest boys and girls and accept wearily as a manifestation of the "system."

There are, to be fair, some observers who have consistently remarked upon the considerable energy and "life" they see in slum children. They have seen openness, humor, real and winning vitality. Many ghetto children I know have a flesh and blood loyalty to one another, a disarming code of honor, a sharp, critical eye for the fake and pretentious, a delightful capacity to laugh, yell, shout, sing, congratulate themselves, and tickle others. Their language is often strong and expressive, their drawings full of action, feeling, and even searing social criticism. I have to contrast all of that to the rigid, long-winded "experts" who are quick to call slum people everything ominous under the sun.

One thing is certain, though: ghetto childhood tends to be short and swift. The fast-moving, animated children I see every day soon enough grow old rather than grow up, and begin to show every sign of the resignation described by writer after writer. At twelve or thirteen these children feel that schools lead nowhere, that there will be jobs for only a few, that ahead of them is the prospect of an increasingly futile and bitter struggle to hold on to whatever health, possessions, and shelter they have.

"They is alive, and you bet they is, and then they goes off and quits," said one mother, summing it up for me. . . . "There comes a day when they ask you why it's like it is for us, and all you can do is shrug your shoulders, or sometimes you scream. But they know already, and they're just asking for the record. And it don't take but a few months to see that they're no longer kids, and they've lost all the hope and the life you tried to give them."

The vitality of each new child restores at least the possibility of hope in a parent; and so life in the ghetto not only persists but seeks after purpose and coherence. . . .

Thus, though we may console ourselves with the programs we offer the poor, some of them are not only condescending and self-defeating, but they overlook the very real assets and interests of ghetto children. It has never occurred to some of the welfare workers, educators, or Head Start teachers I have met that "their" programs and policies bore, amuse, or enrage children and parents from the slums.

Consider, for example, one ghetto family I visit twice a week. They are on welfare. Two children were in a Head Start program last summer. An older son took part in an "enrichment" program. A teen-aged cousin is in the Job Corps. At school the children are told by teachers what they already know, that their school is "inadequate." The building is old, the corridors packed with many more students than were ever intended, and the teachers I have observed are disciplinarians at best. The head of the family is a woman of thirty who regularly calls herself "old." Once she added that she was also "sick," and I immediately took notice, expecting to hear about an ache or pain I could diagnose. But she went on to say that she was "tired of everything they try to do to help us. They send us those welfare checks, and with them comes that lady who peeks around every corner here, and gives me those long lectures on how I should do everything—like her, of course. I want to tell her to go charge around and become a spy, or one of those preachers who can find sin in a clean handkerchief.

"Then they take my kids to the Head Start thing, and first thing I hear is the boys' fingernails is dirty, and they isn't eating the proper food, and they don't use the right words, and the words they do use, no one can make them out. It's just like with the older kids. They try to take them to those museums and places, and tell them how sorry life is here at home and in the neighborhood, and how they is no good, and something has to be done to make them better—like the rich ones, I guess.

"But the worst is they just make you feel no good at all. They tell you they want to help you, but if you ask me they want to make you into them, and leave you without a cent of yourself left to hang on to. I keep on asking them, why don't they fix the country up, so that people can *work,* instead of patching up with this and that, and giving us a dollar for *not* working, to keep us from starving right to death. And then you could get out of here, and let us be, and have our lives."

Child-rearing Comparisons

CATHERINE S. CHILMAN

Child-rearing patterns reported to be more characteristic of families of children who are emotionally healthy [are here] compared with relevant patterns reported to be more characteristic of very poor families.

Conducive	Low-income
1. Respect for child as individual whose behavior is caused by a mul-	1. Misbehavior regarded as such in terms of concrete pragmatic out-

FROM Catherine S. Chilman, Welfare Administration, U.S. Department of Health, Education, and Welfare, *Growing Up Poor* (Washington, D.C.: U.S. Department of Health, Education, and Welfare, 1966), pp. 28–29.

Conducive	*Low-income*
tiple of factors. Acceptance of own role in events that occur.	comes; reasons for behavior not considered. Projection of blame on others.
2. Commitment to slow development of child from infancy to maturity; stresses and pressures of each stage accepted by parent because of perceived worth of ultimate goal of raising "happy," successful son or daughter.	2. Lack of goal commitment and of belief in long-range success; a main object for parent and child is to "keep out of trouble"; orientation toward fatalism, impulse gratification, and sense of alienation.
3. Relative sense of competence in handling child's behavior.	3. Sense of impotence in handling children's behavior, as well as in other areas.
4. Discipline chiefly verbal, mild, reasonable, consistent, based on needs of child and family and of society; more emphasis on rewarding good behavior than on punishing bad behavior.	4. Discipline harsh, inconsistent, physical, makes use of ridicule; based on whether child's behavior does or does not annoy parent.
5. Open, free, verbal communication between parent and child; control largely verbal.	5. Limited verbal communication; control largely physical.
6. Democratic rather than autocratic or laissez faire methods of rearing, with both parents in equalitarian but not necessarily interchangeable roles. Companionship between parents and children.	6. Authoritarian rearing methods; mother chief child-care agent; father, when in home, mainly a punitive figure. Little support and acceptance of child as an individual.
7. Parents view selves as generally competent adults, and are generally satisfied with themselves and their situation.	7. Low parental self-esteem, sense of defeat.
8. Intimate, expressive, warm relationship between parent and child, allowing for gradually increasing independence. Sense of continuing responsibility.	8. Large families; more impulsive, narcissistic parent behavior. Orientation to "excitement." Abrupt, early yielding of independence.
9. Presence of father in home and lack of severe marital conflict.	9. Father out of home (under certain circumstances).

10. Free verbal communication about sex, acceptance of child's sex needs, channeling of sex drive through "healthy" psychological defenses, acceptance of slow growth toward impulse control and sex satisfaction in marriage; sex education by both father and mother.

10. Repressive, punitive attitude about sex, sex questioning, and experimentation. Sex viewed as exploitative relationship.

11. Acceptance of child's drive for aggression but channeling it into socially approved outlets.

11. Alternating encouragement and restriction of aggression, primarily related to consequences of aggression for parents.

12. In favor of new experiences; flexible.

12. Distrust of new experiences. Constricted life, rigidity.

13. Happiness of parental marriage.

13. High rates of marital conflict and family breakdown.

husband unhappy w/ himself

The Youth

The Gap from School to Work

U.S. DEPARTMENT OF LABOR

The essence of the problem is reflected in the paradox that emerges from the following two positions: The United States keeps larger proportions of its children in school longer than does any other nation, to insure their preparation for lifetime activity. Yet the unemployment rate among youth is far higher here than in any other industrial nation and had been rising sharply until the introduction of the Government's youth programs over the last 4 years.

Unemployment rates among youth, while highest for those in low-

FROM U.S. Department of Labor, *Manpower Report of the President, 1968* (Washington, D.C.: U.S. Government Printing Office, 1968), pp. 111–14.

income minority group families, are substantially higher in all income groups than those considered desirable by any concept of acceptable unemployment rates that has been developed in our Nation. Thus, youth in the 14- to 19-year-old bracket from families with incomes of less than $3,000 have unemployment rates of 17.4 percent, an extraordinarily high level. But even youth from families with incomes of $10,000 and over have unemployment rates of 7.7 percent—rates that are about double the national average and quadruple the rates of adults.

The differentials between youth and adult unemployment rates have persisted despite marked improvements in the overall employment situation. Examination of the character and dimensions of youth programs undertaken in the last 4 years, of the rise in youth unemployment rates before that, and of the demographic and economic factors at work suggests that the introduction of these special programs has been a key factor in keeping youth unemployment rates from rising even further in relation to adult rates.

The pattern of high unemployment rates among youth has become more pronounced in recent years. Though some differential between adult and youth rates has existed for decades, the gap has widened with the passage of time. . . .

While unemployment rates give some indication of why the school-to-work problem commands public attention, they are by no means the sole indicator of its dimensions. Unemployment rates do not reflect discouraged abstention from the job market, underemployment, or frustrating occupational misfits that may lead to quits and unemployment—problems on which there is, as yet, no adequate information. . . .

The youth for whom bridges to work are now most adequate are those with the intensive preparation provided by professional training at the college level or beyond. For them, careers are virtually assured and unemployment is at or very close to minimum levels. In fact, in many specialties there are numerous opportunities open for people with professional training. But sizable proportions of all other groups of youth—high school dropouts, high school graduates, and college dropouts—face serious uncertainties as they leave the academic world and begin the work for which school was to have prepared them.

The tremendous advantage college graduates have in entering the world of work can be seen from the unemployment rates for young adults. In March 1967, for example, 20- to 24-year-olds with a college degree had an unemployment rate of only 1.4 percent, compared with

5.3 percent for those with a high school diploma, and a completely unacceptable 10.5 percent for those who had completed only 8 years of school.

Vocational preparation at the secondary and postsecondary levels has been progressively strengthened, however, under the impetus of the Vocational Education Act of 1963. This act has made possible extensive improvements in both the quantity and quality of vocational education offerings, which should mean better job preparation for many youth.

The problem of building bridges between school and work involves many fundamental elements in American life in addition to educational preparation. No one institution has or can have sole responsibility for helping youth to prepare for and make the transition from school to work without unreasonable and discouraging spells of unemployment. Some young people get help from teachers; some get help from school counselors, especially "if they are college material" and will therefore cross into the work world with greater ease at a later point. Many are placed by the Employment Service system. Others get help from social workers, police, neighborhood centers, youth programs, or individual employers to whom they apply. Personal contact (through acquaintances, friends, and relatives), which has always been a strong feature of the job market in this country, is one of the most frequent ways of finding jobs. . . .

Recent studies suggest that we do not fully understand what the function of the parent is in preparing children for work, whether through education, training, or other means. Nor do we know what this parental activity contributes to the Nation's economy. The importance of parental influence in determining the ultimate place of the child in society is suggested by various census data relating the education of parents to the education of their children. Where the father had graduated from high school, about 87 percent of sons aged 25 to 34 were also graduates. On the other hand, where the father did not graduate from high school, less than 60 percent of sons in this age group received high school diplomas. . . .

The need to supplement the activities of the parents through various parent-surrogate activities such as Head Start cannot be overestimated. Services that middle and upper income families provide their children as a matter of course are all too often missing in the low-income home. The availability of adequate substitutes may help break the intergenerational chains of poverty for many children from disadvantaged environments.

FROM Mollie Orshansky, "Who's Who Among the Poor: A Demographic View of Poverty," *Social Security Bulletin* (July 1965), p. 19.

School and Labor-Force Status of Teenagers

(Poor versus non-poor families)

School attendance and labor-force status in March 1964	All children aged 14–19				Children aged 18–19			
	Families with male head		Families with female head		Families with male head		Families with female head	
	Poor	Non-poor	Poor	Non-poor	Poor	Non-poor	Poor	Non-poor
Total number (in thousands)	1,930	12,980	870	1,120	330	2,730	120	300
Percent	100.0	100.0	100.0	100.0	100.0	100.0	100.0	100.0
Attending school	81.8	89.0	83.5	82.7	47.7	62.5	46.3	50.1
Employed	9.2	16.7	8.2	17.9	10.2	16.1	7.3	15.3
Unemployed	1.6	2.4	2.2	2.1	3.7	2.5	4.1	1.3
Not in labor force	71.0	69.9	73.1	62.6	33.8	43.9	34.9	33.5
Not in school	18.2	11.0	16.5	17.3	52.3	37.5	53.7	49.9
Employed	8.8	7.4	4.6	11.0	27.4	28.1	18.7	35.9
Unemployed	3.1	1.5	4.6	3.0	12.0	5.6	13.0	8.0
Not in labor force	6.3	2.1	7.3	3.3	12.9	3.8	22.0	6.0
Keeping house	2.9	.7	5.1	1.2	8.0	1.0	16.3	2.4
Not high school graduate	14.4	5.4	14.1	7.5	30.8	11.6	39.9	13.6
Employed	7.1	2.9	3.6	2.9	17.5	7.4	13.8	5.6
Unemployed	2.2	.9	4.5	1.6	6.8	2.5	11.4	3.7
Not in labor force	5.1	1.6	6.0	3.0	6.5	1.6	14.6	4.3
Keeping house	2.2	.6	4.2	.9	4.3	.5	11.4	.7
High school graduate	3.8	5.6	2.4	9.8	21.5	25.9	13.8	36.2
Employed	1.7	4.4	1.0	8.0	9.8	20.8	4.9	30.2
Unemployed	.9	.7	.1	1.5	5.2	3.1	1.6	4.3
Not in labor force	1.2	.5	1.3	.3	6.5	2.2	7.3	1.7
Keeping house	.7	.1	.9	.3	3.7	.5	4.9	1.7

Income and College Attendance

WILLARD WIRTZ

The most important source of data on the relationship between family income and college attendance, among high school students with various levels of academic aptitude, is "Project Talent," a cooperative research study carried out by the University of Pittsburgh and the American Institute for Research, and financed primarily by the U.S. Office of Education. In the overall project, about 440,000 students in grades 9 to 12 were tested with a battery of tests measuring general intelligence, various specific aptitudes, personality and social maturity, etc. Information was also obtained on scholastic performance, economic and social characteristics of the student's family, and characteristics of the school attended.

In one special study undertaken by Project Talent, high school graduates who were in the project's sample of 12th grade pupils were contacted by mail questionnaire to determine which of them had entered college within 1 year after completing the 12th grade. For the approximately 60,000 graduates who responded (about 67 percent of the sample) it was then possible to relate the data on college attendance to other information, including the income of the student's family and the individual's relative rating on academic aptitude. Academic aptitude was measured by a composite of four Project Talent tests, and respondents were ranked in percentiles based on a representative sample of pupils in grade 12. Those in the 90th to 100th percentile, for example, represent high school graduates whose academic aptitude falls in the top 10 percent of all 12th grade students. . . .

Table 1 shows the percentage of male high school graduates, classified by family income and by percentile ranking on academic aptitude, who had not entered college within 1 year after completing high school. Among those with an extremely high level of general college aptitude (the upper 2 percent) nearly all male high school graduates entered college, regardless of family income. In every in-

FROM testimony of Willard Wirtz, U.S. Secretary of Labor, *Hearings on the Employment Opportunity Act of 1964,* Subcommittee on the War on Poverty Program, House Committee on Education and Labor, 88th Congress, 2nd Session (March 19, 1964), pp. 205–07.

TABLE 1

Percentages of Male High School Graduates Who Responded to Mail Questionnaire and Who Did Not Enter College Within 1 Year After Completing Grade 12

(*By aptitude percentile and family income*)

Aptitude level percentile	Less than $3,000	$3,000 to $5,999	$6,000 to $8,999	$9,000 to $11,999	$12,000 and up
98 to 100	0	3.9	4.8	4.1	1.5
90 to 97.9	12.1	13.3	11.4	7.5	3.3
75 to 89.9	24.6	26.7	19.4	16.1	9.9
50 to 74.9	51.8	47.5	40.3	33.2	20.3
0 to 49.9	80.4	72.7	68.1	59.8	50.3

Source: Data are taken from Project Talent in U.S. Office of Education cooperative research program, project 2333.

come class, more than 95 percent entered college, and because of the small numbers in the sample for some income classes, the differences between income levels are not significant.

At every other level of aptitude, however, there is a marked relationship between reported family income and college entry. Of the boys in the second quartile for general college aptitude (50th to 74th percentile) about 52 percent of those from families with incomes below $3,000 per year failed to enter college, while only 20 percent of those from families with incomes above $12,000 failed to enter college. In fact, boys with below-average college aptitude who came from families in the highest income group were actually more likely to enter college than boys in the second quarter of the aptitude ranking who come from families with incomes of less than $3,000.

Table 2 presents similar data for female high school graduates. Since more of the girls than the boys were unable to estimate their family income, the trends for girls are a little less consistent than for boys. At every level of aptitude, however, the proportion of girl high school graduates who failed to enter college was much higher for those who came from the lowest income families than for those who came from high-income families. Among girls in the second quartile of the aptitude range, for example, 70 percent of those from the highest income families went to college, while only 25 percent of those from the lowest income families did so.

TABLE 2

Percentages of Female High School Graduates Who Responded to Mail Questionnaire and Who Did Not Enter College Within 1 Year After Completing Grade 12

(*By aptitude percentile and family income*)

Aptitude level percentile	Less than $3,000	$3,000 to $5,999	$6,000 to $8,999	$9,000 to $11,999	$12,000 and up
98 to 100.0	10.5	2.5	6.7	6.0	3.2
90 to 97.9	36.7	19.2	16.1	14.9	4.8
75 to 89.9	38.9	43.2	30.2	28.2	10.1
50 to 74.9	74.8	64.2	57.4	40.8	29.2
0 to 49.9	82.6	81.8	77.2	69.6	52.1

Source: Data are taken from Project Talent in U.S. Office of Education cooperative research program, project 2333.

The following additional comments on the findings of Project Talent are from a memorandum prepared by the program director, Dr. John T. Dailey:

The accompanying exhibits show that boys and girls from low-income families, except those in the upper 2 percent of ability, have a much poorer chance of going to college than do those from high-income families. . . .

Nearly all students in the upper 2 percent in ability enter college, regardless of level of family income. This is a most remarkable exception to the general association of low family income and talent loss and perhaps indicates that the availability of student aid today is adequate —for 2 percent of our youth. For the other 98 percent, and even for the 8 percent just below the top 2 percent, family income is an important determiner of who will enter college and rise to positions of leadership and personal fulfillment.

Our success with the top 2 percent should give us hope and determination to extend the adequacy of student aid downward to meet the needs of our highly talented youth—not just the top 2 percent.

However, the problem is not just one of student aid and family resources. The opportunities for attending college vary greatly from one part of the country to another. Large regional differences were found in the proportion of high school graduates at the same level of academic aptitude who went to college. Among pupils at about the 75th percentile in academic aptitude, 70 percent of the high school graduates in the Southwest and Far West entered college, while only 50 percent

Characteristics of Draft Rejectees and Their Families, 1963

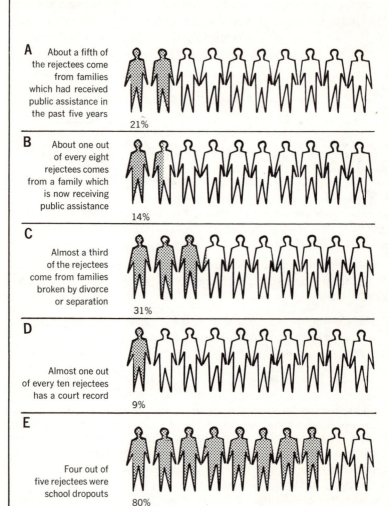

A About a fifth of the rejectees come from families which had received public assistance in the past five years

21%

B About one out of every eight rejectees comes from a family which is now receiving public assistance

14%

C Almost a third of the rejectees come from families broken by divorce or separation

31%

D Almost one out of every ten rejectees has a court record

9%

E Four out of five rejectees were school dropouts

80%

FROM Selective Service System, "Some Socio-Economic Characteristics of the Rejectees and Their Families," *Survey, 1963* (Washington, D.C.: U.S. Government Printing Office, 1964).

of those in the Northeastern and Midwestern States did so. Significant regional differences in the rate of college entry were found at every aptitude level, although they were less pronounced among very bright graduates. Rated according to the proportion of high school graduates who went to college, four large regions are in this order: (1) Southwest, Far West; (2) Southeast; (3) Great Lakes, Plains, Rocky Mountain; (4) New England, Mideast.

Low-cost junior colleges and State colleges that offer programs suited to the needs of students whose interests and aptitudes vary widely are more widely available in regions where college attendance is high.

Providing adequate college programs of this sort in all areas of the country could help eliminate much of the talent loss of our youth.

Education of People Employed in Different Occupations

	Percent with	
	Less than high school	Some college training
Professional and technical workers	6	75
Clerical or sales workers	25	22
Unskilled workers	80	3

FROM Arthur Mauch, *Education and Training* (Ames, Iowa: Center for Agricultural and Economic Development, Iowa State University), p. 3.

The Unemployed and the Underpaid

Casual and Chronic Unemployment

U.S. DEPARTMENT OF LABOR

Over 11 million American workers were jobless and looking for work at some time during the prosperous year 1966. This was almost four

FROM U.S. Department of Labor, *Manpower Report of the President, 1968* (Washington, D.C.: U.S. Government Printing Office, 1968), pp. 18–20.

times the average number (2.9 million) unemployed in any one week of the year. The total number out of work during 1967 was probably somewhat higher. Great progress in reducing unemployment has been made, however, since 1961, when the current economic upturn began. During that recession year, about 15 million workers had periods of unemployment.

The period without work was short (1 to 4 weeks) for over 45 percent of the workers unemployed in 1966. Presumably, unemployment for many of them was due largely to voluntary job changes, some delay in finding work upon entry or reentry into the labor force, and the usual seasonal layoffs. Many secured jobs without outside help. And for those who sought or needed assistance through manpower programs, this help was limited in most cases to job placement services.

The 3.4 million workers with 5 to 14 weeks of unemployment in 1966 may be regarded as an "in between" group. For many of these workers—as well as for those with still briefer periods without work—unemployment was a transitional experience, often cushioned to some extent by unemployment insurance and other benefits. But this group undoubtedly included many workers for whom unemployment of 14 weeks, or even 5 weeks, had serious financial consequences.

Joblessness had hard and unequivocal implications, however, for the 2.7 million workers who were out of work for 15 or more weeks in 1966—over a fourth of the year. More than 1 million of these workers—in cities, towns, and rural areas across the country—spent half or more of 1966 jobless and looking for work.

Any complacency as to the limited impact of extended unemployment among men in the central age groups, who are generally the most employable and have the heaviest family responsibilities, should be ended by these data. Close to 1.3 million men aged 25 to 44 had 5 or more weeks of unemployment during 1966, almost six times the number (226,000) shown by the monthly surveys. For men of this age group out of work 15 to 26 weeks, the differential between the two estimates was even greater (more than sevenfold—342,000, compared with 48,000). Clearly, the number of men of prime working age who are severely affected by joblessness is much higher than is indicated by the monthly unemployment data. And, to a lesser degree, the same is true for women.

With respect to the groups most affected by unemployment—the young, the poorly educated, the unskilled, older workers, and minority groups—the unemployment data based on experience during the year as a whole tell roughly the same comparative story as do the monthly estimates. However, the incidence of extended unemployment is shown to be greater in all groups than is suggested by the monthly figures for these groups. . . .

The widely noted 2-to-1 ratio in the extent of unemployment between nonwhite and white workers is borne out once more by these data. About 12 percent of all nonwhite workers had 5 weeks or more of unemployment in 1966, compared with 6 percent of all white workers. Most seriously affected were the nonwhites who were unskilled laborers—1 out of every 5 was unemployed for 5 or more weeks during 1966.

The major achievements of the past 5 years in reducing unemployment—particularly long-term unemployment—must not be lost sight of, however. Despite very large additions to the work force between 1961 and 1966, the proportion of workers unemployed for 5 or more weeks of the year was cut nearly in half (from 11.6 to 6.4 percent). The general expansion in employment—aided by training and other programs focused on workers with persistent difficulty in finding jobs —brought an even sharper drop in the proportion of workers unemployed 15 weeks or more (from 6.3 percent in 1961 to 2.8 percent in 1966). The improvement was sharpest in the proportion unemployed 27 weeks or more (which fell from 2.8 to 1 percent). Both white and nonwhite workers benefited from this reduction in extended unemployment.

The proportion of workers experiencing repeated spells of joblessness has also dropped significantly. Whereas in 1961, 6.2 percent of the work force had two or more periods of unemployment during the year, by 1966 the figure had fallen to 4 percent. And the proportion of workers reporting at least three spells of unemployment decreased nearly as much (from 3.3 to 2.3 percent).

Nevertheless, the proportion of workers with repeated spells of unemployment did not decline as much, in relative terms, as the overall proportion of workers with many weeks of joblessness. This statistical finding has both economic and policy significance. The improvement in economic conditions, reinforced by manpower programs, has been particularly effective in reducing the number of workers continuously unemployed for long periods; it has, for example, made it much easier for displaced workers to find new jobs. But apparently there has been less progress in reducing irregular or casual employment of unskilled workers or, as yet, in mitigating seasonal layoffs.

Most workers who experience extended unemployment are out of work two or more times during the year. Of the men out of work 15 or more weeks in 1966, 7 out of every 10 were unemployed at least twice during the year. Of those with 27 weeks or more of unemployment, also 7 out of 10 had at least two spells of unemployment, and 4 out of every 10 had three or more spells. These findings underline the need for enlarged efforts to enable the chronically unemployed to qualify for and obtain jobs that promise continuity of employment. There is also a need to explore ways of helping these workers to keep the jobs they get.

The Sub-employed

U.S. DEPARTMENT OF LABOR

The present measures of unemployment—limited, broadly, to persons who have no work at all and are actively seeking a job—are particularly inadequate for assessing the economic situation of disadvantaged workers in urban slums, and also rural areas. A broader, more useful concept for analysis of the problems of these groups—that of sub-employment—was introduced in 1967.

The concept of sub-employment broadens the traditional notions of attachment to the labor force and availability for work, and it introduces the issue of the quality of employment as represented by the level of wages. This is especially important for the development of manpower policy in poverty areas. The employed poor—with earnings below the poverty line even for full-time work—now represent a larger problem, at least in terms of numbers, than the unemployed. Yet they are a group which has so far received comparatively little attention.

Separate consideration of the different kinds of people included among the sub-employed is also essential. The sub-employed are a diverse group, with varied problems requiring different remedial approaches. No one policy will deal effectively with the employment problems of all the sub-employed, nor with all aspects of their problems.

Some of the sub-employed are unable to get or keep a job because of social-psychological characteristics or low motivation. But such

FROM U.S. Department of Labor, *Manpower Report of the President, 1968* (Washington, D.C.: U.S. Government Printing Office, 1968), pp. 35, 83–84.

difficulties must not be considered as characteristic of all the sub-employed. Nor can social-psychological barriers to employment be analyzed apart from the context of available opportunities.

Two obvious but crucial questions are: What are the reasons for the continuing high sub-employment among Negroes and other minority groups in large cities? What can be done to decrease it further? . . .

Sub-employment has declined sharply since 1961. The sub-employment rate, as presently measured, fell from 17 percent in 1961 to 10 percent in 1966.

Low earners were by far the larger of the two groups included in the index—6.7 million, as compared with 2.4 million with 15 or more weeks of unemployment in 1966. And although the number of low

FIGURE 1

Sharp Decline in Sub-employment Rates
for Men and Women Between 1961 and 1966

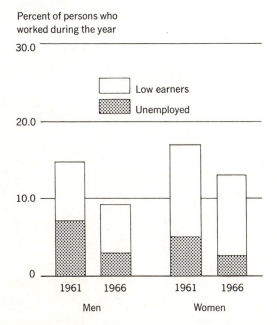

earners declined substantially between 1961 and 1966 (by 16 percent), the improvement was not nearly as sharp as in the number with extensive unemployment (which decreased by more than 50 per-

Nonsupervisory Employees Earning Less Than Specified Wages per Hour, 1968

(Numbers in thousands, est.)

Industry	Total number of nonsupervisory employees	Employees earning cash wages of less than							
		$1.60		$1.30		$1.15		$1.00	
		Number	Percent	Number	Percent	Number	Percent	Number	Percent
Total	51,866	10,123	19.5	7,302	14.1	4,663	9.0	3,422	6.6
Agriculture, forestry, and fisheries	1,513	1,154	76.3	828	54.7	509	33.6	281	18.6
Retail trade (including eating and drinking places)	9,150	3,278	35.8	2,040	22.3	1,094	12.0	553	6.0
Service	7,589	3,259	42.9	2,185	28.8	1,056	13.9	647	8.5
Domestic service	2,223	2,045	92.0	2,005	90.2	1,925	86.6	1,912	86.0
All other	31,391	387	1.2	244	.8	79	.3	29	.1

FROM U.S. Department of Labor, *Manpower Report of the President, 1968* (Washington, D.C.: U.S. Government Printing Office, 1968), p. 27.

cent). Plainly, the problem of low earnings has been less responsive to the economic upturn than extended unemployment and, so far, has been less affected by manpower and antipoverty programs.

Slightly over half of the sub-employed were men despite the fact that their rate was considerably lower than that for women (9 percent, compared with 13 percent). Among both men and women, low earnings was a much more common problem than unemployment of 15 or more weeks; the disparity was greater for women.

The economic disadvantage suffered by non-white men is sharply portrayed by the sub-employment data. Their sub-employment rate was 22 percent, compared with 8 percent for white men. Coupled with an unemployment rate almost three times as high as for white men was an equally disproportionate low-earnings rate. . . .

Willing to Work but Not Seeking Jobs

U.S. DEPARTMENT OF LABOR

Many people who are neither working nor seeking work want and need jobs. Evidence to this effect has accumulated in recent years. For example:

• The proportion of men below normal retirement age who are out of the work force has been rising, especially among nonwhites.

• A high proportion of youth in slum areas who have dropped out of school are neither working nor seeking work.

• Persons with limited education are more likely to be out of the labor force than those with more education.

• A large number of older workers—including many with retirement benefits—both need and wish to continue in paid employment.

• Many women who want to work, either to support themselves and their families or to supplement their husband's income, report that they cannot do so for lack of child-care facilities.

• Illness and disability prevent many persons from working in physically demanding occupations and sometimes keep them from working at any job. Long-term disabilities also tend to discourage persons from even looking for work.

FROM U.S. Department of Labor, *Manpower Report of the President, 1968* (Washington, D.C.: U.S. Government Printing Office, 1968), pp. 22–24.

To get more definite information on how many people not in the labor force want to work and the reasons why they are not seeking jobs, the Department of Labor recently made a series of special studies. The most comprehensive of these studies showed that, in September 1966, 5.3 million men and women—1 out of every 10 of those outside the labor force—wanted a job. The other 9 out of 10 said they did not desire a regular job. However, the information obtained from the latter group did not permit probing into the conditions under which they might consider working nor into their possible need for additional income.

TABLE 1

Reasons for Not Seeking Work Among Those Desiring Jobs, September 1966

(Numbers in thousands)

Reason	Men		Women	
	Number	Percent distribution	Number	Percent distribution
Total[1]	1,641	100.0	3,651	100.0
Believes it would be impossible to find work[2]	266	16.2	488	13.4
Ill health, physical disability	480	29.3	598	16.4
In school	706	43.0	536	14.7
Family responsibilities			1,080	29.6
Inability to arrange child care			435	11.9
Miscellaneous personal reasons[3]	144	8.8	290	7.9
Expects to be working or seeking work shortly	44	2.7	226	6.2

[1] Detail may not add to totals due to rounding.

[2] Includes employers think too old (or too young); couldn't find or did not believe any job (or any suitable job) was available; lacks skill, experience, education, or training; no transportation; racial discrimination; language difficulties; and pay too low.

[3] Includes old age or retirement, moving, entering or leaving Armed Forces, death in family, planning to go back to school, and no need to work at present time.

When those desiring work were asked why they were not looking for jobs, the reasons most often cited were ill health, school attendance, family responsibilities, or belief that they could not find jobs.

Presumably, the impediments to jobs could be overcome for many of these people by better health care, arrangements for child care, school-work programs, referral to suitable jobs, and other services.

The ¾ million people—over 250,000 men and nearly 500,000 women—who were not looking for work because they believed it would be impossible to find any were the group of probably greatest concern from the viewpoint of manpower policy. Presumably many had given up the search for work after fruitless and discouraging job-finding efforts. In addition, nearly as large a number of women cited inability to arrange for child care as the specific reason why they were not looking for jobs.

It is also significant that close to 400,000 of the group not looking for work because of ill health or physical or mental disabilities said they would take part-time or light work if it were available, or said they would seek work when their health improved. However, it is not possible on the basis of the survey data to distinguish clearly between people who could be helped to enter employment and those with serious and uncorrectable handicaps.

Altogether, these data represent a major contribution to knowledge of the people not currently in the labor force who are potential workers. But the number that should be counted as underutilized is still much in doubt.

The gap in the present effort to develop indicators of employment hardship is not as great as might be inferred, however. Many of the 5.3 million people who wanted work but were not looking for it in a particular week of September 1966 had probably sought jobs earlier in the year and then stopped looking—because of discouragement, increasing ill health, return to school, or other reasons. If they actually looked for jobs during 1966, they have, of course, been counted among the unemployed in the figures presented earlier.

Nevertheless, this is still an area of unfortunate doubt and incompleteness in the data on the Nation's underemployed people. It is an area where further factfinding and exploration are much needed.

The Elderly and the Ill

Incomes of the Elderly

I. M. LABOVITZ

Incomes of elderly families and unrelated individuals are substantially below those of the younger population and derived in much smaller part from current gainful employment. (An "unrelated individual" is one who lives alone or in a household where he has no relatives.)

The latest collection of comprehensive income data for the aged is a Bureau of the Census report on income in 1966 of all families and persons in the United States. It is based on inquiries in the current population survey conducted in March 1967—one of a long series of annual reports derived from field surveys of a representative sample of households. These indicate the size and distribution of money incomes of the whole population in the calendar year 1966 in relation to age and other individual characteristics in March 1967. . . .

One-half of all U.S. families reported money incomes of $7,436 or more for 1966. But for families headed by a person aged 65 or more, the median money income was $3,645—less than half as much as for all families. Money income was less than $2,500 for one of every eight families of all ages—but it was less than $2,500 for one of every three elderly families.

For all unrelated individuals, median money income was $2,270. For these aged 65 and older, the median was $1,443, or less than two-thirds as much.

. . . Whereas median incomes of the elderly in 1966 were significantly below those for the whole population, median incomes for ages 55 to 64 were above the medians for the whole population—and

FROM I. M. Labovitz, specialist in social welfare, Library of Congress, "Incomes of the Elderly," *Federal Programs for the Development of Human Resources* (Washington, D.C.: Joint Economic Committee, Subcommittee on Economic Progress, 1968), pp. 345–52.

especially so for unrelated individuals. The comparative amounts and percentages dramatize the degree to which old age is a period when incomes are sharply below those of younger contemporary families and individuals.

In reporting on family and individual incomes in 1966, the Census Bureau pointed out that median family income, at $7,436, was at a new peak. In current dollars, the median amount in 1966 was 124 percent greater than in 1950. Adjusted for price increases, the gain in real income was about 66 percent from 1950 to 1966.

The new high level for the median of all family incomes was accompanied by a new peak at a much lower level for older families. The median amount in current dollars was almost double that of 1950. Adjusted for price advances, the gain in real income for the median elderly family was 41 percent from 1950 to 1966.

Poverty, as defined by the Social Security Administration for its periodic reports on the numbers and progress of the poor, is measured by an income standard that takes account of family size, composition, and farm or nonfarm place of residence. The Department of Agriculture "economy food plan" is used as a basic element in calculating family needs for food (estimated for 1966 at 75 cents a day for each person in an average four-person family). For all family living items other than food, the SSA index adds twice the minimum amount required for food. The index postulates cash income needs for a farm family at 30 percent less than for a similar nonfarm family. For living arrangements that typify the elderly—individuals living alone and two-person families—some allowance is made for the fact that consumption needs are not strictly proportionate to household size. Except to allow for rising prices, the poverty index has been applied without change to income data for each year since 1959.

In 1966, among nearly 30 million persons living in households with incomes below the poverty level, 18 percent were 65 or older. This was a disproportionate ratio, in light of the fact that persons 65 or older were only 9.4 percent of the whole population.

More than one-third of the one- or two-person households of the elderly were poor in 1966, compared with less than one-seventh of all other households. Almost half of all elderly households were among the poor and the near poor.

In nonfarm households of persons 65 or older, poverty in 1966 was much more frequent in households headed by women than in those headed by men. . . . In nonfarm households of persons 65 or older, income in 1966 was below the poverty line in one-fourth of all households headed by white men, in one-half of all households headed by white women or by nonwhite men, and in more than two-thirds of all households headed by nonwhite women.

Moreover, although the incidence of poverty diminished in all these categories between 1959 and 1966, the greatest relative decline was in nonfarm households headed by elderly white males. This was the category with the lowest incidence in 1959, as well as 1966.

. . . There was an increase in the number of poor households among the nonfarm elderly—from 3.9 million in 1959 to 4 million in 1966—during a period when the total number of nonfarm households in poverty declined substantially. As a result, households of the elderly comprised an increased proportion of all poor households.

Somewhat more detailed comparisons for 1959 and 1965, covering both farm and nonfarm households, confirm that households of the elderly were a higher proportion of all poor households in 1965 than in 1959—nearly 37 percent, compared with 33 percent. . . .

As the incidence of poverty is narrowed by advancing prosperity, a rising proportion consists of groups who are especially vulnerable. The elderly constitute one of these susceptible groups. The women among them are especially apt to have low incomes—and the older they are, the smaller are their incomes.

The low-income "gap"—the dollar-deficit of actual incomes below amounts needed to reach the threshold of poverty—was estimated for all the poor at $13.7 billion in 1959 and $11 billion for 1965. For households of persons aged 65 and older, the amount was $3.3 billion in 1959 and $2.6 billion in 1965, slightly less than one-fourth of the total in each year. Measured in dollars, the gap declined for both elderly families and unrelated elderly individuals—but the percentage for unrelated elderly individuals was higher in 1965 than 1959. . . .

Elderly persons derived their money incomes not primarily from current earnings but from these and a variety of other sources. Among other sources are old-age, survivors, and disability insurance benefits; railroad retirement benefits; other public retirement or benefit systems; interest on savings or bonds; dividends; distributions from estates or trust funds; property income, such as rentals; public assistance or other welfare payment; and contributions from relatives and others outside their households. . . .

Nowadays, persons of 65 and over typically have less formal schooling than do their juniors. For several population groups there is a positive association between years of schooling and total income from all sources.

For elderly men, total money incomes in 1966 ranged from a

median of $1,738 for those with less than 8 years of elementary school to $6,433 for those who had 5 or more years of college. For elderly women, although the absolute amounts of income were about half as much as for men, the range was proportionately even wider— from a median of $870 for those with less than 8 years of elementary school to $3,500 for those with 5 or more years of college. Quite likely, the amount of money incomes of widows is directly associated with the number of years of schooling completed by their husbands, as well as with their own education.

Persons who were aged 55–64 in March 1967 (when the 1966 income data were collected) typically had considerably more formal education than those 65 and older. The median period of school attendance was 1.4 years longer for men (halfway through high school) and 2.1 years longer for women (nearly through the junior year of high school). Whether this additional schooling will be associated with higher money incomes after age 65 for this next generation of the elderly is necessarily problematical. Available data suggest that a positive correlation will persist. Several factors and relationships are involved. Not least of these are some of the lasting effects of higher levels of income experienced in earlier years. These higher incomes may have been derived in more instances from occupations that permit a longer working life. They have financed better living conditions than were available to the current elderly population, including better nutrition and health care, thus contributing to individual abilities to continue longer in gainful employment. Also, the higher earlier income may serve as a foundation for higher retirement benefits and property income in old age.

Health Services for the Poor:
A Portrait of Failure

HUBERT H. HUMPHREY

Three years ago Dr. George James observed that "poverty is the third leading cause of death in New York City." Dr. James was in a posi-

FROM Vice-President Hubert H. Humphrey, "The Future of Health Services for the Poor," *Public Health Reports* (U.S. Department of Health, Education, and Welfare, January 1968), pp. 1–5.

tion to know—he was the city's health commissioner. His statement was intended to jolt the complacent, and it did.

The shock wave was strong because the statement was true. Poverty never appears on a death certificate. But it takes its toll: through failures in preventive medicine, fatal delays in seeking treatment, care that is inaccessible or inadequate, poor nutrition, congested living, and in many other ways that make disease more likely to happen, less likely to be checked, more likely to kill.

Throughout most of human history, and throughout much of the world today, poverty has been not the third, but the first, cause of death. It is the mark of an affluent society when heart disease and cancer claim more victims than the diseases directly associated with want and misery. . . .

Yet even for us, in our own time, affluence is only an outer shell. Beneath it are the hard facts of poverty's toll as a disabler and a killer.

In the United States today, nearly one out of every three persons in families with incomes under $2,000 per year suffers from a chronic condition that limits his activity; for families with incomes above $7,000, the figure is one in 13.

In the United States today, men in the age-range 45 to 64, the years of top productivity, average 50 days of disability per year among families with incomes under $2,000; for the over $7,000 income group, the figure is 14.3 disability days.

Those who are poor go to the hospital more often. They remain longer—an average of 10.2 days per hospital stay for the under $2,000 group as contrasted with 7.2 days for the group above $7,000. This is true despite the self-evident fact that they are less able to pay, less likely to have insurance which covers the bill.

Another set of statistics tells a similar tragic story. The contrasting mortality and morbidity rates of our white and nonwhite populations confirm the inequality of health services.

A white baby born today can expect a life-span of 70.2 years, while a nonwhite baby has a life expectancy of 63.4 years—10 percent of a lifetime less. Four times as many nonwhite mothers die in childbirth. Twice as many nonwhite babies die in infancy.

When we turn the spotlight on specific diseases, we see further confirmation. Influenza and pneumonia take more than twice as high a toll among the nonwhite population. Tuberculosis—the great scourge of our grandparents' generation—is all but forgotten except among the poor and nonwhite. Venereal disease is now largely concentrated in the core of our great cities. Nearly all the remaining cases of diseases that need no longer occur at all—typhoid, diphtheria, poliomyelitis, and others—strike those who live in poverty.

Indeed, it would be possible to prepare a set of overlays of a map of the United States. One would indicate areas of high incidence of venereal disease, another of tuberculosis, another of high infant and maternal death rates, another of excessive disability rates from chronic disease. These overlays would cover almost identical territory. And that territory would coincide with another set showing where the poor are congregated—in inner cities and isolated rural areas. The shadow of poverty and the shadow of avoidable disease and early death are the same shadow. They beshroud the same land and the same people.

This fact is more than a national tragedy. It is a national reproach. It is more than unfortunate; it is unconscionable.

President Johnson has said:

"Good health services are the right of every citizen, not the privilege of a few. No American should be denied the opportunity for good health care because he lives in a sparsely populated area or deep in the slums of a large city, because he is unemployed or under-privileged, because he is one of poverty's young or very old, because he lacks access to doctors, hospitals, or nursing homes, because he does not know where to find or how to use health services, or because his affliction extends beyond our present knowledge and our current discoveries."

He has also said, in a Special Message to the Congress, that we must aspire to "good health for every citizen, up to the limits of this country's capacity to provide it."

The President believes, and I believe, that this country's capacity is very high indeed. But cold statistical truths as enumerated show how very far below capacity we are performing for a great many of our citizens. . . .

What are the barriers that separate the poor from the health care that they need and that medical science is capable of providing them? What are the obstacles that we, as a society, must tear down?

First, there are barriers of accessibility. For a variety of reasons, good health care is difficult or impossible to obtain for many of our urban and rural poor.

One such barrier is based on actual shortages. As a nation we do not have enough physicians, enough dentists, enough nurses, enough supporting manpower, and enough hospital and nursing home beds to meet the needs of our people. These shortages affect everyone, regardless of socioeconomic status, to a greater or lesser extent.

For the poor the extent is greater, because of the barrier of mal-distribution of the resources we have. In a study of the Watts area of Los Angeles, Dr. Milton Roemer found that 106 of the 251,000 people living in the district surveyed were physicians—a ratio about one-third that for Los Angeles County as a whole. Of these physicians only five were board-certified specialists. Two of the eight small hospitals in the district were approved by the Joint Commission on Accreditation; for most hospital services the people living in the district were dependent on Los Angeles County General, 10 miles and an hour's bus ride away.

Counterparts of these conditions can be found in almost every major city. For the rural poor, the distribution pattern is likely to be even more unfavorable.

Meanwhile, among nonwhites, the rate of recruitment and education of potential physicians and dentists is still dismally low. Students in low-income families are not entering medical and dental schools at anything like the rates necessary to do justice to their own professional interest or to the patients of all races whom they might serve after graduation.

Another barrier is cost of health service.

The price of medical and hospital care is rising faster than any other component of our economy. The advance of private health insurance over the past few years has benefited millions of Americans but few of the poor who are in most urgent need of help. The great legislative advances of Medicare and Medicaid are helping to lift the burden of cost from the shoulders of the aged and medically indigent, but we cannot delude ourselves that the cost barrier has been eliminated.

Finally, there is the problem of not knowing where to turn. Health services for the poor are fragmented and dispersed. Even those that exist are not easy to find. The individual who needs health care has to shop around for it. And, as Surgeon General William Stewart recently pointed out, "Among all the goods and services he purchases, health care is perhaps the most difficult for him to shop for intelligently. The Yellow Pages are of limited help and there is no Consumer's Guide. . . . The price tag is never displayed. . . . He usually has a very vague understanding of the kind of service he needs and a very inadequate basis for judging the quality of service he receives."

Elsewhere, Dr. Stewart has said, "Today the individual gets to the right place at the right time largely by happenstance. Many do not."

Thus, there are numerous barriers that place good health care beyond the convenient reach of the poor. And in addition to these barriers of accessibility, there are also barriers of acceptability.

For the care that our poor people receive leaves a great deal to be desired, even after they have run the obstacle course to obtain it. Dr. Kenneth Clement of Cleveland, in his keynote address at the recent centennial conference of the Howard University College of Medicine, described indigent medical care as seen through the eyes of those who receive it.

"It is delivered in ways that are depersonalized and lacking in continuity. There is no one health professional with whom the family can build a trusted relationship.

"It is fragmented care—if sick, go here; to be immunized, go there; if a specialty problem, go somewhere else.

"The care is rendered without care for the family as a unit. . . .

"It is often inaccessible. . . .

"The institutions are often distant from the poverty areas. . . . The inaccessibility is often increased by the failure of institutions to provide hours that do not require the patient to miss employment— and employment often without sick-time benefits." .

Dr. Clement summed it up this way:

"The patient must often wait long hours at overcrowded clinics in public or voluntary hospitals, and is not infrequently told to return on some other day when those responsible for manning the clinics are not available. His desire for privacy is consistently ignored and his dignity in many ways degraded."

This is not a pleasant portrait of the health services received by one in almost every five Americans. It is a portrait of at least partial failure—by health departments, private medicine, hospitals, medical schools, voluntary agencies. There is plenty of failure to go around.

V

The Poor:
Culture, Subculture, or Underclass?

To Live Miserable We Know Not Why

William Dean Howells said to me recently, after I had told him of a visit to Tolstoy: "It is wonderful what Tolstoy has done. He could do no more. For a nobleman, with the most aristocratic ancestry, to refuse to be supported in idleness, to insist upon working with his own hands, and to share as much as possible the hardship and toil of a peasant class, which, but recently, was a slave class, is the greatest thing he could do. But it is impossible for him to share their poverty, for poverty is not the lack of things; it is the fear and the dread of want. That fear Tolstoy could not know." These remarks of Mr. Howells brought to mind the wonderful words of Thomas Carlyle: "It is not to die, or even to die of hunger, that makes a man wretched; many men have died; all men must die. . . . But it is to live miserable we know not why; to work sore and yet gain nothing; to be heart-worn, weary, yet isolated, unrelated, girt in with a cold, universal Laissez-faire." To live miserable we know not why, to have the dread of hunger, to work sore and yet gain nothing,—this is the essence of poverty.

. . . To thousands and thousands of working-men the dread of public pauperism is the agony of their lives. The mass of working-men on the brink of poverty hate charity. Not only their words convey a knowledge of this fact, but their actions, when in distress, make it absolutely undeniable.

. . . Recently a man who had been unable to find work and in despair committed suicide, left a note to his wife, saying: "I have gone forever; there is one less in the world to feed. Good-bye. God help you to care for Tony; don't put her away." This is the fear and dread of pauperism; "don't put Tony away" is the last thought of the man whose misery caused him to take his own life.

FROM Robert Hunter, *Poverty* (1912).

THE whole concept of poverty has been attacked as too simple and crude when it draws heavily upon the one criterion of low income and too ambiguous when it invokes other criteria such as educational deficiency, weak personal motivation, or lack of family cohesion. It is particularly dangerous to link characteristics such as cohesion with poverty because there is much evidence that middle-income and upper-income families also frequently suffer from internal conflicts and feelings of emptiness, insecurity, and isolation that ultimately break up their homes.

But more than a definition of poverty is involved. Policies toward poverty are appropriate only if the phenomenon is viewed in terms of human experience. The kind of evidence presented in Section IV has convinced many people that raising the income level of the lowest income quintile of the existing population would not solve the poverty problem. These people believe that money alone cannot wipe out an adverse poverty heritage of alienation, indifferent motivation, low aspirations, physical debilitation, dysfunctional behavior, and environmental dearth. Indeed, simply providing money might frustrate more profound efforts to overcome the roots of poverty.

This multidimensional approach leads directly to the notion that the poor constitute a subculture, a group within the larger society that has, in Robin Williams' words, "its own comparatively distinct value system, its special problems, its distinctive social perspectives."[1] We would add that geographic concentration is probably another characteristic of such a subculture. It is easier to think of the Puerto Ricans in New York City as a subculture than it is to think of the elderly as one. The "culture of poverty" described by Oscar Lewis may actually be more relevant for poor whites than for poor Negroes, among whom black consciousness and Afro-awareness are perhaps becoming stronger than identification with the poverty culture. Indeed, the culture-of-poverty concept may be relatively weak among groups with strong native cultures, such as Puerto Ricans, Mexican-Americans, and American Indians. But the question of which culture —the so-called culture of poverty or the native culture—is the stronger factor in shaping the lives of many of our poor remains to be answered. Lewis suggests that poverty's distinctive way of life is passed on "from generation to generation along family lines." If the poor are a genuine subculture, then public and private policy must rest on an integrated multipronged program, certain aspects of which

[1] Robin M. Williams, *American Society: A Sociological Interpretation,* 2d ed. (New York: Knopf, 1960), p. 374.

would be long term and would require a broad spectrum of expertise and of experimentation.

On the other hand, if the poor are not a subculture, as Charles Valentine asserts, and if poverty is merely a multidimensional condition characterizing problem groups whose constituents are otherwise full members of society, then policy need not be so tightly coordinated or comprehensive, though it must still be multifaceted to deal with the varied aspects of poverty. The following selections from Liebow, Ornati, and the President's Manpower Report provide some analytical and empirical evidence on the controversy over the culture-of-poverty approach versus the multidimensional-conditions approach.

To represent the "vicious cycle of poverty" concept, related to both the subculture and the multidimensional-conditions points of view, we have selected the Carmichael-Hamilton reading, which dramatically presents one aspect of the concept. Gunnar Myrdal initially set forth this concept in his *American Dilemma*. An antithetical view is succinctly presented in Blau and Duncan's *American Occupational Structure*.

If we consider a third possibility—that poverty is caused almost entirely by a single factor, inadequate income and assets—then the task of ending poverty is simplified. These policy issues, which underlie the controversy and the evidence presented below, keep the debate from becoming a sterile battle over definitions alone.

The Culture of Poverty

OSCAR LEWIS

As an anthropologist I have tried to understand poverty and its associated traits as a culture or, more accurately, as a subculture[1] with its own structure and rationale, as a way of life which is passed down from generation to generation along family lines. This view directs attention to the fact that the culture of poverty in modern nations is

FROM Oscar Lewis, professor of anthropology, University of Illinois, *La Vida: A Puerto Rican Family in the Culture of Poverty—San Juan and New York*, pp. xliii–xlviii. © Copyright, 1965, 1966 by Oscar Lewis. Reprinted by permission of Random House.

[1] While the term "subculture of poverty" is technically more accurate, I have used "culture of poverty" as a shorter form.

not only a matter of economic deprivation, of disorganization or of the absence of something. It is also something positive and provides some rewards without which the poor could hardly carry on.

Elsewhere I have suggested that the culture of poverty transcends regional, rural-urban and national differences and shows remarkable similarities in family structure, interpersonal relations, time orientation, value systems and spending patterns. These cross-national similarities are examples of independent invention and convergence. They are common adaptations to common problems.

The culture of poverty can come into being in a variety of historical contexts. However, it tends to grow and flourish in societies with the following set of conditions: (1) a cash economy, wage labor and production for profit; (2) a persistently high rate of unemployment and underemployment for unskilled labor; (3) low wages; (4) the failure to provide social, political and economic organization, either on a voluntary basis or by government imposition, for the low-income population; (5) the existence of a bilateral kinship system rather than a unilateral one; and finally, (6) the existence of a set of values in the dominant class which stresses the accumulation of wealth and property, the possibility of upward mobility and thrift, and explains low economic status as the result of personal inadequacy or inferiority.

The way of life which develops among some of the poor under these conditions is the culture of poverty. It can best be studied in urban or rural slums and can be described in terms of some seventy interrelated social, economic and psychological traits. However, the number of traits and the relationships between them may vary from society to society and from family to family. For example, in a highly literate society, illiteracy may be more diagnostic of the culture of poverty than in a society where illiteracy is widespread and where even the well-to-do may be illiterate, as in some Mexican peasant villages before the revolution.

The culture of poverty is both an adaptation and a reaction of the poor to their marginal position in a class-stratified, highly individuated, capitalistic society. It represents an effort to cope with feelings of hopelessness and despair which develop from the realization of the improbability of achieving success in terms of the values and goals of the larger society. Indeed, many of the traits of the culture of poverty can be viewed as attempts at local solutions for problems not met by existing institutions and agencies because the people are not eligible for them, cannot afford them, or are ignorant or suspicious of them. For example, unable to obtain credit from banks, they are thrown upon their own resources and organize informal credit devices without interest.

The culture of poverty, however, is not only an adaptation to a set of objective conditions of the larger society. Once it comes into existence it tends to perpetuate itself from generation to generation because of its effect on the children. By the time slum children are age six or seven they have usually absorbed the basic values and attitudes of their subculture and are not psychologically geared to take full advantage of changing conditions or increased opportunities which may occur in their lifetime.

Most frequently the culture of poverty develops when a stratified social and economic system is breaking down or is being replaced by another, as in the case of the transition from feudalism to capitalism or during periods of rapid technological change. Often it results from imperial conquest in which the native social and economic structure is smashed and the natives are maintained in a servile colonial status, sometimes for many generations. It can also occur in the process of detribalization, such as that now going on in Africa.

The most likely candidates for the culture of poverty are the people who come from the lower strata of a rapidly changing society and are already partially alienated from it. Thus landless rural workers who migrate to the cities can be expected to develop a culture of poverty much more readily than migrants from stable peasant villages with a well-organized traditional culture. In this connection there is a striking contrast between Latin America, where the rural population long ago made the transition from a tribal to a peasant society, and Africa, which is still close to its tribal heritage. The more corporate nature of many of the African tribal societies, in contrast to Latin American rural communities, and the persistence of village ties tend to inhibit or delay the formation of a full-blown culture of poverty in many of the African towns and cities. The special conditions of apartheid in South Africa, where the migrants are segregated into separate "locations" and do not enjoy freedom of movement, create special problems. Here the institutionalization of repression and discrimination tend to develop a greater sense of identity and group consciousness.

The culture of poverty can be studied from various points of view: the relationship between the subculture and the larger society; the nature of the slum community; the nature of the family; and the attitudes, values and character structure of the individual.

1. The lack of effective participation and integration of the poor in the major institutions of the larger society is one of the crucial charac-

teristics of the culture of poverty. This is a complex matter and results from a variety of factors which may include lack of economic resources, segregation and discrimination, fear, suspicion or apathy, and the development of local solutions for problems. However, "participation" in some of the institutions of the larger society—for example, in the jails, the army and the public relief system—does not *per se* eliminate the traits of the culture of poverty. In the case of a relief system which barely keeps people alive, both the basic poverty and the sense of hopelessness are perpetuated rather than eliminated.

Low wages, chronic unemployment and underemployment lead to low income, lack of property ownership, absence of savings, absence of food reserves in the home, and a chronic shortage of cash. These conditions reduce the possibility of effective participation in the larger economic system. And as a response to these conditions we find in the culture of poverty a high incidence of pawning of personal goods, borrowing from local moneylenders at usurious rates of interest, spontaneous informal credit devices organized by neighbors, the use of second-hand clothing and furniture, and the pattern of frequent buying of small quantities of food many times a day as the need arises.

People with a culture of poverty produce very little wealth and receive very little in return. They have a low level of literacy and education, usually do not belong to labor unions, are not members of political parties, generally do not participate in the national welfare agencies, and make very little use of banks, hospitals, department stores, museums or art galleries. They have a critical attitude toward some of the basic institutions of the dominant classes, hatred of the police, mistrust of government and those in high position, and a cynicism which extends even to the church. This gives the culture of poverty a high potential for protest and for being used in political movements aimed against the existing social order.

People with a culture of poverty are aware of middle-class values, talk about them and even claim some of them as their own, but on the whole they do not live by them. Thus it is important to distinguish between what they say and what they do. For example, many will tell you that marriage by law, by the church, or by both, is the ideal form of marriage, but few will marry. To men who have no steady jobs or other sources of income, who do not own property and have no wealth to pass on to their children, who are present-time oriented and who want to avoid the expense and legal difficulties involved in formal marriage and divorce, free unions or consensual marriage makes a lot of sense. Women will often turn down offers of marriage because they feel it ties them down to men who are immature, punishing and generally unreliable. Women feel that consensual union gives them a better break; it gives them some of the freedom and flexibility that men have. By not giving the fathers of their children legal status as husbands, the women have a stronger claim on their children if they decide to leave their men. It also gives women exclusive rights to a house or any other property they may own.

2. When we look at the culture of poverty on the local community level, we find poor housing conditions, crowding, gregariousness, but above all a minimum of organization beyond the level of the nuclear and extended family. Occasionally there are informal, temporary groupings or voluntary associations within slums. The existence of neighborhood gangs which cut across slum settlements represents a considerable advance beyond the zero point of the continuum that I have in mind. Indeed, it is the low level of organization which gives the culture of poverty its marginal and anachronistic quality in our highly complex, specialized, organized society. Most primitive peoples have achieved a higher level of socio-cultural organization than our modern urban slum dwellers.

In spite of the generally low level of organization, there may be a sense of community and *esprit de corps* in urban slums and in slum neighborhoods. This can vary within a single city, or from region to region or country to country. The major factors influencing this variation are the size of the slum, its location and physical characteristics, length of residence, incidence of home and landownership (versus squatter rights), rentals, ethnicity, kinship ties, and freedom or lack of freedom of movement. When slums are separated from the surrounding area by enclosing walls or other physical barriers, when rents are low and fixed and stability of residence is great (twenty or thirty years), when the population constitutes a distinct ethnic, racial or language group, is bound by ties of kinship or *compadrazgo,* and when there are some internal voluntary associations, then the sense of local community approaches that of a village community. In many cases this combination of favorable conditions does not exist. However, even where internal organization and *esprit de corps* is at a bare minimum and people move around a great deal, a sense of territoriality develops which sets off the slum neighborhoods from the rest of the city. In Mexico City and San Juan this sense of territoriality results from the unavailability of low-income housing outside the slum areas. In South Africa the sense of territoriality grows out of the segregation enforced by the government, which confines the rural migrants to specific locations.

3. On the family level the major traits of the culture of poverty are

the absence of childhood as a specially prolonged and protected stage in the life cycle, early initiation into sex, free unions or consensual marriages, a relatively high incidence of the abandonment of wives and children, a trend toward female- or mother-centered families and consequently a much greater knowledge of maternal relatives, a strong predisposition to authoritarianism, lack of privacy, verbal emphasis upon family solidarity which is only rarely achieved because of sibling rivalry, and competition for limited goods and maternal affection.

4. On the level of the individual the major characteristics are a strong feeling of marginality, of helplessness, of dependence and of inferiority. I found this to be true of slum dwellers in Mexico City and San Juan among families who do not constitute a distinct ethnic or racial group and who do not suffer from racial discrimination. In the United States, of course, the culture of poverty of the Negroes has the additional disadvantage of racial discrimination, but as I have already suggested, this additional disadvantage contains a great potential for revolutionary protest and organization which seems to be absent in the slums of Mexico City or among the poor whites in the South.

Other traits include a high incidence of maternal deprivation, of orality, of weak ego structure, confusion of sexual identification, a lack of impulse control, a strong present-time orientation with relatively little ability to defer gratification and to plan for the future, a sense of resignation and fatalism, a widespread belief in male superiority, and a high tolerance for psychological pathology of all sorts.

People with a culture of poverty are provincial and locally oriented and have very little sense of history. They know only their own troubles, their own local conditions, their own neighborhood, their own way of life. Usually they do not have the knowledge, the vision or the ideology to see the similarities between their problems and those of their counterparts elsewhere in the world. They are not class-conscious, although they are very sensitive indeed to status distinctions.

Conditions of Poverty Versus Culture of Poverty

CHARLES A. VALENTINE

The master question must be, does the lower-class subsociety have a distinguishable subculture of its own? Other issues would include the following. What elements or patterns of this subculture are distinctive? What culture traits or configurations are shared by the lower class with the middle class or with the system as a whole? How is the subculture articulated with the whole culture? In lower-class life, should comparable but contrasting subcultural and wider cultural traits be understood as mutually exclusive, coexisting alternatives, or in some other relationship? How are distinctive patterns perpetuated? Are shared patterns perpetuated by similar means in different subsystems? What functions, adaptive or otherwise, do subcultural configurations have?

These questions can be thoroughly answered only by investigating and describing at first hand the entire range of custom and belief that make up the whole culture of representative lower-class populations. The most direct approach to such research would clearly be fully rounded ethnographic studies among the poor. In the study of any subsociety, obviously, an important objective is to determine in what ways its subculture is distinctive. This has indeed been the major goal of most of the published research cited here. It is clear, however, that equally important aims are to discern what cultural features are shared by different but related subsystems, and how subcultures are articulated with universals in the total system. These are the research tasks and analytical problems that have received so little attention, particularly with respect to lower-class subculture. These aspects of the problem have generally been swept under the rug by the expedient of treating distinctively lower-class traits as distortions, incomplete versions, or pathological variants of middle-class patterns. In contrast, an ethnographic approach would aim to comprehend lower-class life as a whole and thus would devote as much attention to cultural commonalities as to contrasts and discontinuities. This is necessary simply

FROM Charles A. Valentine, professor of anthropology, Washington University, *Culture and Poverty: Critique and Counter-Proposals* (Chicago: University of Chicago Press, 1968), pp. 114–20.

because the definition of distinctiveness is quite dependent on an understanding of what is not distinctive.

Hardly separable from the problems of the existence and distinctiveness of a subculture is a further question: whether many of the features presented by Lewis and others as class-distinctive traits are really culture patterns at all. Lewis defines his model of poverty culture as describing "a way of life handed on from generation to generation" which "provides human beings with a design for living," and he correctly notes that this corresponds to "a culture in the traditional anthropological sense." Yet within his catalog of traits are quite a number that fit into this definition with difficulty, if at all. Many of these features seem more like externally imposed conditions or unavoidable matters of situational expediency, rather than cultural creations internal to the subsociety in question. From the list of poverty-culture traits we can abstract three categories of elements posing different sorts of questions for each of these problematical issues. The sets of items here selected from Lewis' trait list are placed in categories designed for present analytical purposes, rather than Lewis' own classification of the traits.

The first set of items consists of *gross indicators or correlates of poverty*. These include unemployment, underemployment, unskilled work, low-status occupations, meager wages, lack of education, crowded living quarters, and deteriorated housing. Whether these phenomena can be correctly understood as parts of a "design for living" "handed on from generation to generation" through socialization seems open to doubt. As we noted earlier, Lewis himself insists on the distinction between poverty and the "culture of poverty." Are these phenomena not better understood as conditions or symptoms of being poor rather than as inculcated patterns of social tradition? Another of Lewis' own formulations may sharpen the issue: he describes culture as "a ready-made set of solutions for human problems." The question can thus perhaps be rephrased: Are unemployment, low wages, and so forth better understood as problems or as solutions for problems?

Lewis, together with the expositors of lower-class subculture, seems to believe that these are the lower-class cultural solutions to the basic bioeconomic problem of survival. Furthermore, they contend that these "solutions" are part of the lower-class "design for living" in the sense that they are supported by subcultural values and attitudes and perpetuated by personality traits that result from lower-class socialization patterns. The alternative interpretation is that lack of work, lack of income, and the rest pose conditions to which the poor must adapt through whatever sociocultural resources they control. That is, these conditions are phenomena of the environment in which the lower class lives, determined not so much by behaviors and values of the poor as by the structure of the total social system. It may be suggested also that this larger structure is perpetuated primarily by the economic and political actions of the non-poor. Then we may view behavior and values peculiar to the poor as responses to the experience of their special socioeconomic environment and as adaptations to this environment. Moreover, this view does not require that distinctive socialization patterns of personality configurations be invoked to explain class-specific beliefs and practices, a point to which we shall return.

Evidence presented in the literature surveyed here seems to provide little basis for a clear choice between these interpretations. To conclude that the two formulations are both valid but not mutually exclusive—that the two causal sequences may be coexistent and perhaps mutually reinforcing—is a position that may ultimately prove well founded. In the present state of the evidence, however, this conclusion has the ring of an evasive eclecticism. New evidence must be found, and much of it can be discovered through ethnography. Much of the answer must come from on-the-spot observation and inquiry into how people actually treat the conditions in question during their daily lives, under both usual and unusual circumstances. Much can be learned about the extent to which people develop and practice individual or collective means for coping with the conditions as problems potentially susceptible to resolution—or, conversely, the ways in which people may learn to accept these conditions as a normal part of the best or only available mode of existence. In the course of such inquiry, much would also come to light on the distinctiveness of lower-class cultural responses.

The second group of traits found in the subcultural model presented by Lewis consists of *behavioral patterns and relationships*. These include practice of consensual marriage, high frequency of female-centered households without resident adult males, absence of a sheltered childhood, authoritarianism in family relationships, lack of family solidarity, and general failure to develop community organization beyond the household. These examples are typical of the whole list in their emphasis on lacks and absences. Such characterizations convey an impression, not of distinctive subcultural patterns, but rather of a highly random, unpatterned social existence. "Indeed," writes Lewis himself in a frankly evaluative passage, "the poverty of culture is one of the crucial aspects of the culture of poverty."

Nevertheless, it seems most unlikely that this culturally barren set of behavioral and relational traits is really intended to be an exhaustive portrayal of social organization among the poor. To begin with, one can again infer from the emphasis on subcultural distinctions that the role of total-system universals has been neglected or perhaps virtually ignored. Also, this is an area in which Lewis' great concentration on family data has probably led naturally to a lack of information on other aspects of social structure. Moreover, there may be many contexts in which relationships or groupings that seem lacking in organization are actually functional adaptations to the circumstances of poverty. Lewis touches on a few of these, such as the advantages of free unions over marriage for the very poor, but there may be many more. An ethnographic attempt to master the whole shape of social existence from within is needed to clear up these and many related questions. That is, it is most necessary for ethnographers studying the poor to look for forms of social organization and patterned relationships that Lewis does not report.

With respect to the relationships and group forms that do appear in Lewis' trait catalog, it is often quite difficult to decide from available information whether these are sanctioned and perpetuated by subcultural values and beliefs that are communicated through socialization. In some cases at least, it seems quite possible that they are situational adaptations with little or no specific subcultural rationale. Wherever this is the case, the social practices involved may stem from motivations that are consistent with value orientations common to the total culture but capable of only distorted or incomplete expression within the limits of a poverty environment. Whatever behavior can be so interpreted may be better understood as an artifact of the total system rather than a response to subcultural rules or standards.

The third set of elements that can be drawn from the trait list associated with the "culture of poverty" belongs to the realm of *values and attitudes*. Here one is struck first of all by a long series of hostile feelings toward institutions and power centers of the dominant classes. Also found here is a substantial list of negative feelings which the poor are said to harbor toward their own group and its place in the social structure. These elements can be summed up as a combination of potential for protest, together with low levels of expectation and aspiration. Various expressions of spatial and temporal provincialism are also emphasized. All these orientations are so strikingly consistent with objective situational factors that it seems hardly necessary to interpret them as ingrained subcultural values. Indeed, for modern Western people these would seem to be almost inevitable emotional responses to the actual conditions of poverty.

A few suggestions of articulations between the subculture and more general values of the total system are advanced by Lewis. Thus he states that people with poverty culture "claim as their own" some middle-class values with respect to marriage but do not practice these values. He further suggests that one finds a "verbal emphasis upon family solidarity" also not lived up to in reality. He notes a few specific values that, it seems to me, have a definite place in dominant American traditions, quite apart from any lower-class subculture. These include a sense of neighborhood community and a belief in male dominance. All this seems far from adding up to a separate subsystem of values. It would certainly be difficult to find in this catalog a sufficient body of subcultural value orientations to provide rationales and sanctions for all the distinctive traits set forth in other aspects of social life. It seems that much remains to be specified here. The operative patterns still to be discovered may turn out to be some combination of total-system themes and class-specific values. Many of these can be specified through ethnographic research combining observation of much behavior with many recorded expressions of attitudes, both solicited and spontaneous.

One further consideration has received little attention in the relevant literature, probably because the stress on subcultural distinctiveness has inhibited its exploration. This is the possibility that commitment to values, norms, and other cultural themes may often involve ambiguity, ambivalence, and the simultaneous holding of alternative or contradictory beliefs. Some of these possibilities are suggested by Rodman's ingenious idea of "value-stretch." Lee Rainwater has recently followed this up by exploring thoughtfully how "conventional society manages somehow to inculcate its norms even in those persons who are not able to achieve successfully in terms of them," including groups who are thought to live within a poverty subculture. This consideration needs empirical development through ethnographic field work so that we may see more clearly how subcultural elements and total-system universals can coexist as simultaneously available alternatives.

Such investigation may free us from the strain—so evident in the literature—of explaining all class-specific behavior in terms of putative or hypothetical sets of subgroup beliefs and values. These suggested lines of inquiry may also make it easier to perceive and appreciate how cultural resources of various proveniences may be flexibly combined in creative responses to the imperative of adaptation under stressful circumstances, including the deprivations of poverty. Hopefully such reflections may weaken the now seemingly well-nigh tyrannical power of the association between poverty and pathology in the minds of social scientists concerned with under-standing their own social system. If this point is reached, the way will be open for field investigations more free of preconceptions and therefore more likely to produce a valid picture of social and cultural order in the life of the poor. . . .

Life on the Streetcorner

ELLIOT LIEBOW

This study has been primarily concerned with the inside world of the streetcorner Negro man, the world of daily, face-to-face relationships with wives, children, friends, lovers, kinsmen and neighbors. An attempt was made to see the man as he sees himself, to compare what he says with what he does, and to explain his behavior as a direct response to the conditions of lower-class Negro life rather than as mute compliance with historical or cultural imperatives. . . .

Transience is perhaps the most striking and pervasive characteristic of this streetcorner world. It characterizes not only the subtler social relationships but the more obvious spatial relationships as well. It characterizes not only the relationships of those within the network of interlocking and overlapping personal communities at any given time but also the movement into and out of these networks. Some men come into this particular area to escape police who have chased them out from another. Some men leave for the same reason. Some men, like Tally, leave the area because they have used up their friendships and alliances and have to start anew elsewhere. But at the same time, another Tally has moved out of his old area and into this one for the same reasons. Here a family is evicted and the sidewalk becomes a staging area for the allocation of the individual family members to households in the same area or in a distant state. The next day or the same day, the same room or apartment is taken over by members of a family evicted from another part of the city. Here a man loses a job and moves out; another finds one and moves in. Here is a man released from prison after seven years and there goes a man who

FROM Elliot Liebow, research anthropologist, National Institute of Mental Health, *Tally's Corner: A Study of Negro Streetcorner Men* (Boston: Little, Brown, 1967), pp. 208, 218–24.

wants to try his luck in New York. Traffic is heavy in all directions.

Thus, this streetcorner world does not at all fit the traditional characterization of the lower-class neighborhood as a tightly knit community whose members share the feeling that "we are all in this together." Nor does it seem profitable—especially for those who would see it changed—to look at it as a self-supporting, on-going social system with its own distinctive "design for living," principles of organization, and system of values.

Whether the world of the lower-class Negro should be seen as a distinctive subculture or as an integral part of the larger society (at the bottom of it, perhaps, but as much a part of it as those in the middle or on top) is much more than an academic question and has important consequences for "intervention." Marriage among lower-class Negroes, for example, has been described as "serial monogamy," a pattern in which the woman of childbearing age has a succession of mates during her procreative years. The label "serial monogamy" clearly has a cultural referent, deriving as it does from the traditional nomenclature used to designate culturally distinctive patterns of marriage, such as polygyny, polyandry, monogamy, and so on. "Serial monogamy," then, as against the unqualified monogamous ideal of American society at large, refers to and *is used as evidence for* the cultural separateness and distinctiveness of the urban, lower-class Negro.

When these same phenomena are examined directly in the larger context of American life, both "serial monogamy" and cultural distinctiveness tend to disappear. In their place is the same pattern of monogamous marriage found elsewhere in our society but one that is characterized by failure. The woman does not have a simple "succession of mates during her procreative years." She has a husband and he a wife, and their hopes and their intentions—if not their expectations—are that this will be a durable, permanent union. More often, however, it is their fears rather than their hopes which materialize. The marriage fails and they part, he to become one of a "succession of mates" taken by another woman whose husband has left her, and she to accept one or more men. While these secondary and subsequent liaisons are, for the most part, somewhat pale reflections of the formal marriage relationship, each is modeled after it and fails for much the same reasons as does marriage itself. From this perspective, then, the succession of mates which characterizes marriage among lower-class Negroes does not constitute a distinctive cultural pattern "with an integrity of its own." It is rather the cultural model of the larger society as seen through the prism of repeated failure. Indeed, it might be more profitable—again, especially for those concerned with changing it—to look on marriage here as a succession of failures rather than as a succession of mates.

In summary, what is challenged here is not that the marriage pattern among urban low-income Negroes does not involve a "succession of mates" but the implication that this succession of mates constitutes prima facie evidence for the cultural distinctiveness of those to whom it is attributed.

From this perspective, the streetcorner man does not appear as a carrier of an independent cultural tradition. His behavior appears not so much as a way of realizing the distinctive goals and values of his own subculture, or of conforming to its methods, but rather as his way of trying to achieve many of the goals and values of the larger society, of failing to do this, and of concealing his failure from others and from himself as best he can.

If, in the course of concealing his failure, or of concealing his fear of even trying, he pretends—through the device of public fictions—that he did not want these things in the first place and claims that he has all along been responding to a different set of rules and prizes, we do not do him or ourselves any good by accepting this claim at face value.

Such a frame of reference, I believe, can bring into clearer focus the practical points of leverage for social change in this area. We do not have to see the problem in terms of breaking into a puncture proof circle, of trying to change values, of disrupting the lines of communication between parent and child so that parents cannot make children in their own image, thereby transmitting their culture inexorably, ad infinitum. No doubt, each generation does provide role models for each succeeding one. Of much greater importance for the possibilities of change, however, is the fact that many similarities between the lower-class Negro father and son (or mother and daughter) do not result from "cultural transmission" but from the fact that the son goes out and independently experiences the same failures, in the same areas, and for much the same reasons as his father. What appears as a dynamic, self-sustaining cultural process is, in part at least, a relatively simple piece of social machinery which turns out, in rather mechanical fashion, independently produced look-alikes. The problem is how to change the conditions which, by guaranteeing failure, cause the son to be made in the image of the father.

Taking this viewpoint does not reduce the magnitude of the problem but does serve to place it in the more tractable context of economics, politics and social welfare. It suggests that poverty is, indeed, a proper target in the attempt to bring lower-class Negroes "into the mainstream of American life," and it supports the long line of social scientists, from E. Franklin Frazier and Gunnar Myrdal down through Kenneth Clark and Richard Cloward, in seeing the inability of the Negro man to earn a living and support his family as the central fact of lower-class Negro life. If there is to be a change in this way of life, this central fact must be changed; the Negro man, along with everyone else, must be given the skills to earn a living and an opportunity to put these skills to work.

The Convergence of
Poverty-linked Characteristics

OSCAR ORNATI

The demographic characteristics [of low-income families] obviously overlap; being non-white may also mean being a farmer, or being aged, or being a female head of family. The poor do not usually have only one problem and many poor families are classified as "multi-problem" families. Available data point clearly to low education and shrinking occupational mobility as one of the major causes of poverty. Here the increased requirements in education for employment are one of the major causes of poverty. In addition, bad physical and mental health contribute to poverty to an undetermined but clearly significant degree.

Our rough estimate is that of the 20 million abject poor more than two-thirds, or somewhere between 12 and 14 million, are deficient in either health, mental or physical, or education, and a very large number of individuals are affected by more than one disadvantage. The proportions do not change significantly at the $3,500 or $4,500 level.

If we are to move against poverty, we must understand the dynamics of the process. Then we can move from the broad discussions of complex causality which determines an individual's risk of being poor to the isolation of characteristics which, in the aggregate, appear to contribute more, and of those that contribute less, to poverty.

FROM Oscar Ornati, professor of economics, New York University, *Poverty in America* (Washington, D.C.: National Policy Committee on Pockets of Poverty, 1964), pp. 12–18.

Analysis of the 1960 census data allows, at least for that year, a precise count, at different levels of income, of population units which had one or more of four key poverty-linked characteristics. It also provides a set of major preliminary clues as to how to move against poverty along the lines suggested above. Fifteen different poverty-linked family populations were constructed, ranging from units possessing one characteristic to those with all four. Here the problem of overlapping characteristics is eliminated. A non-white family is only non-white. There is no aged family head, no female family head, and no rural-farm resident. The same for the other characteristics. The cumulative total of all families with one characteristic holds no duplication—each family is counted only once. Nor is there duplication when families with two or more characteristics are examined.

As expected, by correcting for overlap, we note that: (1) there are more families with only one poverty characteristic than with two, with three or four, (2) the risk of poverty increases with the number of characteristics. The data in Table 1 indicate that while the relationship is not perfect, the possession of two characteristics means a greater chance of very low income than the possession of one, three a greater chance than two, etc. The degree of poverty, measured by the proportion of families below the three budget levels, varies considerably.

Families that have only one characteristic find between 30 and 40 percent of their membership at or below subsistence, between 55 and 60 percent below the minimum adequacy level and roughly 70 percent below minimum comfort.

Possessing two characteristics condemns a considerably larger portion of the population to subsistence living. For all but one of the six sub-populations with two attributes the proportion below $2,500 is better than half. For non-white families with the added characteristic of rural farm residence, the probability of abject poverty is three out of four. The chance of living at or below the minimum adequacy level is 75 percent or better for all but one of these twice-cursed families. Ninety percent of all non-white farm families, 80 percent of all the non-white aged and 82 percent of all the non-white families with female heads lived under this level. For all but one of these combinations the chance of escaping from the poverty band is less than 2 in 10. Conversely, families with two poverty-linked attributes rarely have incomes placing them above the poverty level. Extreme poverty is the fate of families with 3 or 4 poverty attributes. For three groups the figure is 8 in 10, for one, 7 in 10, and for one 5 in 10.

The policy implications of the data and the analysis presented so

TABLE 1

Percentage of Each Poverty-linked Population Below
Three Low Income Levels, 1960

Characteristics of family head	Number of units	Per-cent	Percent below		
			2,500	4,500	5,500
One characteristic					
Aged	4,276,016	100	39.6	60.2	70.5
Female	2,387,443	100	38.0	60.4	73.3
Rural-farm	2,434,041	100	34.5	57.5	71.0
Non-white	2,786,211	100	28.6	54.7	70.9
Two characteristics					
Non-white, Female	743,115	100	64.6	82.2	88.4
Aged, Female	787,975	100	37.2	56.1	68.4
Aged, Rural-farm	489,732	100	54.9	74.7	83.2
Aged, Non-white	331,316	100	62.6	80.1	87.5
Non-white, Rural-farm	208,047	100	78.3	90.8	94.8
Rural-farm, Female	73,842	100	54.8	73.9	83.1
Three characteristics					
Non-white, Aged, Female	115,444	100	67.5	83.5	89.8
Non-white, Rural-farm, Aged	40,901	100	81.1	91.9	95.4
Rural-farm, Aged, Female	55,444	100	52.5	70.8	80.3
Rural-farm, Non-white, Female	22,784	100	86.6	94.9	97.8
Four characteristics					
Non-white, Rural-farm, Aged, Female	7,698	100	84.0	93.9	97.0

far should be clear. On the one hand, families with one poverty characteristic make up the largest part of the low income population; on the other hand, families with more than one attribute, although less numerous, suffer the heavier burdens. Noting that they are less numerous in no way means they are insignificant. Families with two characteristics involve roughly ten million men, women and children. Half of these live below the contemporary subsistence level. Another quarter of a million families are marked by the even more extreme poverty associated with three or four characteristics. They contribute another million human exceptions to American affluence.

Examination of the differential impact of particular characteristics sharpens the focus of policy. Not only does this provide guidelines for the future, it also gives insight into the effect of past policies.

Table 2 measures the income effect of removing one poverty-linked characteristic from the population of families with three such characteristics. The table shows how, in every case, the removal of the characteristic non-white reduces the percentage of families below subsistence to a greater degree than removing the characteristic rural-farm. The effect is least marked in terms of removing any third characteristic from families with rural-farm as one of their three poverty-linked characteristics.

Table 3 shows—in a manner similar to Table 2—the effect of removing one poverty-linked characteristic from families with two. The pattern that emerges throws some light on the success of a past policy, Social Security. In the first set of percentages and the fifth set we find that subtracting the aged has a modifying rather than a depressing effect on the percentage of extremely low income units. Rural-farm families headed by aged females were slightly better off than rural-farm families headed by non-aged females. Age is the one area where, adequate or not, there does exist a national policy and program of insurance. Removing the non-white characteristic helps here, too, but less so.

Defining poverty through poverty-linked characteristics leads to the following major conclusions: First, the poverty population is characterized by identifying specific socio-demographic attributes. Families that are aged, rural-farm, non-white, headed by females, or

TABLE 2

The Effect of Removing a Poverty-linked Characteristic from a Family Possessing Three Characteristics

(*Changes in percentages of families below the subsistence level*)

Characteristic	*Percent*	*Characteristic*	*Percent*
Non-white, Rural-farm Female	86.6	Non-white, Rural-farm, Aged	81.1
Minus		Minus	
Non-white	54.8	Non-white	54.9
Rural-farm	64.6	Rural-farm	62.6
Female	78.3	Aged	78.3
Non-white, Aged, Female	67.5	Aged, Rural-farm, Female	52.5
Minus		Minus	
Non-white	37.2	Rural-farm	37.2
Aged	64.6	Aged	54.8
Female	62.6	Female	54.9

TABLE 3

The Effect of Removing a Poverty-linked Characteristic from
a Family Possessing Two Characteristics

(Changes in percentages of families below subsistence level)

Characteristic	Percent	Characteristic	Percent
Non-white, Rural-farm	78.3	Non-white, Female	64.6
Minus		Minus	
Rural-farm	28.6	Female	28.6
Non-white	34.5	Non-white	38.0
Non-white, Aged	62.6	Rural-farm, Aged	54.9
Minus		Minus	
Aged	28.6	Aged	34.5
Non-white	39.6	Rural-farm	39.6
Rural-farm, Female	54.8	Aged, Female	37.2
Minus		Minus	
Female	34.5	Aged	38.0
Rural-farm	38.0	Female	39.6

combinations of these, account for 70 percent of the abject poor. Second, in absolute terms, the largest groups are those families possessing only one characteristic. Third, the most severe poverty exists among families with more than one attribute and, fourth, among the multi-characteristic families, non-whiteness is most damaging.

A World of Trouble:
The Pruitt-Igoe Housing Project

LEE RAINWATER

The Pruitt-Igoe Housing Project is in St. Louis. Built in 1954, the project was the first high-rise public housing in the city. It consists of

FROM Lee Rainwater, professor of sociology and anthropology, Washington University, "The Lessons of Pruitt-Igoe," *The Public Interest* (Summer 1967), pp. 116–23.

33 eleven-story slab-shaped buildings designed to provide housing for about 2800 families. At present, it houses about 10,000 Negroes in 2,000 households. What started out as a precedent-breaking project to improve the lives of the poor in St. Louis, a project hailed not only by the local newspapers but by *Architectural Forum,* has become an embarrassment to all concerned. In the last few years the project has at all times had a vacancy rate of over 20 percent. News of crime and accidents in the project makes a regular appearance in the newspapers, and the words "Pruitt-Igoe" have become a household term—in lower class Negro homes as well as in the larger community—for the worst in ghetto living.

The description of Pruitt-Igoe which follows and the implications drawn, are based on a three-year study which I, together with a dozen colleagues, have been conducting. Pruitt-Igoe is not offered as typical of slum conditions in the ghetto—no other public housing project in the country approaches it in terms of vacancies, tenant concerns and anxieties, physical deterioration. Rather, Pruitt-Igoe is interesting precisely because it condenses into one 57-acre tract all of the problems and difficulties that arise from race and poverty, and all of the impotence, indifference, and hostility with which our society has so far dealt with these problems. Processes that are sometimes beneath the surface in less virulent slums are readily apparent in Pruitt-Igoe. And because Pruitt-Igoe exists as one kind of Federal Government response to the problems of poverty, the failure of that response is worth contemplating.

THE DUMPING GROUND

Pruitt-Igoe houses families for which our society seems to have no other place. The original tenants were drawn very heavily from several land-clearance areas in the inner city. Although there were originally some white tenants (Igoe was built for whites, Pruitt for Negroes, but a Supreme Court decision outlawing segregated public housing resulted in an "integrated" project in its earlier years), all of the whites have moved out and the population is now all Negro. Only those Negroes who are desperate for housing are willing to live in Pruitt-Igoe—over half of the households are headed by women and over half derive their principal income from public assistance of one kind or another. The project has proved particularly unappealing to "average" families, that is, families in which there is both a mother and father and a small number of children. Thus, while the overall vacancy rate has run between 20 and 25 percent for several years, the vacancy rate in two-bedroom apartments has been in the 35–40 percent range.

Life in Pruitt-Igoe, and in the St. Louis ghetto generally, is not quite as flamboyant as in Harlem, but it has the same essential characteristics. As sociologists have discovered each time they have examined a particular lower class community in detail, the lower class lives in "a world of trouble."

In the slum, people are continually confronted with dangers from both human and non-human sources. Public housing removes some of the non-human sources of danger (like rats, or faulty electrical wiring), but can replace them by others, as when children fall out of windows or into elevator shafts in Pruitt-Igoe's high-rise buildings, or burn themselves on exposed steam pipes, or cut themselves on the broken glass outside. After about two years of intensive field observation in the Pruitt-Igoe project, our research team administered a questionnaire to a representative sample of tenants to discover how extensive were some of the difficulties we had noticed. Let me list some of the troubles which over half of this representative sample of tenants characterized as "a very big problem" in the project.

A few of these problems had to do with the design and maintenance of the project:

There's too much broken glass and trash around outside.
The elevators are dangerous.
The elevators don't stop on every floor, so many people have to walk up or down to get to their apartments.
There are mice and cockroaches in the buildings.
People use the elevators and halls to go to the bathroom.

However, by far the greatest number of troubles that people complained about had as much to do with the behavior of their fellow tenants as it did with design and maintenance problems *per se*:

Bottles and other dangerous things get thrown out of windows and hurt people.
People who don't live in the project come in and make a lot of trouble with fights, stealing, drinking and the like.
People don't keep the area around the incinerator clean.
The laundry rooms aren't safe: clothes get stolen and people get attacked.
The children run wild and cause all kinds of damage.
People use the stairwells and laundry rooms for drinking and things like that.
A woman isn't safe in the halls, stairways or elevators.

Given these kinds of experiences it's hardly surprising that, although the great majority of the tenants feel that their *apartments* are better than their previous dwelling units, only a minority demonstrate any real attachment to the project community, and most would very much like to move out to a neighborhood that would be nicer and safer.

It is also understandable that a good many of them develop a rather jaundiced view of the public housing program. Thus, when we asked tenants what the government was trying to accomplish by building public housing and how well this had in fact been accomplished, we got answers like these:

"They were trying to put a whole bunch of people in a little bitty space. They did a pretty good job—there's a lot of people here."

"They were trying to better poor people (but) they tore down one slum and built another; put all kinds of people together; made a filthy place and so on."

"They were trying to get rid of the slum, but they didn't accomplish too much. Inside the apartment they did, but not outside."

Other troubles also make life difficult for the project tenants. For example, we asked our sample to indicate from a list of various kinds of aggressive and deviant behaviors how serious and how frequent they felt such behavior to be. One cluster of items turned out to be judged by the tenants as both highly serious and very frequent (over half of the people characterizing these behaviors as very frequent):

Holding somebody up and robbing them.
Being a wino or alcoholic.
Stealing from somebody.
Teenagers yelling curse words at adults.
Breaking windows.
Drinking a lot and fooling around on the streets.
Teenagers getting in fights.
Boys or girls having sexual relations with a lot of different boys or girls.

In short, though some social scientists have quarreled with Kenneth Clark's emphasis on the "tangle of pathology" in the ghetto, it would seem that at least this sample from one federally-supported ghetto shares his views.

THE LOWER CLASS ADAPTATION

The observer who examines the lower class community in any detail perceives an almost bewildering variety of difficulties that confront its inhabitants. But if one wishes to move from simple observation to understanding and on to practical action, it is necessary to bring some order into this chaos of troubles, problems, pains, and failure. That is, one must move from a description of *what* lower class life is like to an understanding of *why* it is that way.

Let us start with an inventory of behavior in the lower class community that middle class people think of as hallmarks of the "tangle of pathology" of slum and ghetto worlds:

High rates of school dropouts.

Poor school accomplishment for those who do stay in.

Difficulties in establishing stable work habits on the part of those who get jobs.

High rates of dropping out of the labor force.

Apathy and passive resistance in contacts with people who are "trying to help" (social workers, teachers, etc.).

Hostility and distrust toward neighbors.

Poor consumer skills—carelessness or ignorance in the use of money.

High rates of mental illness.

Marital disruptions and female-headed homes.

Illegitimacy.

Child abuse or indifference to children's welfare.

Property and personal crimes.

Dope addiction, alcoholism.

Destructiveness and carelessness toward property, one's own and other people's.

All of this behavior is highly disturbing to middle class people—and most of it is even more disturbing to the lower class people who must live with it. It is not necessary to assume that all lower class families engage in even some of these practices to regard such practices as hallmarks of the pathology of the lower class world. Lower class people are forced to live in an environment in which the probability of either becoming involved in such behavior, or being the victim of it, is much higher than it is in other kinds of neighborhoods. From the point of view of social epidemiology, then, this is a high-risk population.

Behavior of this kind is very difficult for most middle class observers to understand. If, however, this behavior is seen in the context of the ways of life lower class people develop in order to cope with their punishing and depriving milieu, then it becomes much easier to understand. Much of the social science research dealing with lower class life in general, or with particular forms of deviant behavior such as juvenile delinquency, has sought to place these kinds of behavior in their contexts. As a result of these studies, we now understand that the "unreasonable" behavior which so often perplexes outsiders generally arises as a logical extension of the styles of life that are available to lower class people in their efforts to adapt to their world.

The ways people live represent their efforts to cope with the predicaments and opportunities that they find in the world as they experience it. The immediately experienced world of lower class adults presents them with two kinds of problems:

1. They are not able to find enough money to live in what they, and everyone else, would regard as the average American way. Because of inability to find work or only work at very low pay, they learn that the best they can hope for if they are "sensible" is despised housing, an inferior diet, a very few pleasures.

2. Because of their poverty, they are constrained to live among other individuals similarly situated—individuals who, the experience of their daily lives teaches them, are dangerous, difficult, out to exploit or hurt them in petty or significant ways. And they learn that in their communities they can expect only poor and inferior service and protection from such institutions as the police, the courts, the schools, the sanitation department, the landlords, and the merchants.

It is to this world that they must adapt. Further, as they grow up, they learn from their experiences with those around them that persons such as they can expect nothing better. From infancy on, they begin to adapt to that world in ways that allow them to sustain themselves—but at the same time often interfere with the possibility of adapting to a different world, should such a different world become available to them. Thus, in Pruitt-Igoe, eight-year-old girls are quite competent to inform the field worker that boys and men are no damn good, are not to be trusted, and that it isn't necessary to listen to or obey your mother because she's made such a mess of her life.

We know from sociological studies of unemployment that even stable middle or working class persons are likely to begin to show some of these lower class adaptive techniques under the stress of long-term unemployment. In the lower class itself, there is never a question of responding to the stress of sudden deprivation, since a depriving world is often all that the individual ever experiences in his life, and his whole lifetime is taken up in perfecting his adaptation to it, in striving to protect himself in that world and to squeeze out of it whatever gratification he can.

STRATEGIES FOR SURVIVAL

It is in terms of these two cardinal characteristics of lower class life—poverty and a potentially destructive community—that lower class individuals work out their strategies for living.

In most of American society two grand strategies seem to attract the allegiance of its members and guide their day-to-day actions. These are the strategies of the good life and of career-success. A good-life strategy involves efforts to get along with others and not to rock the boat; it rests on a comfortable family environment with a stable vocation for husbands which enables them to be good providers. The strategy of career-success is the choice of ambitious men and women who see life as providing opportunities to move from a lower to a higher status, to "accomplish something," to achieve greater than ordinary material well-being, prestige, and social recognition. Both of these strategies are predicated on the assumption that the world is inherently rewarding if one behaves properly and does his part. The rewards of the world may come easily or only at the cost of great effort, but at least they are there for the individual who tries.

In slum worlds, little in the experience that individuals have as they grow up sustains a belief in a rewarding world. The strategies that seem appropriate are *strategies for survival.*

Three broad categories of lower class survival strategies can be observed. One is the strategy of the *expressive life style.* In response to the fact that the individual derives little security and reward from his membership in a family which can provide for and protect him, or from his experiences in the institutions in which he is expected to achieve (the school, later the job), individuals develop an exploitative strategy toward others. This strategy seeks to elicit rewards by making oneself interesting and attractive. In its benign forms, the expressive style is what attracts so many middle class people to the lower class—the fun, the singing, the dancing, the lively slang, the spontaneous gratification of impulse. But underneath the apparent spontaneity, the expressive style of lower class people is deadly serious business. It is by virtue of their ability to manipulate others by making themselves interesting and dramatic that the individual has an opportunity to get some of the few rewards that are available to him—whether these be gifts of money, a gambling bet won, the affections of a girl, or the right to participate in a community of peers, to drink with them, bum around with them, gain status in their eyes.

The individual learns by his expressive ability to "work game" on his peers, to "sound" on them, to "put them in a trick" (thereby raising his status by lowering the other fellow's). While the expressive style is central to preserving the stability and sanity of many (particularly younger) members of the lower class, the pursuit of expressive and self-dramatizing goals often results in behavior which makes trouble for the individual both from his own community and from representatives of conventional society. Dope addiction, drunkenness, illegitimacy, "spendthrift behavior," lack of interest in school on the part of adolescents—all can arise in part as a result of commitment to a strategy of "cool." For example, in Pruitt-Igoe teen-age boys drink, and some smoke marijuana, in order to be able to loosen up enough to develop a "strong game" (i.e., a really persuasive line with peers or girls).

When the expressive strategy fails—because the individual cannot develop the required skills or because the audience is unappreciative—there is a great temptation to adopt a *violent strategy* in which you force others to give you what you need. The violent strategy is not a very popular one among lower class people. There is little really cold-blooded violence either toward persons or property in the slum world; most of it is undertaken out of a sense of desperation, a sense of deep insult to the self. Yet this strategy does not seem as distant and impossible to them as it does to the most prosperous.

Finally, there is the *depressive strategy* in which goals are increasingly constricted to the bare necessities for survival (not as a social being, but simply as an organism). This is the strategy of "I don't bother anybody and I hope nobody's gonna bother me; I'm simply going through the motions of keeping body (but not soul) together." Apparently this strategy of retreat and self-isolation is one that is adopted by more and more lower class men and women as they grow older, as the pay-offs from more expressive strategies begin to decline.

HOPES AND ASPIRATIONS

And along with these survival strategies, lower class people make efforts to move in the direction of the more conventional strategies of the good life or (occasionally) of career-success. One can observe in the lives of individual families (or in whole groups, during times of extraordinary demand for lower class labor) a gradual shift away from the more destructive components of these survival strategies. It is from observations such as these, as well as from interviews about lower class people's hopes and aspirations, that one learns that lower class styles of life are pursued, not because they are viewed as intrinsically desirable, but because the people involved feel constrained to act in those ways given the deprivations and threats to which they find themselves subject. *The lower class does not have a separate system of basic values. Lower class people do not really "reject middle class values." It is simply that their whole experience of life teaches them that it is impossible to achieve a viable sense of self-esteem in terms of those values.*

But lower class people are also intimately alive to how things might be different. They know what they would like if only they had the resources of the average working class man—they would want a quiet, rather "square" life in a quiet neighborhood far from the dangers, seductions, and insults of the world in which they live. In the slums, there is no personal preference for—or sociological value attached to—matrifocal families, or a high incidence of premarital sexual relations resulting in unwanted pregnancies, or living alone as a deserted or divorced wife and having a boyfriend because you're afraid that if you remarry your welfare will be cut off or your new husband will not prove a stable provider. Lower class people are not easily confused between how they must live and how they would like to live. What they might wish to preserve from the expressive heritage of lower class ways (particularly when, as among Negroes, those ways provide a kind of ethnic identity and not just a class identity) they feel that they can preserve while living a more stable kind of life. Lower class people would not find it nearly as agonizing as some intellectuals seem to feel they would to try to reconcile their traditions and their aspirations.

The AFDC Mother

U.S. DEPARTMENT OF LABOR

One way of exploring whether welfare is in fact a way of life, passed on from one generation to another, is to examine the length of time individual recipients remain on welfare. In 1961, the median length of time on AFDC was 27 months for currently active cases and 18

FROM U.S. Department of Labor, *Manpower Report of the President, 1968* (Washington, D.C.: U.S. Government Printing Office, 1968), pp. 96–97.

months for closed cases. But the length of time on assistance varied widely with both race and residence. For closed cases, the median time spent on assistance was higher for Negroes (22 months) than for whites (15 months) and lower in urban areas (16 months) than in rural areas (20 months). Periods of dependency tended to be longer in medium-sized cities (50,000 to 500,000) than in the largest cities. In general, however, the mothers in rural farm and nonfarm areas were those who spent the longest continuous periods of time on assistance.

These figures on "continuous time" on assistance obscure the great turnover in the AFDC rolls. A recent analysis of case turnover showed that 584,000 cases were authorized and 508,000 cases were closed in calendar year 1966, while slightly more than 1 million were carried over from the preceding year. Averaged over the year, about 45,000 new families were added to the rolls each month, while 41,000 left. Certain families have repeated periods on relief; of the cases added in 1966, about 34 percent had received assistance previously.

Since individuals do go on and off welfare, cumulative data showing the total time spent on welfare by an AFDC mother and her children are important in determining how welfare fits into their life cycle. According to the study of cases closed in 1961, 10 percent of the Negro and 7 percent of the white mothers had spent 9 or more years on welfare. Nevertheless, in absolute terms, white families outnumbered Negro families among the very small minority of AFDC cases on assistance for as long as this.

The proportion of their adult life that women spend on AFDC is another significant measure of their dependence on this assistance. A study based on a 1-percent random sample of AFDC cases in Philadelphia (drawn in 1959, and followed through to 1962) showed that the majority (60 percent) had spent slightly less than half (47 percent) of their adult life on welfare. In at least one city, then, welfare was not a permanent or exclusive style of life for all of the women on AFDC during the time they raised their children.

Finally, intergenerational dependency on welfare can also be measured. In the cases closed during early 1961, less than a third both of the white and of the Negro mothers had grown up in families in which their parents had also been on assistance. However, a study in the State of Washington in 1964 yielded a substantially higher figure. About 43 percent of the AFDC mothers in the sample reported that their parents had been on assistance—3 percent said their parents had been dependent for as long as they could remember; 27 percent said that they had been dependent for several years; and 13 percent said that they had received assistance for a brief period.

Altogether, the generalization that welfare becomes a permanent style of life for all or most AFDC recipients is not supported by the available evidence. The people on welfare are a varied group. Many of the families are not involved in long-term or intergenerational dependency. It must be recognized, however, that significant proportions of AFDC families do represent a second generation on welfare. . . .

White Colonialism, Black Power, and the Vicious Circle

STOKELY CARMICHAEL AND CHARLES V. HAMILTON

This is why the society does nothing meaningful about institutional racism: because the black community has been the creation of, and dominated by, a combination of oppressive forces and special interests in the white community. The groups which have access to the necessary resources and the ability to effect change benefit politically and economically from the continued subordinate status of the black community. This is not to say that every single white American consciously oppresses black people. He does not need to. Institutional racism has been maintained deliberately by the power structure and through indifference, inertia and lack of courage on the part of white masses as well as petty officials. Whenever black demands for change become loud and strong, indifference is replaced by active opposition based on fear and self-interest. The line between purposeful suppression and indifference blurs. One way or another, most whites participate in economic colonialism.

Indeed, the colonial white power structure has been a most formidable foe. It has perpetuated a vicious circle—the poverty cycle—in which the black communities are denied good jobs, and therefore

FROM Stokely Carmichael, civil rights leader and black power advocate; and Charles V. Hamilton, professor of political science, Roosevelt University, *Black Power: The Politics of Liberation in America* (Vintage Edition), pp. 22–23. © Copyright, 1967 by Stokely Carmichael and Charles V. Hamilton. Reprinted by permission of Random House.

stuck with a low income and therefore unable to obtain a good education with which to obtain good jobs. They cannot qualify for credit at most reputable places; they then resort to unethical merchants who take advantage of them by charging higher prices for inferior goods. They end up having less funds to buy in bulk, thus unable to reduce overall costs. They remain trapped.

In the face of such realities, it becomes ludicrous to condemn black people for "not showing more initiative." Black people are not in a depressed condition because of some defect in their character. The colonial power structure clamped a boot of oppression on the neck of the black people and then, ironically, said "they are not ready for freedom." Left solely to the good will of the oppressor, the oppressed would never be ready.

And no one accepts blame. And there is no "white power structure" doing it to them. And they are in that condition "because they are lazy and don't want to work." And this is not colonialism. And this is the land of opportunity, and the home of the free. And people should not become alienated.

But people *do* become alienated.

VI

Policy Issues and Alternatives

Never To Be Employed

Anthony Rocha, 17, of Atlanta, Ga., is a small, slight youngster who exudes a nail-chewing nervousness; he is a high-school dropout; he has never had a real job. Of average intelligence, but two years behind his class because of illness and accidents, Rocha quit Atlanta's Fulton High School two weeks before Christmas while in the ninth grade, against his parents' wishes.

Dressed in a white shirt and tan, tight-legged trousers, lounging on a couch in his modest home, he tried to explain why. "Some people find an interest in school, but I just didn't. [So] me and a friend of mine decided we would just quit and get us a job. I didn't realize it would be so hard to find one. I've tried to get jobs at service stations, a bakery, and all the grocery stores out here, but there just aren't any jobs for a person like me."

There were other reasons, of course, for his leaving school. Anthony's stepfather, who never finished high school himself, is a warehouse stockman who earns only $62.50 a week, with which he must support a family of five.

"All I wanted to know when I quit school," adds Rocha, "was that I could support myself and stop mooching on my mother and father. I realize now I definitely made a mistake."

But the wisdom came too late, as it frequently does. . . . "What can a kid do about unemployment," asks [former Secretary of Labor] Willard Wirtz, "pick up his phone and call his congressman?"

FROM *Newsweek* (April 1, 1963).

THE Annual Report of the President's Council of Economic Advisers declared in January 1968 that "poverty in the United States has been declining at an appreciable rate. With continued overall prosperity and well designed comprehensive programs . . . poverty can be reduced even more effectively in the future—to the point where it will survive only as an unpleasant memory." Although we are still far from the condition hoped for in this statement, some progress has been made. Poor nonfarm households as a percentage of total households declined from 22.5 per cent in 1959 to 17.6 per cent (or 10.3 million households) in 1966. This decline may be attributed partly to the antipoverty war and partly to the long "cyclical" expansion of the total economy in the 1960s, although we cannot determine the precise influence of each factor. It is true that the ratio of "social welfare expenditures" to gross national product rose from .105 in 1959–60 to .130 in 1966–67, as the Merriam selection indicates; but we cannot ignore the contribution of economic expansion, particularly evident in the drop in our unemployment rate. The overall unemployment rate in the base year 1959 was 5.5 per cent; in 1966 it had fallen to 3.8 per cent. Had the unemployment rate in 1966 remained at 5.5 per cent there would have been about 1.3 million more persons unemployed than was actually the case, which would no doubt have added substantially to the number of poor households.

We strongly support the view that full employment (not just "maximum" employment) is the best single means of attacking poverty, and perhaps, as Harry Johnson has argued, it may also prove useful in attacking discrimination against blacks, women, and the aged. A burgeoning demand for labor is also an important means of drawing into the labor market those who want to work but do not actively seek jobs. We would like the government to assume its full responsibility as employer of last resort. This commitment is implicit in the Employment Act of 1946, and it is explored more fully in the Mangum selection. Our society must decide, of course, what rate of inflation is acceptable in order to attempt a full-employment attack on poverty, for it seems likely that some inflation will accompany unemployment rates below 3 per cent.

Full employment, however, would not help even most of the poor. It would not lift all the underpaid out of poverty, nor would it help the aged and the ill, female family heads, or unskilled and unmotivated youths. It would not necessarily eliminate or even reduce poverty-generating environmental conditions of both urban and rural life such as crippling school conditions, adverse housing, and broken families.

Much would depend on whether full employment were maintained and whether it were maintained largely through government military outlays or through welfare expenditures addressed to these environmental conditions. *Any antipoverty program must include what Lee Rainwater has called "structural" components*—that is, services designed to help specific groups among the poor who cannot be reached by programs with an aggregative emphasis.

The inadequacies of a full-employment program can also be found in income maintenance strategies such as a guaranteed annual income through a negative income tax. However, we believe that a combination of full employment and income maintenance would reduce the service, or structural, components of the nation's antipoverty effort to a tolerable minimum.

Not only do we believe in the efficacy and the efficiency of a guaranteed minimum income through the federal tax mechanism, but we anticipate the adoption of such a plan in the foreseeable future. A popular consensus in favor of such a plan, spurred on by the defects of the existing welfare system and remarkable agreement on income maintenance among liberals and conservatives, rapidly crystallized during 1969 as President Nixon proposed a "family assistance system" through what was in effect a negative income tax. Excerpts from his television speech, concentrating on the income maintenance aspect, are reproduced in this section. His *de facto* income maintenance plan, in which he formally abjured a "guaranteed income," was further elaborated in a message to Congress three days later.

Despite a doubling of public outlays for educational purposes from 1959–60 to 1966–67, as indicated in Merriam's social welfare expenditures table, the antipoverty portions of those funds have not been allocated in the best way. The critique of Head Start in this section points to one weakness, and the selections by Coles and Kozol in Section IV indicate other weaknesses. These defects probably could not be corrected by any program that simply grants funds to educational institutions, particularly at the elementary and preschool levels. One of the greatest defects in our educational programs is the failure to establish a vast network of government-subsidized nursery schools for AFDC and working mothers, creches operated by a newly trained generation of humanistic teachers. On the other hand, if our social consensus is that these mothers belong at home until their children are older, how can we fail to guarantee them a comfortable income?

The almost fourfold growth of public funds devoted to vocational education since 1959–60 is gratifying. But the financing of on-the-job training for the unskilled poor has been left too much to private employers, who usually find the payoff unsatisfactory in terms of maximizing profits. On-the-job training could make an enormous contribution to developing marketable skills among the poor, especially those who are eager to work, such as Anthony Rocha of the opening vignette, but such a contribution will not materialize unless our society is prepared to underwrite it with substantial public funds. On-the-job training is essentially vocational training, and it need not be confined to the public schools or left to the vagaries of private financing.

In education, progress will be severely inhibited, as much of the material in this book shows, until we tackle the low level of motivation generated by the poverty environment, particularly in the black ghetto. The Community Council of Greater New York, for example, has placed great emphasis upon training programs in the ghettos that pay workers during training and guarantee them employment upon completion of the program. Hence the educational component of the future antipoverty effort will have to employ an integrated, structural approach coordinated with an aggregative income and employment approach. Indeed, the potential timebomb inherent in the mutually reinforcing problems of poverty, race, and urban deterioration can be defused only by adopting a comprehensive strategy that mobilizes all the resources of our society, as we have done in facing major international conflicts in the past.

The poverty war has sharply delineated for the American people the question of how resources should be allocated between the private and the public sectors, as pointed out in the March selection. In this connection, it is interesting to note that since World War II the allocation of massive cash transfer funds for expansion of private employee benefit and pension plans, generally accruing to the comfortably well-off workers, has been greater than that for public social insurance benefits and assistance, accruing mostly to the poor.[1] But in general, as John Kenneth Galbraith has argued, we must overcome a hallowed resistance to the shifting of activities toward the public (especially the federal) sector. This is not the case with military expenditures, most of which go to private firms, for these outlays are considered sacrosanct. There are those, such as Howard J. Samuels, who have the temerity to argue for the importance of expanded welfare outlays even in the face of increased military expenditures. But this perfectly "rational" view seems to be only a voice crying in the congressional wilderness.

---

[1] Ida C. Merriam, "Social Welfare Expenditures, 1929–67," *Social Security Bulletin,* vol. 30, no. 12 (December 1967), p. 16.

Coverage, Gaps, and
Future Directions of Public Programs

MICHAEL S. MARCH

Public attention in the "war on poverty" tends to focus on the $2 billion budget for the Office of Economic Opportunity (OEO). Funds from public programs to assist the poor, however, are on the order of 20 times the amount budgeted for OEO. This paper analyzes how much Federal, State, and local governments are spending to help the poor, what kinds of programs they are supporting, and looks ahead at some of the fundamental choices that we face in the future on these programs.

PRESENT PUBLIC PROGRAMS FOR THE POOR

Federal Programs.   The OEO has imparted a new and significant thrust to the war on poverty, but the Federal antipoverty effort is much broader and larger. The President's budget message for fiscal year 1968 indicated that 10 Federal agencies would devote an estimated $25.6 billion to help the 30 million poor people in our Nation. Table 1 provides information on the programs included in this total. The figures are based on the January 1967 budget. . . .

First, a few words should be said about the content of this analysis:

The tabulation is designed to measure program levels. For administrative budget accounts, the figures are largely new obligational authority. For the trust fund programs, expenditure data are used because they are the best measure of program level. Trust funds, such as social security (OASDI) are included where appropriate because the benefits they provide directly assist the poor. The ravages of poverty were a major factor motivating the creation of the social security programs in 1935. A report at that time indicated that at least one-half of the 7.5 million people then over 65 years of age were dependent.

The analysis includes only those Federal programs which make a

FROM Michael S. March, Resources Planning Staff, U.S. Bureau of the Budget, "Federal Programs for Human Resource Development," *Federal Programs for the Development of Human Resources* (Washington, D.C.: Joint Economic Committee, Subcommittee on Economic Progress, 1968), pp. 143–53.

direct impact on low-income people. Only the funds which benefit people with incomes below the poverty line are counted. The income levels used to measure the poverty line were worked out in a special joint study by the Social Security Administration and the OEO. The levels vary as among single people, married couples, small families, and large families, et cetera. For example, the poverty line for a single person was $1,540, while for a family of four it was $3,130 in calendar 1963.

The figures are necessarily statistical estimates rather than precise accounting data. Survey data from many different sources—HEW, VA, Labor, Census, other agencies—were used by Bureau of the Budget staff to estimate the proportions of benefits going to the poor from individual programs. More than 100 programs with funds totaling $59 billion in 1968 were included in the analysis. Only a few of the programs, such as the OEO funds, the public assistance, and the Indian health and education programs, were counted 100 percent as assisting the poor. For the great bulk of the programs, only portions of the funds were counted as going to the poor. For example, about one-third of social security (OASDI) benefits were counted; 40 percent of the health insurance for the aged; 30 percent of hospital care by the Veterans' Administration; 20 percent of unemployment compensation benefits by Labor; two-thirds of public housing by the Department of Housing and Urban Development; 95 percent of title I grants and 30 percent of other programs under the Elementary and Secondary Education Act.

Many other programs which indirectly help to provide jobs or serve the poor or help the poor insofar as they are members of the general population are entirely excluded from the analysis. For example, most public works programs, including the entire Federal-aid highway program, are excluded. Recreation and park programs, which make it possible for poor people to have some recreation, are not counted. None of the substantial expenditures for Defense contracts or for military personnel which provide jobs and incomes for many people below the poverty line are included. Finally, this analysis makes no effort to take account of the benefits to the poor from fiscal and economic policies which maintain high employment and make it possible for unemployed individuals to secure jobs or for the underemployed to secure better jobs.

Now, let us turn to the substance of the data in table 1. The following points stand out:

1. Total Federal aid for the poor has nearly doubled in the last 6 years, rising from $13 billion in fiscal 1963 to an estimated $25.6

billion in the 1968 budget. The programs under the Economic Opportunity Act contribute $2 billion toward this increase.

2. Cash benefits for maintenance of incomes in 1968 are estimated at $14.6 billion, or 57 percent of all aid to the poor. They include OASDI benefits of $8.5 billion, of which $1.6 billion was under proposed legislation, still pending in the Congress.

3. Education and training programs, including work training programs, will total $3.8 billion in 1968, an increase of more than twelvefold since 1960 and 1963. Programs initiated under the Economic Opportunity Act of 1964 and the Elementary and Secondary Education Act of 1965 account for the bulk of the increase.

4. Health programs are estimated at $4.2 billion in 1968, a sixfold increase over 1960. Health insurance for the aged and grants to States for medical assistance programs under title 19 of the Social Security Act, as enacted by the Social Security Amendments of 1965, are large factors in the rise in this category.

5. Social services, aid for economic and community development, special food programs, public housing, and urban renewal programs, etc., provide the bulk of the last catchall category. In total they were projected to increase more than fourfold, from $0.7 billion in 1960 to an estimated $3.1 billion in 1968.

Two main points stand out in table 1 about the Federal programs for aid to the poor.

First, the 2½-fold increase from $9.9 billion in 1960 to a projected $25.6 billion in 1968 represents distinct progress. In relation to the cash payments budget, this represented an increase from 10.5 percent in 1960 to 14.8 percent in 1968.

Second, and even more important, is the change in the nature of assistance provided. In fiscal 1960, nearly 84 percent of the Federal aid of $9.9 billion was through cash benefit payments. Education, health, service, and community development programs comprised only $1.6 billion or 16 percent.

Although the proposed program for 1968 included $14.6 billion of cash benefit payments, 76 percent more than in 1960, this category had declined to 57 percent of the total. Education, health, service, and economic and community development programs had increased more than sixfold since 1960 to $11.0 billion in 1968 and comprised 43 percent of the total. There has been a clear shift toward human investment programs as a major weapon in the war against poverty.

A third principal point is demonstrated by table 2, which classifies the Federal funds for the poor by agency. The Office of Economic Opportunity, which is in the Executive Office of the President and

TABLE 1

Estimated Federal Funds for Programs Assisting the Poor, Fiscal Years 1960–68

(*Administrative budget and trust funds, billions of dollars*)

Category	1960 actual	1963 actual	1966 actual	1967 estimate	1968 estimate
Education and training					
HEW: Elementary and Secondary Education Act of 1965			1.0	1.1	1.3
Other	0.1	0.2	.5	.7	.7
OEO-NYC, Job Corps, CAP, etc			.7	.9	1.3
Labor-MDTA, etc.		(1)	.1	.2	.3
Interior	.1	.1	.1	.1	.1
VA	.1	(1)	(1)	.1	.1
Subtotal	.3	.3	2.5	3.1	3.8
Health					
HEW: Health insurance for the aged and disabled (HI and SMI)			(1)	1.4	1.7
Public assistance medical care	.2	.4	.7	1.0	1.2
Other	.2	.3	.6	.7	.8
VA: Hospital and domiciliary care	.3	.4	.4	.4	.4
OEO: CAP, etc.			.1	.1	.1
Subtotal	.7	1.0	1.8	3.6	4.2
Cash benefit payments					
HEW: OASDI	4.0	5.3	6.8	6.8	8.5
Public assistance	1.8	2.3	2.8	2.9	3.0
Railroad retirement	.3	.3	.3	.3	.4
Labor: Unemployment benefits	.5	.6	.4	.4	.4
VA: Compensation and pensions	1.6	2.0	2.3	2.4	2.4
Subtotal	8.3	10.4	12.7	12.8	14.6
Services, economic and community development, etc.:					
Agriculture: Food programs	.2	.3	.4	.4	.5
Other	.2	.3	.5	.3	.2
Commerce: EDA and Appalachia		.1	.2	.3	.2

Note: Figures may not add because of rounding.
[1] Less than $50,000,000.

TABLE 1 (continued)

Category	1960 actual	1963 actual	1966 actual	1967 estimate	1968 estimate
OEO: CAP and other			.6	.6	.6
HEW: VRA, WA, etc.	(1)	.1	.1	.1	.1
HUD:					
Public housing and rent supplements	.1	.1	.1	.2	.2
Urban renewal and other	.1	(1)	.3	.3	.8
Interior: Services to Indians, etc.	.1	.2	.2	.2	.3
Labor: Employment, youth and other services	(1)	.1	.1	.2	.1
SBA (economic opportunity loans)					
Subtotal	.7	1.2	2.6	2.5	3.1
Total					
Administrative budget	5.1	6.8	11.8	13.0	14.6
Trust funds	4.9	6.2	7.7	9.1	11.1
Grand total	9.9	13.0	19.6	22.0	25.6

has the principal coordinating role in the effort against poverty, provides less than 8 percent of all the Federal funds for this effort—mostly for innovative and gap-filling programs. The Department of Health, Education, and Welfare provides $17.3 billion, or 68 percent of all the funds, including $8.1 billion from the administrative budget. The Veterans' Administration is the second largest agency provider of funds, accounting for $2.9 billion or 11 percent. Six other agencies provide a total of $3.4 billion or 13 percent.

STATE AND LOCAL GOVERNMENT AND PRIVATE VOLUNTARY OUTLAYS

Only the roughest estimates of State and local government and private voluntary agency expenditures for assistance to the poor are available. A contract study made for the Office of Economic Opportunity soon after it was established indicated that in the fiscal year 1964 (some of the figures were for 1963) a total of $12.9 billion expended by State and local governments assisted the poor. This total does not include the State-local share of federally aided public assistance programs which, at that time, was on the order of $2 billion.

The emphasis, however, was somewhat different from that of the Federal Government. Only about $4 billion was for financial assistance, including public assistance, and about $11 billion was for education, health, community facilities, and other programs. This tabulation assumes that expenditures for building highways and utilities assist the poor, and so is less restrictive than the Federal estimates.

An additional $2.4 billion was estimated as being provided by private voluntary agencies, of which only about $200 million was financial assistance and the remainder was for education and training, health, and other programs. (See table 3.)

It would be reasonable to assume that the $17 billion—including public assistance—which was provided by State and local governments and private organizations for aid to the poor in 1964 has not diminished in the last 4 years and probably has increased substantially.

Thus, aid to the poor in 1968 from Federal, State and local, and private sources must exceed $40 billion, and probably all but $2–$3 billion of this comes from public funds. The total represents about 5 percent of GNP and approximates $1,350 per poor person.

GAPS IN POVERTY PROGRAMS

Judging from pronouncements by groups, conferences, committees, and individuals, public and private, who propose additions and improvements in poverty programs and other closely related areas, some people believe the biggest gap in the antipoverty effort is the lack of sufficient spending. Among the suggestions have been proposals which could readily result in doubling or tripling the present Federal antipoverty effort. They include the following:

• A "Freedom Budget" by the A. Philip Randolph Institute proposing additional expenditures of $185 billion in 10 years, 1966–75, for social investment. It would be designed to abolish poverty, provide guaranteed jobs, guaranteed incomes, decent homes, modern health services, and full educational opportunity for all, as well as achieve other objectives. A large part of the strategy is to heat up the economy to provide lots of opportunities for minorities.

• The report of the Advisory Council on Public Welfare, which proposed a national minimum standard for public assistance payments geared to the cost of a modest but adequate family budget and provision of such aid and social services as a matter of right. These plus the many other proposals in the report, although not priced, clearly added up to a multibillion dollar effort.

TABLE 2

Estimated Federal Agency Funds for Programs Assisting
the Poor, Fiscal Years 1960–68

(*Administrative budget and trust funds, billions of dollars*)

Agency	1960 actual	1963 actual	1966 actual	1967 estimate	1968 estimate
Agriculture	0.4	0.6	0.9	0.7	0.7
Commerce		.1	.2	.3	.2
Health, Education, and Welfare	6.3	8.6	12.9	14.7	17.3
	(4.0)	(5.3)	(6.8)	(8.2)	(10.2)
Housing and Urban Development	.2	.1	.4	.5	1.0
Interior	.2	.3	.3	.3	.4
Labor	.5	.7	.6	.7	.6
	(.5)	(.7)	(.5)	(.6)	(.5)
Office of Economic Opportunity			1.4	1.6	2.0
Railroad Retirement Board	.3	.3	.3	.3	.4
	(.3)	(.3)	(.3)	(.3)	(.4)
Veterans' Administration	2.0	2.4	2.7	2.9	2.9
Total	9.9	13.0	19.6	22.0	25.6
	(4.9)	(6.2)	(7.7)	(9.1)	(11.1)

Note: Figures in parentheses represent amounts of trust fund expenditures
included in each respective total. Figures may not add because of rounding.

TABLE 3

Estimated Expenditures by State and Local Governments and
Private Voluntary Agencies for Aid to the Poor

(*Mostly fiscal year 1964; in billions of dollars*)

Program category	State and local governments	Private voluntary agencies
Education and training[1]	4.8	1.2
Health, including mental health[1]	2.1	.5
Financial assistance	2.0[2]	.2
Other		
Community facilities[3]	2.2	.1
All other	1.8	.4
Total	12.9[2]	2.4

[1] Adjusted to include capital facilities.
[2] In addition, States and localities spent approximately $2,000,000,000 in
matching grants for the federally aided public assistance programs.
[3] Includes highways, utilities, etc.

• A symposium on guaranteed income plans, hosted by the Chamber of Commerce of the United States, at which the merits of "negative income tax" plans costing $10 billion or more a year were debated.

• Proposals by the Council for the White House Conference on Civil Rights which made many recommendations for economic security and welfare, housing, justice, and education, including a suggestion that the then average public expenditure of $533 per pupil be increased to a goal of $1,000 per child. There are about 43 million public school children, so the implied outlay for this single proposal was on the order of $20 billion.

• A $3-billion, 2-year, emergency slum job and riot damage program approved by the Senate Poverty Subcommittee as an add-on to the 1967 extension of the Economic Opportunity Act.

• Senate bill 2088, 90th Congress, first session, by Senator Robert F. Kennedy and 20 others—the Urban Employment Opportunities Development Act—to allow tax credits, accelerated depreciation, and extra deductions for wages, etc., to firms creating jobs in ghettos. The initial cost is not large but the proposal is interesting for its use of the tax side of the budget and its probable expansibility.

• A $9-billion-a-year program of children's allowances. If all the 80 million children and youth were made eligible for such payments, as was apparently intended, this would work out to less than $10 a month for each—about enough to pay for lunch at school.

• Various studies indicate that rural America lags behind urbanized areas in income and in vital social services and that large resources will be needed to redress the balance. A President's National Advisory Commission on Rural Poverty has been asked to study and make recommendations on the entire gamut of policies and programs affecting rural life.

• Mayor Jerome P. Cavanagh, president of the National League of Cities and also of the U.S. Conference of Mayors, has testified that price tags in congressional hearings for seven programs which affected cities totaled $242 billion over the next 10 years.

• Among the scores or even hundreds of specific ways of spending more money to help the poor, some large contenders include:

• The negative income tax, guaranteed income, or an equivalent restructuring of the public assistance programs, that would cost $10 or $12 billion a year—and much more if they spread, as would be natural, to some people now above the poverty line.

• Job opportunity or "manpower" programs which could range all the way from a few hundred millions to several billions more per year.

• Cities programs to rebuild the physical facilities and services systems of ghettos and to create opportunities in them for the minority groups at costs that range up to or exceed the entire present Federal outlay for aid to the poor.

• Programs to restructure education for the underprivileged completely by as much as doubling the present per student outlay.

In addition, there are, of course, all sorts of proposals to expand on-going programs of the agencies listed in table 2 in the health, community action, economic development, rural life, and other fields.

FUTURE DIRECTIONS FOR POVERTY PROGRAMS

One need not believe Pareto's "law" concerning the persistence of inequality in the distribution of incomes to recognize that the elimination of poverty is indeed a difficult problem. Neither natural abilities of men nor the play of fortune on their lives are so uniform that the extremes of the normal distribution are canceled out. One of the functions of society is to moderate the ill effects upon the unfortunate minority who are poor. How can the public do this best?

Where public programs are being formulated for an effort such as combating poverty, it is natural to ask: How much? However, perhaps even more fundamental, are the questions:

What kinds of tools shall be used?

Who should receive the assistance?

By whom should the action be taken?

While resources are always limited, today the future directions of the war on poverty are covered by extremely murky clouds of fiscal uncertainty. The fiscal situation places a very large premium on careful planning and programming of the resources that are currently dedicated to the antipoverty effort and careful scrutiny of new programs.

Both fiscal policy tools of macroeconomics and structural measures have been used in the antipoverty effort in recent years, and their efforts are intertwined. The number of poor, according to the Bureau of the Census and the Department of Health, Education, and Welfare, has declined from 40 million in calendar 1960 to approximately 34 million in 1964 and then to about 29.7 million in calendar 1966. By any standard 29.7 million people are still a very large group of poor in an affluent society which is enjoying high employment.

Out of the large number of existing programs and proposals for new programs and expanded programs to fight poverty, how do we find the best ways to speed up the permanent removal of these 29.7 million poor from poverty? How can we break the vicious inter-generational cycle of poverty?

One way for those seeking to design better solutions and to direct resources to more effective channels might be to address the following types of tradeoffs or alternatives:

1. *Cash benefits versus human resource development.* An ex-tremely significant contribution toward alleviating poverty has been made by the income maintenance programs which were initiated in the depths of the great depression. Public income maintenance pro-grams in fiscal year 1966 totaled $39.8 billion, compared to $25.3 billion in 1960 and $8.9 billion in 1950. In 1966, Federal funds pro-vided $34 billion and State and local governments, $5.8 billion. These programs have raised millions of people above the poverty line.

Yet poverty was far from abolished. One possible reason appeared in estimates by the Council of Economic Advisers that in fiscal year 1965 only about one-fourth of all the public transfer payments went to persons who were below the poverty line. In the future, if there are no drastic changes in the structure of present public income main-tenance programs, a declining proportion of benefits will go to the poor, particularly in the social insurance category. About half the poor today cannot qualify for cash benefits of any sort.

Recognition of the importance of investment in human resources, particularly through education and health, is a recent phenomenon among economists. This awareness has been accompanied by a major thrust in Federal programs in the last several years toward increasing education and health programs, especially for the poor.

The choice between these two sets of tools is not an easy one. In-come maintenance payments, if properly directed, can produce an immediate effect in lifting people out of poverty. But some believe that they may have adverse incentive effects, and there seems to be a con-siderable reluctance to provide funds for welfare benefits. The struc-turing of income maintenance programs to direct the funds to the poor is, moreover, not an easy matter.

Human resource programs, according to the evidence adduced by T. W. Schultz, Edward F. Denison, and others, produce a good cost-benefit return and play a large role in economic growth. However, they operate in the long run, and our knowledge of how to direct them effectively to assist those who live in the subculture of poverty is still limited.

In passing, it should be noted that cash benefits can be traded off against jobs or jobs with training. This is currently under active debate in the Congress on the program for aid to families with dependent children.

There is, in effect, a whole continuum of possible programs ranging from solid rehabilitation by means of education and training and other measures to equip people for *bona fide* jobs in the competitive job market; so-called "work training" which prepares people by exposing them temporarily to the responsibilities of a regular job; "make work" or sheltered work which could provide permanent jobs for individuals who are not employable in the regular labor economy; and outright cash support. When and to what extent is each type appropriate?

2. *The aged versus the youth.*   When the Social Security Act of 1935 was first being structured, two groups were clearly recognized as being prime targets requiring protection against deprivation: the aged and the children. The evolution of public programs since then largely favored the aged, at least in the Federal arena. The fiscal year 1968 budget contains benefits and services estimated at $29 billion for persons over age 65 and on the order of $12.5 billion for children and youth under 21. No breakdown by age is available on the funds for the poor in table 1, although it is clear that major portions of both the cash benefits and health categories are directed to assisting the aged. On the other hand, the education and training category is largely directed toward assisting children and youth. Substantial new legislative advances have been made for both groups since 1964.

Of the approximately 29.7 million Americans who were below the poverty line in 1966, some 5 million were over age 65 and 14 million were children and youth under age 21. What would be the comparative social and economic returns from additional allocations of resources to these two groups? Through what sorts of programs can assistance be targeted to the poor in each of these categories without great leakages of resources to the much larger numbers of nonpoor who are in both these categories? And what, also, should be done for the other 11 million American poor who are age 22 to 64, many of whom are in families with children?

3. *Negroes versus the rest of the poor.*   Data from the March 1966 Current Population Survey indicated that 69 percent of the poor were white. Yet, of the 22.6 million nonwhites, 45 percent were below the poverty line and Negroes made up 31 percent of the poor. Only 13 percent of the whites were poor.

The problem of poverty among the Negroes is exacerbated and complicated by the legacies of past discrimination and the effects of remaining discrimination. Solution of this deep problem is further complicated by the riots which have injected factors that go far beyond that of poverty. How does the policymaker and allocator of resources address the interlinked problems of reducing poverty and achieving full rights for the Negro in our society? And what comparative priority should be accorded to the poverty-stricken whites who constitute 69 percent of the poor and many of whom fear the competition of the rising Negro?

4. *Cities versus rural areas.* The March 1965 Current Population Survey indicated that 43 percent of all the poor lived in rural areas. In the early years of the OEO effort, the rural areas did not receive their share of the OEO dollar, although efforts are being made to redress this.

Recently, there has been strong emphasis on the problems of the urban ghettos. Yet it is also being recognized increasingly that many of the people who are the residents of the ghettos had migrated from the rural slums. One poverty-laden area in Chicago has more residents born on the Mississippi Delta than it has natives of Chicago.

What is an appropriate national strategy for meeting equitably and effectively the problems of poverty in both rural and urban areas?

5. *Self-help versus massive aid.* The OEO programs are built on the principle that individuals and communities should be given opportunities to help themselves. Development of individual abilities and skills and active community organization and development are viewed as steps toward a lasting improvement in the lot of the poor.

Many suggestions are made, however, for large direct assistance through cash grants or make-work. What are the tradeoffs of these approaches in speed, social and economic effect, public acceptability, and ultimate cost/effectiveness?

6. *Direct aid to individuals versus environmental improvement.* The great bulk of the Federal, as well as State-local and private efforts for assisting the poor, has been for programs which are designed to provide services and cash benefit payments to individuals and families. The proportion of funds for reshaping the urban ghettos and rural slums in a physical sense has been modest.

What role does a new environment play in helping the deprived? How should brick and mortar programs which are designed to change the physical environment for the poor be articulated with service programs? What are the relative payoffs of aid to the poor through providing new housing or new community facilities as opposed to using the funds for services? How can the poor be buffered against the possible ill-effects of reconstruction programs which require their relocation?

7. *Private versus public action.*   Although the relative role of private voluntary agencies is diminishing as large public programs are created to assist the poor, the function of nonprofit agencies and of business enterprise in the effort against poverty remains a key consideration. Despite the large numbers of proposals for huge Federal programs, it is doubtful that few serious students of the body politic would thrust the whole burden of combating poverty on governmental agencies.

The relationships and roles of public and private organizations in this effort, however, are far from settled. What imaginative ways can be devised to encourage private businesses to use the untrained and to help create better conditions for the poor? What is the role of mixed public-private agencies such as the community action programs (CAP's) which are emerging under the Economic Opportunity Act programs? How can incentives be structured into programs so that administering agencies and recipients will adopt the socially beneficial and productive courses of action rather than wasteful nonproductive roles? Can the general public be educated so it will elect to invest its resources in fundamental preventive and rehabilitative measures that strike at the roots of poverty but have a deferred yield? Or must public policy wait until it is too late to use all but the stopgap and palliative measures?

8. *Fragmented programs or concerted programs?*   The OEO *Catalog of Federal Assistance Programs* for June 1967 lists a total of 459 programs which are designed to assist American people in furthering their social and economic progress. These programs are administered by 15 different Federal agencies or departments and by many bureaus within them. The Federal administrative structure in a large number of cases is paralleled by similar organizations at the State and at local level.

The existence of these many categorical programs and compartmentalized agencies makes it difficult to concert services for the poor. Promotion of services for the poor is further handicapped because in many instances the State or local agencies have not been decentralized to poverty areas. Although financial assistance programs are also categorical, it has proved easier to spend large amounts for cash transfers than for the provision of preventive and rehabilitative services. Technology and organization for the delivery of concerted services in communities is still largely in the horse-and-buggy stage.

The creation of CAP's under the aegis of the OEO and the drive toward decentralization of services into the poverty neighborhoods through neighborhood centers has brought a refreshing new thrust to the effort against poverty. This has, of course, also been accompanied by a good deal of static as new institutions confronted old institutions, or as submerged peoples found a voice through which they could express their desires and their views. The question remains unanswered, however: How ready are our governmental agencies and institutions to administer effectively large additional amounts of resources to assist the poor? Can we perhaps find improved patterns of service-delivery, both responsive to the poor and cost/effective—and devise new methods of providing governmental financial assistance—which permit concerted services for individuals, family centered services, and grassroots community or neighborhood action to solve the fundamental problems of poverty?

There is a healthy omen in the plethora of proposals which are being debated. Debate and, beyond debate, critical testing of all proposals is essential, for perhaps the biggest gap in the poverty programs is the gap in knowledge. We know little about the causes of poverty and even less about its cures. Basic research has been neglected and cost/effectiveness research—especially in the interprogram area—is still in its infancy. Yet the problem of poverty is a central issue of our society.

Manpower Policy:
A Critique and a Proposal

GARTH L. MANGUM

Summarizing 2 years of effort in 3,500 words indicates either low output or high discipline. The task can best be accomplished in summary form with a few generalizations about the state of manpower policy and a brief evaluation of specific programs. . . .

The thrust of the manpower programs of the past 5 years has been to aid those who face various disadvantages in competing for jobs. This emphasis is attested to more by legislative and administrative

FROM Garth L. Mangum, professor of economics, George Washington University, "Evaluating Federal Manpower Programs," and "Government as Employer of Last Resort," *Federal Programs for the Development of Human Resources* (Washington, D.C.: Joint Economic Committee, Subcommittee on Economic Progress, 1968), pp. 187–90, 441–43.

efforts and public discussion than by expenditures of less than $2 billion per year.

OVERALL CRITIQUE OF FEDERAL MANPOWER POLICY

The relevant manpower programs which emphasize in varying degrees services for the competitively disadvantaged are the Manpower Development and Training Act, the Vocational Education Act of 1963, the vocational rehabilitation program, and the several manpower components of the Economic Opportunity Act. . . .

This array of programs did not emerge as part of any systematic effort to identify and provide each of the services needed by various disadvantaged groups or by all the disadvantaged. Instead individual acts were written, considered, and amended in rapid succession to meet current crises, real or imagined, with little attention to their interrelations. Though overall objectives are reasonably clear, the objectives of some of the individual programs are not.

The resources and enrollments in all of these programs are too small relative to the size of the labor force and the magnitude of needs to have had an appreciable impact on the problems they were intended to "solve." Remedial programs for the disadvantaged currently enroll an average of only 300,000 people at any point in time—this in an economy where in prosperous 1966, 2.5 million persons were unemployed 15 weeks or more, 850,000 were unemployed over half the year, 1.3 million looked for but did not find any work, 1.3 million males 25 to 64 years of age did not seek work and more than 5 million persons worked for less than the Federal minimum wage. . . .

The 1961–67 period is most appropriately viewed as an experimental one during which many things were tried with varying degrees of success and failure. A positive contribution of these efforts was the identification of a number of services which have proven useful in lowering the obstacles to employment and retention of the disadvantaged. A few of these are:

1. Outreach to seek the discouraged and undermotivated and encourage them to partake of available services.
2. Adult basic education, to remedy the lack of obsolescence of earlier schooling and prevocational orientation to expose those with limited experience to alternative occupational choices.
3. Training for entry level skills, for those unprepared to profit

from the normally more advanced training which assumes mastery of rudimentary education.

4. Training allowances, to provide support and an incentive for those undergoing training and residential facilities for youth whose home environment precludes successful rehabilitation.

5. Work experience, for those accustomed to the discipline of the workplace.

6. Job development, efforts to solicit job opportunities suited to the abilities of the disadvantaged jobseeker.

7. Relocation and transportation assistance to bring the workers to where the jobs are.

8. Subsidization of private employment of the disadvantaged.

9. Job coaching to work out supervisor-worker adjustments after a job is found.

10. Creation of public-service jobs tailored to the needs of job-seekers not absorbed in the competitive market.

Essential as these services are, they are available through no one program, agency, or labor market institution. The various programs are limited in the services they can offer. The budgetary commitments for the various services are not rationally related to need. For instance, there are currently more slots for work relief than for training when training should probably stand above work relief in the hierarchy of remedial services.

The administrative capability to deliver these services has yet to be developed. At the local level, there is no single agency or combination of easily accessible institutions where those seeking help can find it. Neither has any community the resources to provide some type of service to all who need it. A multiplicity of Federal funding sources encourages interagency competition at the Federal level and a proliferation at the local level, placing a premium on "grantsmanship." Coordination has been tried with little success and consolidation of programs has been limited. Existing agencies have changed their orientation and biases but slowly and only under considerable outside pressure. New agencies have yet to learn effective practices. Surprisingly little has been done, considering the number of programs and the level of expenditures, to develop or train capable staffs at any level of government.

The currently approved model for delivering comprehensive manpower services is the concentrated employment program (CEP). It attempts to concentrate and integrate the efforts of existing programs on behalf of target populations. It appears to have two premises: (1) The complex of programs and agencies can be integrated and focused through a single local institution; (2) while sufficient resources cannot be marshaled for a measurable national impact, concentration of both financial resources and administrative capability on narrowly defined targets may make an appreciable difference in a limited number of big-city slums and rural depressed areas. The brief CEP experience argues for both technical assistance for planning and management capability and augmented resources to avoid becoming one more link in a chain of unfulfilled promises.

Administration officials and Members of Congress have been too impatient to await the results of new and existing programs and to allow for restructuring, removal of negative elements, and finally their expansion into effective programs. As a result, there has been an excessive resort to gimmicks and to attempts to devise "instant policies for instant success." The procedure has become a familiar one. New approaches are designed intuitively rather than empirically. They are launched with public relations fanfare, complete with numerical goals and early target dates. Manipulation of numbers to "prove" success then becomes a major staff function until a quiet burial of the goals and targets can be devised. The favored gimmicks of the moment are the CEP approach and private enterprise involvement. Both have promise as part of the manpower policy arsenal of weapons but the experiences of neither to date has earned the warmth with which they are being embraced.

For no program are there adequate valid data for evaluation of strengths and weaknesses and no program currently has a reporting system capable of producing such data. Data on the characteristics of enrollees are adequate in some but not all programs. Data on services provided are weak and followup data on program results are grossly inadequate and undependable. *Ad hoc* internal evaluations have been made of several programs, either in-house or by contract, but for the most part their coverage is limited, their data weak, and their investigations not probing.

Nevertheless, one concludes from observation, available data, and piecing together other fragmentary evidence, that some programs are at least moderately successful and merit expansion. None is a clearly proven failure, though in several cases the funds could have been better spent elsewhere. Through this necessary experimental process many lessons have been learned, needs probed, and useful services identified. Congress has demonstrated a willingness to change and adapt programs in light of administrative experience. Expansion of programs has been slower than anticipated but less because of congressional reluctance than absence of aggressive administration requests. . . .

THE NEED FOR AN EMPLOYMENT GUARANTEE

As experience with manpower programs for the disadvantaged grows, so does the recognition of the primacy of job opportunities. Followup surveys of MDTA completers find one in seven unemployed when last contacted following training. NYC and Job Corps graduates face the same job markets after leaving the programs that they faced before; one-half of the public assistance recipients who enter work experience and training programs return to public assistance when they leave it. Special Labor Department surveys discover ghetto unemployment three times the national average along with extraordinarily high rates of nonparticipation in the labor force and low wage employment, resulting in a "subemployment" rate of 34 percent. A 1966 job order for 3,000 automobile workers attracted 16,000 applicants to the employment service in Detroit. More than twice as many Washington, D.C., youths responded to 1967 publicity than there were jobs available. A "jobmobile" touring Philadelphia slums in July 1967 to advertise 500 low paid city jobs resulted in 2,700 applicants, some of whom had stood in line for hours.

Someday, absent the inflationary potential of war, general levels of employment may absorb a higher proportion of the available labor force. Education and training efforts may make a significant contribution to the number who can be employed without unacceptable price level impacts. The political balance may even change to increase the tolerance to inflation. Ways may be found to attract employers to depressed areas and neighborhoods, or to get the unemployed and underemployed out of them. Until then—and the day appears far off—reasonably adequate solutions to the social and personal problems of the employable but competitively disadvantaged will require the Government to act as "employer of last resort." A significant start has been made in this direction but the ambivalence with which work programs have approached their objectives has limited the value of the experience. We now know more about what doesn't work well than what does. We can only guess how many require an employment guarantee but clearly the number exceeds the willingness of the public to foot the bill. Advocacy requires an estimate of the universe of need and an exploration of administrative problems.

Even with the relatively low levels of unemployment which prevailed during 1966, 2.4 million persons were unemployed at least 15 weeks during the year and 840,000 were unemployed more than half the time during the year. An additional 1.2 million looked but did not find work at any time. An average of 2 million persons was working part time but sought full-time jobs. There were 1.8 million men between the ages of 25 and 64 who, though able to work, were neither working nor seeking jobs; 500,000 were between 25 and 49. Nearly three-quarters of a million households were headed by men who were not workers. At least 5 million persons were working at wages below the Federal minimum.

It would be from these persons, and those women and youth now outside the labor force who would prefer to work, that a program to guarantee employment opportunities would draw its clientele. The number taking advantage of such a program would depend upon the pay, location, working conditions, and eligibility rules. Experience upon which to make a judgment is totally lacking, but speculation can provide a budgetary estimate.

Many of those who experienced a total of between 15 and 26 weeks of unemployment at some time during the year may have been reasonably satisfied with their situation. However, a larger proportion of those unemployed continually for between 15 and 26 weeks and most of the 840,000 who were unemployed at least half the year might consider themselves better off in a guaranteed employment program. The one-half million prime working age males, able to work but out of the labor force, may be a reasonable estimate of all of those out of the labor force who would re-enter. The one-half of the involuntary part-time employed who customarily work full time are a reasonable estimate of the potential applicants among that group.

Based on 1966 labor force data, the potential clients of an employment guarantee would appear to be the following:

Unemployed more than 26 weeks	840,000
Unemployed continuously, 15 to 26 weeks	295,000
Males, 25 to 49 years of age, out of labor force but able to work	500,000
Involuntary part time who usually work full time (nonagriculture)	1,183,000
Total	2,818,000

An estimate of nearly 3 million potential applicants is probably conservative, particularly in view of the 5 million low wage workers who have demonstrated their commitment to the labor force and might apply if wages were significantly higher than their current ones.

Some of the part year employed might prefer the public program for the remainder. Thus a larger estimate might be defended but, considering the odds against a program of that magnitude being undertaken in the near future, it is a reasonable outside boundary for program and budgetary consideration. Adding likely overhead costs to annual employment at, for instance, $1.50 an hour would bring the total budgetary cost to $12 billion a year. . . .

Useful jobs can be created commensurate with the abilities of almost anyone simply by the expenditure of public funds to purchase their services. However, there is no assurance that supervisors will use free labor wisely. Making the jobs lead to the mainstream of the job market is a difficult and as yet unsolved task. The redistribution of jobs in favor of the disadvantaged is more difficult. Employers, whether public or private, have a natural preference for the best qualified workers available and no current program has a sufficiently attractive "carrot" to substantially effect recruiting decisions. While alternatives merit continued experimentation, current experience would suggest that, for those for whom remedial education, training and better labor market services are inadequate to make successful job market competition possible, direct public expenditure, either for public employment or subsidized private employment is the only dependable road to jobs. However, maintenance of dignity requires both that the jobs be productive and that all stigma of dependency be absent.

The foray into social philosophy suggests three principles which make the design and implementation of programs more difficult: (1) The Government as employer of last resort must be the last resort for the Government as well as the individual; (2) every possible bridge into regular competitive employment must be supplied and its crossing encouraged; and (3) if the guaranteed employment is identified and stigmatized it will have failed its purpose. Since the goal is income with dignity, the criteria should not be family income but employability and the need for a productive role. Willingness to expend funds is only the first step to guaranteeing employment opportunities. More ingenuity and imagination are needed than that required for the relatively simple task of providing a competitive job in the private economy.

Economic Growth as a Promising Cure

HARRY G. JOHNSON

An important factor is mental or physical incapacity of the individual to render productive services of sufficient value to raise him or his household above the poverty line. This factor in poverty is interrelated with the level of unemployment, in the sense that the scarcer is labour in general, the more economic incentive there is to devise square holes in the economic system to accommodate the square pegs available. The alleviation of poverty attributable to this source requires the assistance of social workers, the maintenance of an adequate health service, and, probably most important, the provision of adequate social assistance transfers.

A number of other causal factors in poverty can be grouped under the general heading of discrimination, which denies particular groups the opportunity either to acquire or to use the capacity to make valuable productive contributions. From the economic point of view, discrimination is equivalent to the imposition of a special tax on those discriminated against. The denial or restriction of educational opportunities to the children of the lower income groups, and the use of educational qualifications to restrict entry to particular occupations or careers, are probably the most obvious examples to a British audience: but there are other important forms of discrimination that promote poverty. Discrimination on grounds of colour is a far less important source of poverty in this country than in the United States, partly because coloured people are as a result of a deliberately discriminatory immigration policy a far smaller proportion of the population, but it is by no means a negligible influence. Discrimination by age and by sex are also important, though their presence and effects are disguised by moral and emotional rationalizations. Discrimination by age operates at both ends of the spectrum, severely restricting the ability of the young to take gainful employment, and forcing the old to retire from employment whether they so desire or not; if society believes that children should be in school and the elderly in the limbo of retirement, it has an obligation to provide family allowances and

FROM Harry G. Johnson, professor of economics, London School of Economics and Political Science and the University of Chicago, "The Economic Approach to Social Questions," Inaugural Lecture, London School of Economics and Political Science, October 12, 1967.

old-age pensions on a scale generous enough to allow them to dwell there in adequate comfort. Discrimination against the female sex runs through both the education system and the labour market, and is rationalized by the conventional assignment of females to the role of housekeeper for the family; an important consequence is a high incidence of poverty among unmarried, separated, divorced, or prematurely widowed mothers of families, whose capacity to render productive services is too low, as a result of systematic discrimination, to sustain the responsibilities of head of a household unexpectedly thrust on them: again, if society wishes to push women into housekeeping, it has a responsibility to shield that role against the risks of poverty. Finally, considerable discrimination of a poverty-promoting kind is exercised by trade unions, which in their efforts to improve their members' wages and working conditions restrict the demand for skilled labour and force non-members to resort to lower-paid employment elsewhere in the economy.

The economic analysis of poverty indicates—as is indeed implied by the fact that poverty, being defined simply as an insufficiency of income to meet expenses, has innumerable causes—that the social attack on the poverty problem should take a variety of forms. To the pure theorist of the classical tradition, the problem is of course incalculably simpler: if some people have more and others less money than they are deemed to need, take money away from the former and give it to the latter. Unfortunately, this simple prescription has left its mark on those of the other social sciences that pride themselves on the directness of their concern with the poverty issue, and assume that economics (or the economic system) has solved the problem of generating enough money income so that no one need be poor. But neither the economic system nor the political is so simple: economically, poverty has deep social roots; and the political system is constrained by the same social foundations to limit the degree of rectification of poverty by income transfers that it will tolerate. That being so, the most promising—though also the most difficult—cures for poverty lie in the direction of providing increased opportunity to earn adequate incomes, rather than in the direction of recapturing and redistributing incomes after they have been earned. The cures are difficult both because they involve sacrificing many of our conventional notions of what is good and what is bad for social equality, and because they require serious thought about social causation; but they are promising because they seek to remedy poverty not by transferring income between individuals in society, but by making such transfers no longer necessary, except in cases where the justice of transfers is clearly evident to all as a matter of social conscience.

Education and Vocation

BEN B. SELIGMAN

Despite efforts to the contrary, especially in recent years, children from families trapped in poverty have had little chance of reaping the harvest promised by education. Such children do badly in school because they are prepared by the school for a poor performance. The school, it is said, cannot counteract the harmful physical and emotional influences of the urban slum. Although many a ghetto child comes to school with as much motivation as the middle-class child, within two or three years he discovers that he is expected by the teacher to do poorly, and poorly he does. He becomes "alienated" and "withdrawn," a slow reader, uninterested in the school environment, a "problem," a "delinquent." The sociologist says the slum child lacks a sufficient variety of experiences because he is insufficiently stimulated, that his language skills are inadequate because there is little "verbalizing" in a poor home, and that he has a poor memory because external pressures teach him to be inattentive. All too often such characterizations merely reflect the anticipations of the sociologist and tell us nothing about the child from the ghetto. When teachers speak of their charges as "them," they confess to an expectation of failure, and with such an expectation the children do fail. They come to believe that collusion exists among the teachers to generate failure, and the conflict between teacher and slum child becomes intense. For the fact is that the schools freeze the poor kid into a lower-class style of life. That the children are poor is all too often an excuse for not educating them at all. Why else the "highfalutin' " terminology of "psychological unreadiness" and "cultural deprivation"? Given a chance to be direct and honest about their feelings, slum children can give vivid descriptions of their schools, teachers, blocks, and families.

FROM Ben B. Seligman, professor of labor economics, University of Massachusetts, *Permanent Poverty: An American Syndrome* (Chicago: Quadrangle Books, 1968), pp. 84–89.

They search for words that can become live symbols of their experience. The sociologist is apt to know little about poor youth because he has confused boredom with stupidity. . . .

More likely, slum children and slum youth show no achievement because of the general oppressiveness of school, street, and home. Each part of the environment corrupts others. The sum is a profound disaffection that no amount of "socialization" can remedy. As Paul Goodman remarks, there are no objects in the larger environment to which a youth can react in ways meaningful to him. Moreover, the affluent society has provided no goals, so that poor youth begin to wonder whether anyone seriously wants to make a place for them. It is not surprising that they spend their time doing nothing. Teachers come from the colleges with a sense of idealism, with a hope of dedication, and soon discover they must spend most of their time disciplining the rowdy. The street and the school support each other to create attitudes that keep youth in slums and eventually in poverty. The inequality that develops acquires a tinge of caste as well as class. . . .

Vocational education, unfortunately, does not yet provide an effective channel for the move out of poverty. In many school systems vocational students are looked upon as inferior. There doesn't seem to be much worthwhile in being a plumber or a carpenter, and with attention focused almost entirely on academic work, the vocational student feels completely left out. The fact is that the entire educational system is out of balance, for it is geared to the 20 or 30 per cent of those who go on to college. Most are pushed out of school: 35 per cent of students are lost in high school, and 45 per cent of high school students are lost in the sense that they wind up in dead-end jobs. Despite federal government efforts dating back to 1917 in providing funds to the states for vocational education, only a fraction of full-time high school students are pursuing vocational careers. In 1963 more than 60 per cent of that fraction was enrolled in home economics and agriculture courses; the rest were in distributive education and nursing courses.

Nevertheless, vocational enrollments seem to be rising, from 3.7 million in 1959 to 5.3 million in 1965. The expenditures are also increasing—they are now running at some $600 million a year—but this has been due mainly to the flow of funds from Washington under the Vocational Education Act of 1963. In some schools new courses have been introduced and an effort has been made to fit the curriculum to the requirements of both student and industry. Perhaps vocational training can help to reduce dropout problems, at least in the sense that it promises future financial gains to those who stick it out.

. . . It was not surprising that the government's War on Poverty should make such an intensive effort to deal with educational handicaps. Education was indeed woven into most of the eleven poverty programs and sub-programs financed by the OEO and the five others operated by other departments with OEO money. Project Head Start was directed to some 560,000 poor children of pre-school age at 13,400 centers in 2,500 communities. The objective was to reach these children as early as possible before they were absorbed by a traditional school system for which they were ill prepared. These were children who had never seen a book, who could not identify colors or distinguish between long and short. Unfortunately, the critical follow-up into the school years often failed to materialize—there was a palpable lack of funds, facilities, staff, and imagination. The teen-age equivalent of Head Start, Project Upward Bound, put two thousand poor bright youths who had failed to respond to the usual high school routine onto college campuses. Some "caught fire" and were able to pass college entrance examinations which they had failed earlier.

Is Head Start a Slow Start?

SAR A. LEVITAN

The Head Start program has sustained its original popularity, managing to avoid the disenchantment that has beset other poverty projects. But popularity does not necessarily connote program effectiveness; and despite congressional and public support, many basic questions regarding Head Start's value, scope, and direction remain unanswered. For example, should the limited resources be concentrated upon summer programs preparing poor children for school entry, maximizing the number of participants? Or should the funds be devoted to year-round facilities? Would cost effectiveness be maximized by restricting participation to even fewer children and providing them

FROM Sar A. Levitan, Center for Manpower Policy Studies, George Washington University, "Head Start: It Is Never Too Early to Fight Poverty," *Federal Programs for the Development of Human Resources* (Washington, D.C.: Joint Economic Committee, Subcommittee on Economic Progress, 1968), pp. 425–28.

preschool facilities beginning with age 3 or even lower? And, assuming a determination to concentrate resources on a limited number of children, should the resources be restricted to preschool facilities or should they be devoted to enriching the primary grade education of poor children? . . .

During its early phases Head Start was able to capitalize on research that indicated significant educational advancements. Dr. Leon Eisenberg of Johns Hopkins University found improvements of eight to ten points in the IQ's of 480 children who took part in Baltimore's 1965 Head Start project. These findings were supported by additional studies during the following year. Followup studies of the 1965 summer program participants indicated, however, that benefits of the Head Start program soon faded. A widely publicized study by Max Wolff and Annie Stein of Yeshiva University among kindergartens in four public New York City elementary schools showed that, 6 months after the Head Start program ended, participants scored no higher on achievement tests than nonparticipants from similar socioeconomic backgrounds. A later study by the Office of Education also indicated that several months after completion of the 1965 summer program, discernible gains could be detected only among those participants from the most disadvantaged backgrounds—especially among the rural Negroes of the South. For most Head Start children achievement level gains were not appreciably different than those of non-Head Start children. These studies do not indicate that Head Start in any way harms the children, but only that their classmates from similar backgrounds soon catch up to the Head Start children.

Most studies of the effect of Head Start have focused on the cognitive achievements of participants. Because Head Start aspires to broader goals, however, consideration must also be given to other factors in appraising the total impact of the program. Most significant, perhaps, is the fact that Head Start children are frequently observed to be more motivated and responsive than their non-Head Start peers. More than 90 percent of a sample of Head Start parents and workers testified that the children gained self-confidence and developed new interests, according to the Census Bureau survey. The Wolff and Stein study, as well as the Office of Education survey, also indicated that Head Start participants showed much more noticeable gains in educational motivation than in achievement levels several months after the 1965 summer program.

The rapid "fadeout" effect in achievement levels, together with the realization that a short summer course is often inadequate to meet the comprehensive needs of the preschool children, have provided the major impetus for the creation of full-year Head Start programs. These projects, with a median length of 9 months, are expected to have greater impact on the achievement levels of disadvantaged children. The study conducted by the Office of Education showed that first-grade children from almost all socioeconomic backgrounds who attended kindergarten had significantly higher achievement levels than comparable first graders who had not attended kindergarten. The Head Start program, which is generally conceded to be of higher quality than kindergarten, might be anticipated to produce even better results. But the benefits of the longer Head Start program may not be sustained unless the primary school programs the children enter are similarly enriched.

In terms of their impact on the children, then, full-year Head Start projects would seem preferable to the shorter summer programs. Though a summer's exposure is beneficial in some respects, it is not long enough to leave an indelible effect and its benefits (at least in terms of achievement levels) soon fade. . . . Why has OEO not been quicker to shift its resources to the full-year concept? The answer is as much political as programmatic. Because they are much more expensive, full-year programs cannot serve nearly as many children as the summer programs—given current levels of spending. The administration has shown a distinct penchant for the "numbers racket," and the huge numbers of children who have passed through summer Head Start projects unquestionably provide impressive publicity. In this case, however, it has probably amounted to a sacrifice of quality for quantity—a result no doubt regretted by Head Start officials themselves. Aside from these political considerations, it is also more difficult to mount full-year projects than summer programs, when school facilities are unutilized and regular teachers are available. . . .

A significant innovation—first initiated on a large scale by Head Start and now being adopted by educational systems throughout the country—is the use of subprofessional aids to provide individual attention to students, to relieve teachers of routine tasks and to provide employment to the poor. In fiscal year 1966, title I money was used to employ 73,000 teachers' aids and 44,000 other subprofessionals, equaling more than one-quarter of all new staff positions created by title I funds. It should be noted, however, that the maximum potential of many subprofessionals has not been utilized; they are often assigned routine duties—as lunchroom monitors or keepers of simple records. Rarely have they been allowed to contribute to the educational process as Head Start planners would prefer.

Head Start's broad approach to services for children is another concept which has been widely and profitably copied. The Council on the Education of Disadvantaged Children reports that provision of breakfasts and lunches, basic medical care and eyeglasses, shoes and overcoats—the most elemental bodily requisites for learning—is one of the most rapidly spreading practices under title I. Only a few years ago one major southern city refused to provide free lunches to poor children on the ground that food had no relation to the child's education. Today, that southern city provides free lunches.

There is also increasing concern among local educational authorities for improving teachers' attitudes toward poor children and increasing the flexibility of the curriculum. Although these changes cannot be attributed entirely to Head Start, appropriate credit must be given to its emphasis on innovative techniques dealing with each child as a developing individual. . . .

Head Start programs have increased demands for State support of public kindergartens. Virginia has established free public kindergartens, using Head Start money to finance the costs allocated to special services for poor children. Several States are now considering legislation for statewide kindergartens. . . .

The Head Start preschool program has also stimulated inquiry and research into the educational needs of 2- and 3-year-olds. A project sponsored by the National Institutes of Health found that after a year of tutoring for an hour a day, the average IQ of a group of 30 slum children was substantially raised while the average IQ of a control group of untutored poor children actually dropped. . . .

Riots: Causes and Future Choices

KERNER COMMISSION

The record before this Commission reveals that the causes of recent racial disorders are imbedded in a massive tangle of issues and circumstances—social, economic, political, and psychological—which

FROM Kerner Commission, *Report of the National Advisory Commission on Civil Disorders* (Washington, D.C.: U.S. Government Printing Office, 1968), pp. 91–93, 218–19.

arise out of the historical pattern of Negro-white relations in America. . . .

Despite these complexities, certain fundamental matters are clear. Of these, the most fundamental is the racial attitude and behavior of white Americans toward black Americans. Race prejudice has shaped our history decisively in the past; it now threatens to do so again. White racism is essentially responsible for the explosive mixture which has been accumulating in our cities since the end of World War II. At the base of this mixture are three of the most bitter fruits of white attitudes:

Pervasive Discrimination and Segregation. The first is surely the continuing exclusion of great numbers of Negroes from the benefits of economic progress through discrimination in employment and education and their enforced confinement in segregated housing and schools. The corrosive and degrading effects of this condition and the attitudes that underlie it are the source of the deepest bitterness and lie at the center of the problem of racial disorder.

Black Migration and White Exodus. The second is the massive and growing concentration of impoverished Negroes in our major cities resulting from Negro migration from the rural South, rapid population growth, and the continuing movement of the white middle class to the suburbs. The consequence is a greatly increased burden on the already depleted resources of cities, creating a growing crisis of deteriorating facilities and services and unmet human needs.

Black Ghettos. Third, in the teeming racial ghettos, segregation and poverty have intersected to destroy opportunity and hope and to enforce failure. The ghettos too often mean men and women without jobs, families without men, and schools where children are processed instead of educated, until they return to the street—to crime, to narcotics, to dependency on welfare, and to bitterness and resentment against society in general and white society in particular.

These three forces have converged on the inner city in recent years and on the people who inhabit it. At the same time, most whites and many Negroes outside the ghetto have prospered to a degree unparalleled in the history of civilization. Through television—the universal appliance in the ghetto—and the other media of mass communications, this affluence has been endlessly flaunted before the eyes of the Negro poor and the jobless ghetto youth.

As Americans, most Negro citizens carry within themselves two basic aspirations of our society. They seek to share in both the material resources of our system and its intangible benefits—dignity, respect, and acceptance. Outside the ghetto, many have succeeded in achieving a decent standard of life and in developing the inner resources which give life meaning and direction. Within the ghetto, however, it is rare that either aspiration is achieved.

Yet these facts alone—fundamental as they are—cannot be said to have caused the disorders. Other and more immediate factors help explain why these events happened now.

Recently, three powerful ingredients have begun to catalyze the mixture.

Frustrated Hopes.   The expectations aroused by the great judicial and legislative victories of the civil rights movement have led to frustration, hostility, and cynicism in the face of the persistent gap between promise and fulfillment. The dramatic struggle for equal rights in the South has sensitized northern Negroes to the economic inequalities reflected in the deprivations of ghetto life.

Legitimation of Violence.   A climate that tends toward the approval and encouragement of violence as a form of protest has been created by white terrorism directed against nonviolent protest, including instances of abuse and even murder of some civil rights workers in the South, by the open defiance of law and Federal authority by state and local officials resisting desegregation, and by some protest groups engaging in civil disobedience who turn their backs on nonviolence, go beyond the constitutionally protected rights of petition and free assembly and resort to violence to attempt to compel alteration of laws and policies with which they disagree. This condition has been reinforced by a general erosion of respect for authority in American society and the reduced effectiveness of social standards and community restraints on violence and crime. This in turn has largely resulted from rapid urbanization and the dramatic reduction in the average age of the total population.

Powerlessness.   Finally, many Negroes have come to believe that they are being exploited politically and economically by the white "power structure." Negroes, like people in poverty everywhere, in fact lack the channels of communication, influence, and appeal that traditionally have been available to ethnic minorities within the city and which enabled them—unburdened by color—to scale the walls of the white ghettos in an earlier era. The frustrations of powerlessness have led some to the conviction that there is no effective alternative to violence as a means of expression and redress, as a way of "moving the system." More generally, the result is alienation and hostility toward the institutions of law and government and the white society which controls them. This is reflected in the reach toward racial consciousness and solidarity reflected in the slogan "Black Power."

These facts have combined to inspire a new mood among Negroes, particularly among the young. Self-esteem and enhanced racial pride are replacing apathy and submission to "the system." Moreover, Negro youth, who make up over half of the ghetto population, share the growing sense of alienation felt by many white youth in our country. Thus, their role in recent civil disorders reflects not only a shared sense of deprivation and victimization by white society but also the rising incidence of disruptive conduct by a segment of American youth throughout the society.

Incitement and Encouragement of Violence. These conditions have created a volatile mixture of attitudes and beliefs which needs only a spark to ignite mass violence. Strident appeals to violence, first heard from white racists, were echoed and reinforced last summer in the inflammatory rhetoric of black racists and militants. Throughout the year, extremists crisscrossed the country preaching a doctrine of violence. Their rhetoric was widely reported in the mass media; it was echoed by local "militants" and organizations; it became the ugly background noise of the violent summer.

We cannot measure with any precision the influence of these organizations and individuals in the ghetto, but we think it clear that the intolerable and unconscionable encouragement of violence heightened tensions, created a mood of acceptance and an expectation of violence and thus contributed to the eruption of the disorders last summer.

The Police. It is the convergence of all these factors that makes the role of the police so difficult and so significant. Almost invariably the incident that ignites disorder arises from police action. Harlem, Watts, Newark, and Detroit—all the major outbursts of recent years were precipitated by arrests of Negroes by white police for minor offenses.

But the police are not merely the spark. In discharge of their obligation to maintain order and insure public safety in the disruptive conditions of ghetto life, they are inevitably involved in sharper and more frequent conflicts with ghetto residents than with the residents of other areas. Thus, to many Negroes, police have come to symbolize white power, white racism, and white repression. And the fact is that many police do reflect and express these white attitudes. The atmosphere of hostility and cynicism is reinforced by a widespread perception among Negroes of the existence of police brutality and corruption and of a "double standard" of justice and protection—one for Negroes and one for whites. . . .

The complexity of American society offers many choices for the future of relations between central cities and suburbs and patterns of

Social Welfare Expenditures, 1929–1967

(In millions; revised estimates as of October 1967)

Program	1928–29	1934–35	1939–40	1944–45	1949–50	1954–55	1959–60	1964–65	1965–66	1966–67
					Total expenditures					
Total	$3,921.2	$6,548.3	$8,795.1	$9,205.3	$23,508.4	$32,639.9	$52,293.3	$77,261.5	$87,973.3	$100,238.5
Social insurance	342.4	406.3	1,271.8	1,409.4	4,946.6	9,834.9	19,306.7	28,090.0	31,905.0	37,377.1
Old-age, survivors, disability, and health insurance			40.4	266.8	784.1	4,436.3	11,032.3	16,997.5	20,295.3	24,579.3
Health insurance for the aged									63.6	3,393.1
Railroad retirement			116.8	145.0	306.4	556.0	934.7	1,128.1	1,211.6	1,272.3
Public employee retirement	113.1	208.8	283.4	355.0	817.9	1,388.5	2,569.9	4,520.5	5,145.4	6,021.0
Unemployment insurance		9.2	553.0	216.7	2,190.1	2,080.6	2,829.6	3,002.6	2,662.3	2,752.1
Railroad unemployment insurance			18.9	4.3	119.6	158.7	215.2	76.7	52.4	38.7
Railroad temporary disability insurance					31.1	54.2	68.5	46.5	42.6	38.7
State temporary disability insurance				5.1	72.1	217.5	347.9	483.3	507.3	520.0
Hospital and medical benefits					2.2	20.0	40.2	50.9	54.3	56.0
Workmen's compensation	229.3	188.4	259.2	416.6	625.1	943.0	1,308.5	1,834.8	1,988.2	2,155.0
Hospital and medical benefits	75.0	65.0	90.0	122.0	193.0	315.0	420.0	580.0	630.0	685.0
Public aid	60.0	2,997.6	3,597.0	1,030.6	2,496.2	3,003.0	4,101.1	6,283.4	7,301.4	8,901.6
Public assistance	59.9	623.9	1,124.3	1,028.8	2,490.2	2,941.1	4,041.7	5,874.9	6,497.5	7,780.4
Vendor medical payments					51.3	211.9	492.7	1,367.1	1,709.9	2,318.3
Other	.1	2,373.7	2,472.7	1.7	6.0	61.9	59.4	408.5	803.9	1,121.2
Health and medical programs	351.1	427.2	615.5	2,354.2	2,063.5	3,103.1	4,463.8	6,418.5	7,161.0	8,113.3
Hospital and medical care	146.3	253.1	343.0	1,995.9	1,222.3	2,042.4	2,853.3	3,629.9	4,069.9	4,513.4
Civilian programs	117.1	225.3	297.6	364.8	886.1	1,297.6	1,973.2	2,514.8	2,720.3	2,790.8
Defense Department	29.2	27.7	45.4	1,631.1	336.2	744.8	880.1	1,115.1	1,349.5	1,722.6
Maternal and child health programs	6.2	6.9	13.8	62.1	29.8	92.9	141.3	227.5	281.5	312.8
Medical research						.2	.6	4.3	5.3	6.0
Medical research		.3	2.6	2.5	69.2	132.8	448.9	1,165.6	1,305.9	1,456.5
School health (educational agencies)	9.4	10.0	16.4	23.3	30.6	65.9	101.0	132.0	135.0	140.0

Program										
Other public health activities	88.8	112.2	154.5	178.0	350.8	383.7	401.2	671.5	723.8	900.9
Medical-facilities construction	100.4	44.8	85.2	92.4	360.8	385.4	518.1	592.0	645.0	789.6
Defense Department				38.9	1.1	33.0	40.0	34.8	28.6	58.5
Other	100.4	44.8	85.2	53.5	359.8	352.4	478.1	557.2	616.4	731.2
Veterans programs	657.9	597.5	629.0	1,125.8	6,865.7	4,833.5	5,479.2	6,038.8	6,360.3	7,011.7
Pensions and compensation	434.7	386.5	443.3	766.6	2,092.1	2,689.7	3,402.7	4,156.0	4,423.8	4,554.8
Health and medical programs	50.9	50.8	75.8	101.8	748.0	761.1	954.0	1,239.0	1,301.9	1,369.2
Hospital and medical care	46.7	47.8	61.5	85.5	582.8	721.5	879.4	1,120.9	1,175.2	1,271.3
Hospital construction	4.2	3.0	14.3	16.3	161.5	34.1	59.6	81.2	86.0	51.0
Medical and prosthetic research					3.7	5.6	15.1	36.9	40.7	46.9
Education				9.8	2,691.6	706.1	409.6	43.4	36.9	378.3
Life insurance	136.4	122.8	77.0	201.2	475.7	490.2	494.1	446.9	455.4	557.5
Welfare and other	35.8	37.5	32.9	46.4	858.3	186.5	218.8	153.6	142.3	151.5
Education	2,433.7	2,007.5	2,561.2	3,076.3	6,674.1	11,157.2	17,626.2	28,050.2	32,566.9	35,632.7
Elementary and secondary	2,216.2	1,820.1	2,267.4	2,620.6	5,596.2	9,734.3	15,109.0	22,353.9	25,054.9	27,427.1
Construction	377.0	123.3	258.0	82.5	1,019.4	2,231.9	2,661.8	3,267.0	3,449.9	3,600.6
Higher	182.1	147.9	217.6	314.4	914.7	1,214.4	2,190.7	4,784.6	6,319.6	6,943.4
Construction	.2		20.6	42.3	310.3	198.6	357.9	1,229.0	1,814.3	1,813.0
Vocational and adult	34.9	39.1	75.4	139.2	160.8	204.9	298.0	852.4	1,067.1	1,121.7
Housing	13.2	13.2	4.2	11.1	14.6	89.3	176.8	318.1	334.8	374.6
Public housing	13.2	13.2	4.2	11.1	14.5	74.7	143.5	234.5	249.2	277.7
Other					.1	14.6	33.2	83.6	85.6	96.8
Other social welfare	76.2	99.0	116.4	197.9	447.7	619.0	1,139.4	2,062.4	2,343.8	2,827.5
Vocational rehabilitation	1.6	2.3	4.2	10.2	30.0	42.4	96.3	210.5	298.6	411.3
Medical services	.1	.2	.3	1.4	7.4	9.1	17.7	34.2	48.0	80.5
Medical research						.3	6.6	22.4	27.9	31.0
Institutional care	74.7	70.7	62.4	82.9	145.5	195.3	420.5	784.4	766.7	840.1
School meals			4.0	47.4	160.2	239.6	398.7	617.4	537.4	582.6
Child welfare		26.0	45.0	55.5	104.9	135.1	211.5	356.1	399.5	445.8
Special OEO programs								51.7	287.3	464.5
Social welfare, not elsewhere classified			.9	2.0	7.1	6.5	12.4	42.3	54.2	83.1

FROM Ida C. Merriam, "Social Welfare Expenditures, 1929–1967," *Social Security Bulletin* (December 1967), p. 5.

white and Negro settlement in metropolitan areas. For practical purposes, however, we see two fundamental questions:

Should future Negro population growth be concentrated in central cities, as in the past 20 years, thereby forcing Negro and white populations to become even more residentially segregated?

Should society provide greatly increased special assistance to Negroes and other relatively disadvantaged population groups?

For purposes of analysis, the Commission has defined three basic choices for the future embodying specific answers to these questions:

THE PRESENT POLICIES CHOICE

Under this course, the Nation would maintain approximately the share of resources now being allocated to programs of assistance for the poor, unemployed and disadvantaged. These programs are likely to grow, given continuing economic growth and rising Federal revenues, but they will not grow fast enough to stop, let alone reverse, the already deteriorating quality of life in central-city ghettos.

This choice carries the highest ultimate price, as we will point out.

THE ENRICHMENT CHOICE

Under this course, the Nation would seek to offset the effects of continued Negro segregation and deprivation in large city ghettos. The enrichment choice would aim at creating dramatic improvements in the quality of life in disadvantaged central-city neighborhoods—both white and Negro. It would require marked increases in Federal spending for education, housing, employment, job training, and social services.

The enrichment choice would seek to lift poor Negroes and whites above poverty status and thereby give them the capacity to enter the mainstream of American life. But it would not, at least for many years, appreciably affect either the increasing concentration of Negroes in the ghetto or racial segregation in residential areas outside the ghetto.

THE INTEGRATION CHOICE

This choice would be aimed at reversing the movement of the country toward societies, separate and unequal.

The integration choice—like the enrichment choice—would call for large-scale improvement in the quality of ghetto life. But it would also involve both creating strong incentives for Negro movement out of central-city ghettos and enlarging freedom of choice concerning housing, employment, and schools.

The result would fall considerably short of full integration. The experience of other ethnic groups indicates that some Negro households would be scattered in largely white residential areas. Others—probably a larger number—would voluntarily cluster together in largely Negro neighborhoods. The integration choice would thus produce both integration and segregation. But the segregation would be voluntary.

Articulating these three choices plainly oversimplifies the possibilities open to the country. We believe, however, that they encompass the basic issues—issues which the American public must face if it is serious in its concern not only about civil disorder, but the future of our democratic society.

Income Guarantee Alternatives

CHRISTOPHER GREEN

Recently, interest has developed in new programs which may have an important impact on the income of poor families in the short as well as the long run. These programs include those that would guarantee a minimum income and supplement the low earnings, property, and transfer income of our low-income population. The logic of guaranteed minimum income programs stems in part from an evaluation of the poverty problems in America. The logic also stems from an examination of our present income transfer programs. At present we are transferring over $40 billion of income through one or another of our public income maintenance programs. These programs include Old-Age, Survivors, Disability, and Health Insurance (OASDHI), certainly the most important of our income maintenance programs; unemployment compensation, the public assistance programs, and

FROM Christopher Green, professor of economics, North Carolina State University, "Improving Income Maintenance Through Negative Taxation," *Federal Programs for the Development of Human Resources* (Washington, D.C.: Joint Economic Committee, Subcommittee on Economic Progress, 1968), pp. 398–403.

veterans' pensions and compensation. Interestingly, it is estimated that only about one-half of these transfer payments go to persons who are poor before having received transfers and a little less than a quarter of total transfers is received by persons who are defined as poor after receiving transfer payments, i.e., on a total money income basis. While few persons would suggest that our income maintenance programs should help only poor people, the statistics perhaps suggest that not enough is now being done for the persons who really need aid.

One of the problems with our income-maintenance system is that none of the programs makes need a sufficient condition for receiving public transfer income. The OASDHI and unemployment compensation programs protect against income loss due to age or involuntary unemployment. Thus they provide varying measures of income security to only some of our poor population while many of the beneficiaries of these programs are in no sense poor. The "welfare" or public assistance programs make need a necessary condition for receipt of public aid, but they do not make need a sufficient condition for receiving assistance payments. Only certain categories of the poor have any claim to public assistance. Assistance is usually available to families or individuals who fall into certain categories, such as the blind, the permanently and totally disabled, dependent children in families lacking a breadwinner, and the indigent aged. However, the statistics on poverty indicate that the poor, who now number nearly 30 million, are a much more diverse group than the public assistance categories and the 8 million recipients of public assistance (including general assistance) would suggest. In fact, the "able-bodied" poor and their dependents make up a substantial portion of the poor population and yet our federally assisted public assistance programs simply bypass this particular group.

Further examination of our present income-maintenance programs suggests that they alone cannot achieve the objectives of effectively improving income maintenance for all of the poor. The reasons for this can be fairly simply stated. The OASDHI program is for the aged but four-fifths of the poor are not aged. The unemployment compensation program is for the insured unemployed and yet many of the poor are living in families with a head who works full year full time. For example, it is estimated that in 1965, 2.4 million poor families were headed by a person who worked full year full time. Another 350,000 heads of poor families worked full year at part-time jobs and they too would not be eligible for unemployment compensation. Moreover, unemployment compensation programs cannot easily be made to meet the needs of many persons with very spotty employment records. The veterans' programs are for veterans with particular disabilities.

The public assistance programs presently aid only certain categories of the poor. While they could be modified to cover all of the poor, two factors suggest that this route would not be a recommended one. One factor is that under the present public assistance program benefits are usually reduced dollar for dollar of any increase in the other income of the recipient. Therefore, earners of income would be "taxed" at a 100 percent rate on their increased earnings. This means that as long as an individual's or family's earnings are below the maximum level of public assistance for which it is eligible there is no monetary gain from earning. Thus, making public assistance available to all of the poor could severely undermine the incentives to work of the poor population, reduce their already meager earnings, and considerably raise the cost of any program aimed at raising the income of poor families. A further objection to the use of public assistance to meet the needs of the able-bodied poor is that the present public assistance programs are already unpopular with the taxpayer and the recipient alike. Therefore, receipt of public assistance by the able-bodied poor may continue to carry with it the stigmas that are attached to the present relief recipient.

In recent years interest has grown in developing new systems of income transfers. One of these systems is called negative income taxation. Negative income taxation is related to the idea of a guaranteed minimum income which has roots that go back at least several decades. The suggestion for a negative income tax can be traced to plans devised during World War II by the Englishwoman Lady Juliet Rhys-Williams. Another system is family allowances which already exist, in practice, in almost every other Western industrialized nation. Family allowances are payments to families with children for the benefit of the children and they are usually paid irrespective of family income. Perhaps the chief difference between negative income taxation and family allowances is that payments under the former are conditioned on family income while those under the latter represent a demogrant to all children irrespective of family income. From the standpoint of public policy toward low-income people this difference is a very important one.

Negative income tax proposals would use the income tax system to transfer income to low-income families. One version of negative income taxation would use the value of exemptions and deductions in the income tax system as a criterion for determining eligibility to receive negative income tax payments. Families with income amounting to less than the value of exemptions (EX) and minimum standard deductions (MSD) allowed them under the present tax system (i.e., families with "unused EX & MSD") would be eligible to receive negative income tax payments equal to some percentage of the shortfall. The percentage would be considerably less than 100 percent in order to preserve incentives to work. To take an example, assume the percentage (i.e., the "negative tax rate") is 50 percent. Under present income tax law a four-person family is allowed $2,400 in personal exemptions plus $600 in minimum standard deductions, or a total of $3,000 in nontaxable income. If the family's income is $1,000 in a given year it would have $2,000 in unused EX & MSD against which is applied the 50-percent negative tax rate. The family would receive a $1,000 payment from the Government.

Another version of negative income taxation is illustrated in table 1. This version specifies a basic allowance, say, $400 for each member of the family and a tax rate(s) applied to total income which indicates what portion of the basic allowance actually comprises a net addition to family disposable income. For example, a five-person family has a total of $2,000 in basic allowances. If the family's income (not including the allowance) is $2,400 and the tax rate is 33⅓ percent, then the family's disposable income is increased by $1,200 ($2,000—.33⅓ ($2,400) = $1,200). This plan, proposed by James Tobin, would "tie in" to the present income tax schedule if taxpayers are allowed to choose either the basic allowance plus the 33⅓-percent schedule *or* the present personal exemptions and standard deductions plus the present tax schedule. . . .

It is useful to ask what are the basic similarities and differences between the two types of negative income tax plans described. In their essentials the proposals are similar. Each has three basic variables. These three variables are: (1) A basic income guarantee—that is, the basic allowance or the level of negative tax payments a family may receive when it has no other income; (2) a tax rate or set of tax rates which reduces the basic guarantee to zero at some level of income; (3) a break-even level of income—that is, the level of income where negative income tax payments are reduced to zero. For example, in the case of the EX & MSD version, the break-even level of income is the value of the tax unit's exemptions and deductions.

Any two of these three basic variables determines the third. For example, in the EX & MSD plan the two variables that are chosen are the break-even level of income and the tax rate or rates. These determine that the guaranteed minimum income for a family of four is $1,500 if the negative tax rate is 50 percent [3000–0)·50]. In the other version of negative income taxation the two variables chosen are the level of basic allowances and the tax rate(s). These two combined determine, as table 1 shows, that the break-even level of income is $4,800 for a family of four.

The fact that these two plans are basically similar suggests that any plan to guarantee a minimum income will be similar to the negative income tax plans described here. That is, any plan to guarantee a minimum income will have three variables: a guarantee, a rate at which that guarantee is reduced as family income rises, and ultimately a break-even level of income at which persons no longer receive *net* benefits under the plan.

The discussion of the three basic variables also suggests something about adoption of family allowances. In most countries, family allowances are paid to all children no matter what the income or wealth of their parents. Many families receive children's allowances even though there is very little need for them. This means that it is necessary to raise income taxes or other taxes in order to pay for what will ultimately be a very costly plan. To some American social planners family allowances seem to make sense, especially when one realizes

TABLE 1

A Negative Income Tax Plan of Tobin Type[1]

Family income before income supplement	Size of family					
	1	2	3	4	5	6
	Income supplement family is entitled to					
0	$400	$800	$1,200	$1,600	$2,000	$2,400
$600	200	600	1,000	1,400	1,800	2,200
$1,200	0	400	800	1,200	1,600	2,000
$1,800		200	600	1,000	1,400	1,800
$2,400		0	400	800	1,200	1,600
$3,000			200	600	1,000	1,400
Breakeven income[2]	1,200	2,400	3,600	4,800	6,000	7,200
Tax breakeven income[3]	1,422	3,000	4,636	6,306	8,050	9,928

[1] Income guarantee or basic allowance of $400 per person and a tax rate of 33⅓ percent.

[2] Level of income at which net allowances are reduced to zero by the 33⅓-percent tax rate.

[3] Level of income at which the tax liability under the Tobin 33⅓-percent schedule equals the tax liability under the present individual income tax schedule.

how unpopular the present aid to dependent children program is. But in a very real sense, family allowances would be an inefficient way of helping the poor, although they may be justified on other grounds such as protecting the security of children. An example of the inefficiency of family allowances is indicated by a proposal to pay monthly allowances of $8 to each child under 6 and $12 to each child between 6 and 17 years of age. Since less than a quarter of all children live in poor families only about $2 to $2½ billion of the $9 billion estimated cost of the proposal would be received by poor families, although perhaps an additional $½ billion to $1 billion would be received by near-poor families. The majority of the payments would be received by families who are reasonably well off.

In a system of family allowances only one basic variable is operative: the level of family allowances. There is no explicit tax rate which reduces the family allowances as family income rises and thus there is no break-even level of income. (There is, however, a tax on income or payrolls which raises revenues to pay for the plan.) Thus the essential difference between family allowances and negative income taxes, aside from the fact that the former applies only to families with children, is that negative income taxation makes *need* a condition for eligibility to receive income transfers. To repeat an earlier point: negative income taxation is an income-condition plan and family allowances are demogrants.

The two negative income tax plans described above differ in an important respect. Aside from differences in cost, the basic difference between these plans lies in the extent to which the income tax system that exists today would need to be reformed in order to accommodate the proposals described above. In the case of the unused EX & MSD plan, only minor reforms are needed. Reforms could be largely if not wholly confined to the negative side of the system. For example, it is important to broaden the definition of income for negative income tax purposes to include all income, not simply that income which is defined as taxable under the present income tax system. An important source of income that should be included is public transfer income which is presently nontaxable. One exception might be the continued exclusion of public assistance payments on the grounds that public assistance is payable only after calculating all family resources including the level of negative income tax payments for which the family is eligible. It is also important to redefine the tax unit to more closely approximate a family or consumer unit. Individuals with no income may not be poor if they are living in a family with a productive breadwinner.

In contrast, the basic allowance plan would necessitate undertaking more general tax reform. This is so, because a much larger portion of the population would be affected by the plan. By effectively substituting a refundable $400 per capita tax credit in place of the present $600 per capita personal exemptions for taxpayers using the 33⅓-percent tax schedule, the Tobin basic allowance plan would alter the present positive tax system and make net allowance recipients of some present taxpayers. Moreover, the cost of the plan, which is estimated at $14 billion on the basis of 1962 data bluntly raises the question of financing negative income taxation. The estimated (1964) cost of the EX & MSD plan is approximately $6 billion—about equal to the annual increase in Federal income tax revenues produced by economic growth. . . .

Welfare Alternatives

RICHARD M. NIXON

Nowhere has the failure of government been more tragically apparent than in its efforts to help the poor, and especially in its system of public welfare. . . .

My purpose tonight, however, is not to review the past record, but to present a new set of reforms—a new set of proposals—a new and drastically different approach to the way in which government cares for those in need, and to the way the responsibilities are shared between the state and Federal Governments.

I have chosen to do so in a direct report to the people because these proposals call for public decisions of the first importance; because they represent a fundamental change in the nation's approach to one of its most pressing social problems; and because, quite deliberately, they also represent the first major reversal of the trend toward ever more centralization of government in Washington. . . .

This new approach is embodied in a package of four measures: first, a complete replacement of the present welfare system; second, a comprehensive new job training and placement program; third, a re-

FROM President Nixon's Address to the Nation on Welfare Reform (August 8, 1969).

vamping of the Office of Economic Opportunity; and fourth, a start on the sharing of the Federal tax revenues with the states. . . .

Whether measured by the anguish of the poor themselves, or by the drastically mounting burden on the taxpayer, the present welfare system has to be judged a colossal failure. . . .

Benefit levels are grossly unequal—for a mother with three children, they range from an average of $263 a month in one state, down to an average of $39 in another state. So great an inequality is wrong; no child is "worth" more in one state than in another. One result of this inequality is to lure thousands more into already overcrowded inner cities, as unprepared for city life as they are for city jobs.

The present system creates an incentive for desertion. In most states, a family is denied welfare payments if a father is present—even though he is unable to support his family. . . .

The present system often makes it possible to receive more money on welfare than on a low-paying job. This creates an incentive not to work; it also is unfair to the working poor. . . .

Any system which makes it more profitable for a man not to work than to work, and which encourages a man to desert his family rather than stay with his family, is wrong and indefensible. . . .

I propose that we abolish the present welfare system and adopt in its place a new family assistance system. Initially, this new system would cost more than welfare. But unlike welfare, it is designed to correct the condition it deals with and thus to lessen the long-range burden.

Under this plan, the so-called "adult categories" of aid—aid to the aged, the blind and disabled—would be set, with the Federal Government contributing to its cost and also sharing the cost of additional state payments above that amount.

But the program now called "Aid to Families with Dependent Children"—the program we normally think of when we think of "welfare"—would be done away with completely. The new family assistance system I propose in its place rests essentially on three principles: equality of treatment, a work requirement and a work incentive.

Its benefits would go to the working poor, as well as the nonworking; to families with dependent children headed by a father, as well as to those headed by a mother; and a basic Federal minimum would be provided, the same in every state.

I propose that the Federal Government build a foundation under the income of every American family with dependent children that cannot care for itself—wherever in America that family may live.

For a family of four now on welfare, with no outside income, the basic Federal payment would be $1,600 a year. States could add to that amount and most would do so. In no case would anyone's present level of benefits be lowered. At the same time, this foundation would be one on which the family itself could build. Outside earnings would be encouraged, not discouraged. The new worker could keep the first $60 a month of outside earnings with no reduction in his benefits, and beyond that the benefits would be reduced by only 50 cents for each dollar earned.

By the same token, a family head already employed at low wages could get a family assistance supplement: those who work would no longer be discriminated against. A family of five in which the father earns $2,000 a year—which is the hard fact of life for many families—would get family assistance payments of $1,260 for a total income of $3,260. A family of seven earning $3,000 a year would have its income raised to $4,360.

Thus, for the first time, the Government would recognize that it has no less of an obligation to the working poor than to the nonworking poor; and for the first time, benefits would be scaled in such a way that it would always pay to work.

With such incentives, most recipients who can work will want to work. This is part of the American character.

But what of the others—those who can work but choose not to?

The answer is very simple.

Under this proposal, everyone who accepts benefits must also accept work or training provided suitable jobs are available either locally or at some distance if transportation is provided. The only exceptions would be those unable to work, and mothers of preschool children. Even mothers of preschool children, however, would have the opportunity to work—because I am also proposing along with this a major expansion of day-care centers to make it possible for mothers to take jobs by which they can support themselves and their children.

This national floor under incomes for working or dependent families is not a "guaranteed income." Under the guaranteed income proposal, everyone would be assured a minimum income, regardless of how much he was capable of earning, regardless of what his need was, regardless of whether or not he was willing to work.

During the Presidential campaign last year I opposed such a plan. I oppose it now, and will continue to oppose it. A guaranteed income would undermine the incentive to work: the family assistance plan increased the incentive to work. A guaranteed income establishes a right without responsibilities: family assistance recognizes a need and establishes a responsibility. It provides help to those in need, and in turn requires that those who receive help work to the extent of their capabilities. There is no reason why one person should be taxed so that another can choose to live idly.

In states that now have benefit levels above the Federal floor, family assistance would help ease the states' financial burdens. But in 20 states—those in which poverty is most widespread—the new Federal floor would be above present average benefit levels, and would mean a leap upward for many thousands of families that cannot care for themselves. . . .

The new family assistance would provide aid for needy families; it would establish a work requirement, and a work incentive; but these in turn require effective programs of job training and job placement —including a chance to qualify not just for any jobs, but for good jobs, that provide both additional self-respect and full self-support.

Therefore, I am also sending a message to Congress calling for a complete overhaul of the nation's manpower training services. . . .

To remedy the confusion, abitrariness and rigidity of the present system. The new manpower training act would basically do three things:

¶It would pull together the jumble of programs that currently exist, and equalize standards of eligibility.

¶It would provide flexible funding—so that Federal money would follow the demands of labor and industry, and flow into those programs that people most want and need.

¶It would decentralize administration, gradually moving it away from the Washington bureaucracy and turning it over to states and localities. . . .

The Manpower Training Act will have other provisions specifically designed to help move people off welfare rolls and onto payrolls:

¶A computerized job bank would be established, to match job seekers with job vacancies.

¶For those on welfare, a $30-a-month bonus would be offered as an incentive to go into job training.

¶For heads of families now on welfare, 150,000 new training slots would be opened.

¶As I mentioned previously, greatly expanded day-care center facilities would be provided for the children of welfare mothers who choose to work. However, these would be day-care centers with a difference. There is no single ideal to which this Administration is more firmly committed than to the enriching of a child's first five years of life, and thus helping lift the poor out of misery at a time when a lift can help the most. Therefore, these day-care centers would offer more than custodial care; they would also be devoted to the development of vigorous young minds and bodies. As a further dividend, the day-care centers would offer employment to many welfare mothers themselves. . . .

For a third of a century, power and responsibility have flowed toward Washington—and Washington has taken for its own the best sources of revenue.

We intend to reverse this tide, and to turn back to the states a greater measure of responsibility—not as a way of avoiding problems, but as a better way of solving problems. Along with this should go a share of Federal revenues. I shall propose to the Congress next week that a set portion of the revenues from Federal income taxes be remitted directly to the states—with a minimum of Federal restrictions on how those dollars are to be used, and with a requirement that a percentage of them be channeled through for the use of local governments. . . .

The first-year costs of the new family assistance program, including the child care centers and job training, would be $4 billion. I deliberated long and hard over whether we could afford such an outlay. I decided in favor of it for two reasons: because the costs would not begin until fiscal 1971, when I expect the funds to be available; and because I concluded that this is a reform we cannot afford not to undertake. The cost of continuing the present system, in financial as well as human terms, is staggering if projected into the nineteen-seventies.

Revenue sharing would begin in the middle of fiscal 1971, at a half-year cost of a half billion dollars. This cuts into the Federal budget, but it represents relief for the equally hard-pressed states. It would help curb the rise in state and local taxes.

Over all, we would be spending more—in the short run—to help people who now are poor and who now are unready for work or unable to find work. . . .

If we do invest in this modernization, the heavily burdened taxpayer at least will see the light at the end of the tunnel. And the man who now looks ahead only to a lifetime of dependency will see hope for a life of work and pride and dignity. . . .

Abolishing poverty and putting an end to dependency—like reaching for the moon a generation ago—may seem impossible. But in the spirit of Apollo, we can lift our sights and marshal our best efforts. We can resolve to make this the year, not that we reached the goal, but that we turned the corner: from a dismal cycle of dependency toward a new birth of independence; from despair toward hope; from an ominously mounting importance of government toward a new effectiveness of government—and toward a full opportunity for every American to share the bounty of this rich land.

VII

Poverty and Political Action

Backlash, Privilege, and Pressure

[Poor people in other countries] are more integrated. The whole history during the past 150 years has been a history of popular uprisings. The people have stood up in great movements. Your poor here have been silent people. They're not even participating much in your voting. Very low participation, not only in the South where Negroes have been kept out, but also in the North. . . .

The fundamental thing is that you have these pockets of poverty and you have become accustomed to them. I'm always wondering—you travel by train into New York or Chicago and you travel through the slums and the funny thing is you don't even see them. And it is because these poor people have never before stood up on their back legs. . . .

When I was here studying the Negro problem back more than a quarter of a century ago, it was supposed by people—and not only by radicals—that it would be natural for the poor to get together. Of course, the fact is just the opposite. It is the poor who are in conflict with each other, who are in competition with each other, who hate each other. The worst enemy the Negro has is the poor white; the only superiority the poor white has is the fact that he is not Negro, and this is the basis for your backlash.

If you attack poverty, you must do it on a broad scale. Martin Luther King knew this. What I have is the fear that the poor people of different ethnic character will fight each other as they have always done; what I also have is the hope that they will stand together and ask for their rights.

No privileged class in history has ever climbed down from its privileges and opened its monopolies just out of good will. I believe very much in idealism. But it plays its role only when there is pressure from below.

FROM Gunnar Myrdal, "Gunnar Myrdal on Poor People's March" (interview by Mike McGrady), Boston *Globe* (May 26, 1968).

THE forecasts in S. M. Miller's 1964 analysis of the political potential of an alliance of the black and white poor, included in the first edition of this book, have proved correct to such large degree that we are pleased to retain the selection in major part in this edition. Miller's prediction of a surge of poor people's political activity is an outstanding example of historical forecasting, and it should have prepared readers for the subsequent evolution of the civil rights movement, the black-white ghetto riots,[1] the emergence of black power, the poor people's march, and the black opposition to the Vietnam war, so vividly expressed in the selection by St. Clair Drake.

Who would deny the impact of that upsurge? We believe that the Model Cities program, for example, was in large part a direct political outcome of these upheavals (particularly the ghetto riots), which are likely to sustain the allocation of welfare antipoverty funds to the public sector. And in the competition between the military and the antipoverty advocates for public funds, these political stirrings will no doubt check somewhat the conservative coalition that "killed the anti-rat bill (and) is determined to kill the antipoverty program altogether."[2]

Nonetheless, as Edward P. Morgan contends, our society appears to be conducting a political retreat from the poverty war. The conservative coalition against the poverty war has succeeded in cutting some appropriations and eliminating others, largely by persuading Congress that fiscal retrenchment was required to compensate for escalated military expenditures and accelerated inflation. The extent to which growing conservative forces at the local level will further weaken poverty programs remains to be seen, although their increase in strength in the 1969–70 mayoral campaigns in the great cities where "law and order" was a major issue is not encouraging. The backlash of the poor white, observed by Myrdal, may unhappily be extending into middle-income working-class families. Some of the related crosscurrents at work in determining the near future fate of antipoverty programs are thoughtfully analyzed in Vincent Burke's prescient discussion of the Poor People's Campaign.

---

[1] See Carl Rowan's reference to an Associated Press dispatch about interracial cooperation among looters and thieves, Portland *Oregonian,* August 2, 1967.

[2] Drew Pearson, Portland *Oregonian,* August 1, 1967.

and resources, on which much of our future economic growth depends:

We spawn new industries that need more and more skilled people, while a fourth of the population drops out of high school before graduation.

The "help wanted" columns grow longer with offers of technical jobs, while the welfare lists grow longer with names of people who don't qualify for those jobs—but could.

We buy more and more portable TV sets to take to the beach—only to find that the water is too polluted for swimming.

Answers to these contradictions must be found. And while "more spending" is not the answer by itself, it is self-deluding to pretend that our public and human needs can be met without public cost.

Simply spurring the economy on to greater growth each year will not solve the problems of the cities if the greater proportion of the new wealth continues to be poured into motorboats, electric carving knives and costume jewelry—while the cities decay—and while millions of people remain undereducated—and unmotivated.

Nor will "turning the problem over to free enterprise" solve it. Private business can and should play a much more significant role, but it should not be expected to educate and motivate four-year-old ghetto kids at its own expense any more than it should build missiles at its own expense.

It is devastating to hear so much of the political dialogue turn on how much spending should be cut, not just today but in the future, while public problems deepen. After the Vietnam war, the argument goes in some quarters, taxes should be reduced a little each year as the means of stimulating growth. There is very little analysis of what kind of growth, growth for what, or even whether that really is the route to growth.

In 1964 we cut taxes in the interest of stimulating the economy, of eliminating the "fiscal drag." And the idea has proved to be valid. But we did not give enough thought to keeping taxes where they were and stimulating the economy by investing more in public needs. It was argued that higher spending instead of a tax cut would have been politically unacceptable; Congress would never have approved. And that may be right. That is why it is important to begin a new discourse now on what our priorities for the future will be.

The time has come to turn the dialogue around, to examine in depth the trade-off in both economic and human terms between future tax cuts and more public investment. The time is coming when that kind of choice will be upon us.

We will have some critical choices to make: Cut taxes and spend our incomes for whatever extra luxuries we wish, or invest more for some of the things we cannot buy as individuals—schools, parks, education of the disadvantaged, economic re-development of decaying areas.

Increasingly the evidence of recent years has pointed to the impressive economic gains from investment in human development. They are harder to measure than investment in steel and concrete, but just as real.

Estimates by some of our experts conclude that about half the growth in output in the last 50 years has come from investment in education, training and health.

Improved education in the past few decades has raised the average quality of labor by a third—quality that is translated daily into higher production.

Or look at the investment in health, in purely economic terms. Since the turn of the century the increase in life expectancy has enlarged the work force by 25%.

The future capacity of this country to produce will depend more on developing "human capital" than on striving for new peaks of affluence. The examples of Germany and Japan have offered striking evidence of the economic importance of human capital. They rose from ashes to affluence in less than 20 years. Their greatest asset: an educated, motivated population.

This country can no longer afford the waste of slums and ghettos. A society cannot expect to prosper indefinitely bedded in social tension so deep that it erupts into riots as predictable as summer. But in more specific terms, society needs the productive capacities of these people as much as they need the help of society.

Few economic analysts fear, as they once did, that automation will flood the country with unusable manpower. The foreseeable problem is one of finding enough qualified people for the more demanding jobs.

A recent Government study predicted that in the decade ending in 1975 employment would grow 26%. The greatest growth will be in jobs calling for higher levels of education. White collar jobs are expected to grow 38% while blue collar jobs grow 17%. Plain laboring jobs will grow scarcely at all.

We have enough experience with man-power training and retraining now to know that a high percentage of those unemployed or under-employed can be fitted for existing jobs. There is some delay on the return, and some waste in the process; but the return when it comes in is manifold.

A man or woman salvaged from idleness and welfare creates a double economic benefit. By earning his own way he saves the public the $2,500 it costs to keep a family of four on welfare, and at the same time contributes $6,000 to the gross national product by his earnings.

. . . Whether a dollar is spent by a private consumer or by the government, the end is still the purchase of goods. A dollar spent for teacher training is promptly transformed into purchasing power by the recipient. However spent, the money still ends up in the cash registers of the private sector.

On top of that, if public spending helps bring into the main stream of the economy—and into the mass market—those people now on the fringes it creates a new source of demand to fuel business growth.

And business incentive would certainly not be shot down by the kind of marginal extra taxes required; it is not that fragile.

The whole conception of "more public spending" is too easily dismissed in boom times like these as being inflationary. It would be, of course, without taxes to pay for it.

But there is nothing inflationary about channeling an increased proportion of national spending into the public instead of the private sector. Quite the contrary. Properly used, public spending can help combat inflation.

Certain sectors of the economy—like construction, medical services—contribute more than their share of inflationary pressure because demand for these services outstrips supply. Funds spent to develop workers and build factories, or foster technological advance, would alleviate the pressure.

Can the U.S. afford to spend more than it does for public needs without taking a cutback in the standard of living? Clearly it can—as long as the economy can be kept growing as well as it has. . . .

The High Price of High Fertility

PHILIP M. HAUSER

Our post-war boom in babies is exacting a high price from the American people—as measured in human as well as financial costs. The

FROM Philip M. Hauser, professor of sociology, University of Chicago, Address at the Annual Meeting of Planned Parenthood–World Population, New York City (October 16, 1963), pp. 1–3.

baby boom will from now on worsen the U.S. unemployment problem, greatly increase the magnitude of juvenile delinquency, exacerbate already dangerous race tensions, inundate the secondary schools and colleges, greatly increase traffic accidents and fatalities, augment urban congestion and further subvert the traditional American governmental system.

Needless to say high fertility is by no means the only factor accounting for these difficult problems. But it is a major factor in making them worse. This is well illustrated by the way in which the baby boom is now contributing to high unemployment. Our post-war babies who reached flood stage after demobilization in 1946, are reaching labor force age in the sixties. The number of new workers under 25 years of age entering the labor force, averaging 600,000 per year during the sixties, is three times the number of new workers who entered the labor force between 1955 and 1960. The bulge in new entrant workers, coming at a time when we are experiencing a high level of chronic unemployment and increasing automation, may constitute the gravest challenge our economy has ever faced in peace time. . . . Under such circumstances it may also be anticipated that consumer demand will slough off in many areas—the teen-age market, the marriage market and other markets oriented to the marriage market including consumer durables; and that general consumer demand may decline as the public interprets mounting unemployment as indicating an uncertain economic outlook. *We have yet to demonstrate that we can generate new jobs as fast as we did babies after the war.* . . .

High fertility does not directly produce internal migration but it does accelerate imbalance between population and resources in the relatively underdeveloped areas of the country and, therefore, stimulates increases in migratory streams. There can be no doubt that high fertility has increased the volume of internal migration from the South to the North and West and from rural to urban areas.

The tremendous range of problems we face in our central cities, furthermore, is being increasingly compounded by the persistence of fertility differentials based primarily on income and educational status. Low income and minority families continue to have more children than they say they want, in large part because of the discriminatory medical services we make available to them so that they are virtually denied access to modern fertility control. The children, in turn, receive inferior and discriminatory educations, and the combination of high fertility and inadequate training is a major deterrent to the economic and social advance of families in the culture of pov-

the latter is subordinated to the former, when man's integrity and his social relationships are turned into instruments of production, then economic life destroys rather than fulfills our spiritual destiny. To the Christian, as we have seen, this must be understood in terms of God's acts of creation and grace. Through these acts, man has been given freedom and the ground to stand upon. Christian response to what God has done involves gratitude and creative service. It involves the attempt to cooperate with God so as to fashion a world more and more hospitable to the covenant community of mankind which is God's intention. Christian response does not involve the withholding of the necessary conditions of life as a means of manipulating the spiritual life of one's fellows.

Whatever one may say concerning the importance of work (and I consider work to be necessary to man's personal and social fulfillment), it loses its Christian significance when it is slavery or when it is an anxious attempt to make oneself worthy. It contributes to genuine fulfillment instead when it is an attempt to do the good or necessary thing because it is good or necessary, as one's free gift in response to God and in love of one's fellow creatures.

In this perspective, the "Protestant ethic" (which as we have received it may be a distortion of both ethics and of Protestantism) represents a half-truth. The true half is the importance of work in human fulfillment. The false half is the subordination of man to work and, worse yet, the attempt to establish whether or not people are deserving of what God has already given them.

We must reject even more emphatically the gross materialism and individualism of many of our inherited economic attitudes. Man was not made for material ends; nor can we limit human creativity to what will bring cash in the marketplace. Any definition of man's nature which treats him as an isolated stranger among his fellows destroys his true humanity just as surely as does any totalitarian effort to dissolve his uniqueness in social conformity. Man is both personal and social by nature.

These perspectives should have much to say to us about such proposals as guaranteed income.

revealing. More than anything else, the members of this movement (mostly mothers on welfare) sought to have their aid payments considered as a basic right, not as a gift. But most other people are accustomed to thinking of anything which is not earned through work as a gift, and it is believed that the recipients should be grateful to the givers.

In a Christian perspective, something can be said for the viewpoint of the apparently ungrateful welfare mothers. If one accepts the idea that creation is given to all of us alike (and apart from our deserving), it is clear that when social provision is made for basic economic well-being the gratitude belongs not so much to other people as to our Creator.

Misplaced gratitude can create the notion that the receiver is somehow inferior to the giver (unless, of course, it is a truly shared experience with mutual giving, mutual gratitude, and mutual respect). Gratitude can therefore lead also to human separation. I am afraid that some of the "warm feeling" which accompanies much of our giving is not so much the inner glow of Christian radiance as it is the pride which comes from playing God and the assuaged conscience which is prematurely content with problems only half-solved. The symbolic Christmas basket has generally made us all feel better. But it leaves the humiliated poor in a scarcely improved condition. There is much to be said for an objective handling of the basic conditions of life, treating them rather as a basic human right for which grateful thanks belong, not to any human agency, but to God alone.

Something is particularly wrong with the use of material giving in order to manipulate the response of others. Years ago we used to speak of the "rice Christians": persons who became Christians in countries like China in order to get more rice. Doubtless they were volubly grateful. It is less certain whether they were very dedicated Christians. And the worst of it was that one could never be sure!

Let there be no misunderstanding at this point. People ought to be grateful. Apart from gratitude we become arrogant and contemptuous of our good gifts. But when gratitude must take the form of being thankful to other men for the conditions of life itself, then the Christian must say that that kind of gratitude belongs rather to God.

How should we summarize this discussion? The most important point to remember is that the basic conditions of human existence ought to be secured prior to all talk about earning or deserving or incentive. The whole point of economics is to create and maintain the material conditions which best *serve* man's true humanity. When

public welfare regulations and the statutory provisions regulating selection of jurors in California. Recommendations for changes in these rules will be made to the State Bar Association and the State Legislature.

Finally, the problem of economic development of the community itself must be faced by the lawyer. Lawyers for the wealthy spend much of their time raising funds, providing business advice and ordering their clients' financial affairs.

CRLA has considered this part of the role of the lawyer for the poor as well. In one region, clients are being assisted in securing small business loans for a number of cooperative business enterprises.

In another area, a group of tenants being evicted from a public housing project are being helped to form their own non-profit corporation and to secure funds for new housing. This has involved negotiations with the Farmer's Home Administration, meetings with real estate specialists and coordination with an architect. From this has developed a pre-fabricated house that can be sold for a price within the client's ability to make the payments.

All of this involves a different kind of cooperation between social agencies, community action programs and legal services in the rural areas. Just as Sam Spender was served by a group of lawyers and non-lawyers so can the client community be served as a whole. Community action and legal action are complementary concepts that can be used to serve each other.

Ethical Guidelines
for Income Guarantees

PHILIP WOGAMAN

One of the striking aspects of most welfare programs, whether public or private, is the expectation that the recipient will humbly acknowledge his indebtedness and properly express his gratitude to the giver. The outraged public response to the Welfare Rights Movement was

FROM Philip Wogaman, professor of Christian social ethics, Wesley Theological Seminary, *Guaranteed Annual Income: The Moral Issues* (Nashville: Abingdon Press, 1968), pp. 76–78.

of what he signs and of the relationship between his economic and marital problems. Certainly for the lawyers, social workers, non-professionals and others who worked for him there will be some new appreciation of the nature and interdependency of their respective roles.

Valuable as are such coordinated efforts, however, they do not raise the most basic problems in really doing something about the Spenders' problem. They involve cooperation around only limited ends.

Sam's situation is probably similar to that of several hundred thousand farm workers and poor residents of rural California. He will soon be out of work after the oranges are picked; he only works an average of 100 days a year. And in fact there probably will be no training program available to him nor is he covered by unemployment insurance.

He will earn less than $1900 a year. In Sam's case he may remain in his house if he can maintain the payments. For many farm workers home is a substandard dormitory owned by the grower where they live as "licensees" without even the same rights as a tenant. Those who wish to see them can and have been arrested for trespassing on "private property." Even the store which fraudulently sold him goods, although they may let him off the hook, will continue to operate in the same fashion.

To cope with these problems, the lawyer's services cannot be limited to the kind that was afforded Sam. If a pattern is established there must be an injunction suit brought against the store to prevent similar practices in the future. In several counties, CRLA attorneys have brought or threatened such suits against companies engaging in such practices.

If investigation of the field in which Sam is working reveals, as so many do, violations of the labor code in failing to provide water or sanitation facilities, a complaint to the Industrial Welfare Commission must be initiated and private legal action discussed with the client.

If complaining to the authorities involves retaliation against the client by the labor contractor or his employer, new remedies must be fashioned to protect him. In one case, pleadings are being drafted to challenge the firing of a picker by a labor contractor for seeing a CRLA attorney.

Nor can the service provided to the poor community be limited to lawsuits. The laws, rules and regulations themselves have to be examined and changes on behalf of the poor urged. CRLA has been studying the operation of wage garnishments, the administration of

of the case. In addition, there is the conflict between him and his wife ostensibly over the management of the family's finances.

Given these problems, the attorneys have turned to the non-lawyers (community workers) on the CRLA staff or social agencies or programs within the community. The landlord must be called and an agreement not to evict negotiated.

The employer must be contacted so that he will be reassured that the problem is being handled. Discussions on family problems and counseling on debt management should probably be initiated.

Ways of bringing additional income to the family must also be explored. In some instances, the offices have assisted the family in getting church or privately sponsored emergency financial assistance. In other instances, the family has been helped in securing welfare. Where eligibility or the level of benefits has become a problem the presence of a lawyer has made a substantial difference. In Sam's case, the family may be entitled to AFDC-U (Aid to Families of Dependent Children where the male is unemployed or employed part time). In several cases, this has involved challenging the regulations determining whether low-paying farm labor is full-time or part time employment.

Sam may also be entitled to medical assistance under Title 19 of the Social Security Act (Aid to the Medically Indigent). He will also be talked to about job retraining for himself and after school employment for his son. In several instances, the offices have aided clients in enrolling in such programs.

In all of these efforts, the skills and knowledge necessary go beyond the lawyer's training and expertise. They also place new burdens on his time although he is already facing an impossible case load. Cooperation with other programs in the community and delegation of many of these roles to the non-professionals working in the offices becomes not only a desirable aspect of the program but a necessity. Handled in this fashion, there may be some relief for Sam Spender's problems. The legal actions may cut his debts and the damage suit by his wife may add to his income. His suit against the finance company might also involve damages for fraud.

He may well be able to get medical assistance and financial aid to cope with his immediate difficulties. Counseling and debt management may, as they have in some cases, prove to be valuable. There may even be some training program available to enable him to leave farm work for more stable and remunerative employment.

He may also come away with a sense that seeking to help himself has value and that the law can be used as a tool to protect and work for him. Perhaps he will be more cognizant of the legal implications

munity action programs or public agencies. He is deeply in debt. He is three months in arrears on a $240 loan on his furniture for which he pays $40 principal and three dollars in interest each month. He owes $150 in medical bills and expects to spend another $50 next month for treatments for his back. He is two months behind on his rent and does not have the money for this month's payment.

He has a job with Fertile Fruit Co. picking oranges where he makes $50 a week. His wife used to work before she was injured falling from a ladder while picking oranges several months ago. He has two children, age 11 and 16, both of whom are in school. He says that the man at the furniture store told him that he didn't have to make any payments for 90 days and that the furniture was entirely new. When the furniture was examined at home, it turned out to be used. Even new it wasn't worth more than $90 dollars.

The Take-Away Finance Co. has now attached Sam's wages on the basis of the contract he signed.

Sam says the real problem is his wife who wastes all his money on "junk." He's about ready "to throw the whole damn thing in."

Even a brief perusal of the case reveals several legal issues. The first legal problem for Sam is the wage attachment which may cause him to lose his job. In California an employee may be entirely exempt from wage attachment if he can show that his family needs exceed his income.

Secondly, it may be possible to avoid the furniture debt if the false statements of the salesman can be proved and some knowledge or participation by the finance company established. CRLA's law offices have already had several cases dismissed or compromised on these grounds.

It also appears that there may have been, in his case, some illegal interest charged by "stuffing" the purchase price; that is, raising the price of goods to credit buyers in order to hide excessive interest charges.

Finally, Sam's wife may have a claim for damages or workman's compensation against the company as a result of her injury. Such a case would be referred to the local bar association's lawyer referral service from which a private attorney would handle the case for a fee. CRLA takes cases only for those who cannot afford a lawyer. Thus far the program has made over 300 referrals.

An analysis of the legal problems faced by the Spenders, however, does little more than scratch the surface. The possible loss of the job, the pending eviction, the problem of future employment are also part

The Hungry World

THE ROYAL BANK OF CANADA

The United Nations Declaration of Human Rights, adopted in 1948, says: "Everyone has the right to a standard of living adequate for the health and well-being of himself and of his family."

To have a good standard of living does not mean becoming encumbered with western world impedimenta. It does mean not having to eat grass, as women have been seen to do near the Persian Gulf; it does mean that the emaciated labourer in China does not have to go for a day on scraps of food that contain only 200 calories while his Canadian counterpart has a regular 2,500-calorie intake.

Owen D. Young said at the University of California: "Let no man think that the living standards of America can be permanently maintained at a measurably higher level than those of the other civilized countries. Either we shall lift theirs to ours or they will drag ours down to theirs." . . .

One thing is certain: The import of food from the wealthier to the less wealthy regions can never provide more than a small part of what is needed. We cannot feed the underdeveloped countries by scraping our bins, borrowing on next year's crops, shipping dried eggs, lard or milk. Pearson and Paalberg point out in their book *Starvation Truths, Half-Truths, Untruths:* if all feeding of wheat to livestock in Canada and the United States were prohibited, and the consumption of wheat by human beings reduced by 25 percent; if the acreage of corn and oats were reduced by 25 percent and planted to wheat; we could produce about 1,000 million additional bushels of grain for human consumption. On the Chinese standard, this would feed about 80 million people for a year. As has been estimated by the United Nations, more than 1,500 million people have to be fed. . . .

So basically influenced are human beings by the need for food that peace and war, international understanding, and the whole fabric of human social life are profoundly affected by it. Prince Philip said in an address to Canadian engineers and scientists in Toronto: "It is recognized that an explosive situation will inevitably develop if the

FROM the Royal Bank of Canada, "The Hungry World," *Monthly Letter* (June 1964), pp. 1–4.

gap between the 'have' nations and the 'have-not' nations grows too big."

The statistics of misery is not, then, a remote economic and technical affair, but one bound up intimately with social policy. Statesmen who are realists will give a high place in their thinking to the elimination of hunger and squalor in all parts of the world as a means to protecting and enhancing the lives of people in their own countries.

Aldous Huxley said in a paper for the Fund for the Republic in 1963: "By shifting our attention from the now completely irrelevant and anachronistic politics of nationalism and military power to the problems of the human species . . . we shall be . . . reducing the threat of sudden destruction by scientific war and at the same time reducing the threat of more gradual biological disaster."

From disappointment, through resentful frustration, to widespread social unrest the road is short. Shorter still is the road from social unrest, through chaos, to dictatorship, possibly of the Communist party, more probably of generals and colonels.

The restlessness in Asia, the Middle East and Africa means among other things an increasing consciousness of the disparity between their people's present living standards and the standards common in more affluent countries. Of democracy they know little, but of hunger they know much.

Since the end of the second world war more than 800 million people in various parts of the world have seized independence, hopefully seeking to become masters of their own destiny in order to escape from poverty. Almost all of them are abysmally poor, with weak capacity for self-sustained economic growth.

Dr. [H. L.] Trueman [Secretary of the Canadian Freedom from Hunger Committee] warns that we must not allow our attention to what is going on in the major part of the world, affecting two-thirds of the world's population, to be distracted by the banging of fists on conference tables, the blast of rockets from launching pads, and the building of walls dividing nations. "What I hear," he says, "is the babble of millions of children's voices in schools where no schools previously existed; the lapping of water in new irrigation channels; the sound of millions of better ploughs moving through the good earth, and the lowing of healthier cattle on a thousand hills."

The common man throughout the world is not seeking Utopia, but a little alleviation of his lot today and that better tomorrow about which Dr. Trueman speaks. Hundreds of millions whose forebears patiently accepted lives of misery are involved in what has been called "the revolution of rising expectations." What has been, up until the past quarter century, a distant dream has now become a passionate demand.

Historian Arnold Toynbee has expressed the hope that this age will be remembered because it is the first generation in history in which mankind dared to believe it practical to make the benefits of civilization available to the whole human race.

0
1
C 2
D 3
E 4
F 5
G 6
H 7
I 8
J 9